# DREAM WARRIOR

## Passages of a Creative - Scholar

### MEL DONALSON

Mechanicsburg, PA USA

Published by Sunbury Press, Inc.
Mechanicsburg, Pennsylvania

SUNBURY PRESS
www.sunburypress.com

Copyright © 2025 by Mel Donalson.
Cover Copyright © 2025 by Sunbury Press, Inc.

Sunbury Press supports copyright. Copyright fuels creativity, encourages diverse voices, promotes free speech, and creates a vibrant culture. Thank you for buying an authorized edition of this book and for complying with copyright laws by not reproducing, scanning, or distributing any part of it in any form without permission. You are supporting writers and allowing Sunbury Press to continue to publish books for every reader. For information contact Sunbury Press, Inc., Subsidiary Rights Dept., PO Box 548, Boiling Springs, PA 17007 USA or legal@sunburypress.com.

For information about special discounts for bulk purchases, please contact Sunbury Press Orders Dept. at (855) 338-8359 or orders@sunburypress.com.

To request one of our authors for speaking engagements or book signings, please contact Sunbury Press Publicity Dept. at publicity@sunburypress.com.

FIRST SUNBURY PRESS EDITION: May 2025

Set in Adobe Garamond | Interior design by Crystal Devine | Cover by Victoria Mitchell | Edited by Anaiah Davis.

Publisher's Cataloging-in-Publication Data
Names: Donalson, Mel, author.
Title: Dream warrior : passages of a creative-scholar / Mel Donalson.
Description: First trade paperback edition. | Mechanicsburg, PA : Sunbury Press, 2025.
Summary: Melvin Donalson's *Dream Warrior: Passages of a Creative-Scholar* is a testament to a Black man's commitment to succeed and find fulfilment in the opposing worlds of academia and entertainment.
Identifiers: ISBN 979-8-88819-267-2 (softcover).
Subjects: BIOGRAPHY & AUTOBIOGRAPHY / African American & Black | BIOGRAPHY & AUTOBIOGRAPHY / Educators | BIOGRAPHY & AUTOBIOGRAPHY / Entertainment & Performing Arts.

Designed in the USA
0 1 1 2 3 5 8 13 21 34 55

*For the Love of Books!*

With my deepest love,
this book is dedicated to
Beverly, my remarkable wife and companion
and to
Derek, my amazing son and friend

# Contents

Acknowledgments — vii
Introduction — 1

**CHAPTERS**

1  The Colored Section — 7
2  Years That Ask, Years That Answer — 20
3  Pieces of a Young Man — 46
4  Wanderlust — 64
5  Like A Winding Sheet — 91
6  Landlocked — 101
7  Dreams, Ideals, and Stars — 117
8  The Cultivation of Talent — 149
9  Seekers and Saints — 160
10  The Symmetry of a Creative-Scholar — 175
11  Perfect Accidents — 187
12  The Crookeds and the Straights — 201
13  Promises and Prayers — 218
14  Nights of Dreams, Mornings of Hope — 228
15  Wrestling with Despair — 244
16  The Echoes of Dreams — 258

Bibliography — 264
About the Author — 265

# Acknowledgments

Having the opportunity to write about my life is a privilege. I am extremely thankful to my family and friends who supported me in my search for the golden fleece of dreams. My parents—Wilbert and Dorothy—were courageous people of faith and hard workers. Their love for me and belief in me provided an enduring foundation for building my life. To my sister, Paulette, and my brother, Brian, we've navigated many life-changing turns in the road, but our shared love remained the compass that showed us the way. Fred Lamster (my brother from another mother) and his wife, Fran, have also been my supportive family during years of ups-and-downs and turn-arounds.

To the many who helped me along the winding road that often circled around to yet another winding road, I have valued you all: Delores and Joe DaLuz; Elaine and Harold Perkins; John Marcelino; James Tobey; Jennifer "JJ" Levine; Walt Toombs; Jill Bruce; Sharon Early Kinney; Liz Mackie; Lynn Fulham; James Carignan; James Leamon; Pam Wansker; Lynn Klamkin; Skye Dent; Michael Whitted; Valerie Sanders; Marcus Bruce; Mari Jo Buhle; Wilfred Samuels; Bill and Virginia Edwards; Rodney Hooks; Beatriz Fox; James and Elizabeth Gawrich; Justin Arnold and Elida Ceja; Nancy Aguilar; Marylu Castillo; Uriel Serrano; Jenny Artiga Lu; Imani Spears; Anibal Serrano; Jenny Hicks; Juan Carlos Parrilla; Kate and Dave Remo; Bill and Laura Paden; Richard and Elaine Doran; Ron and Mary Peterson; Rick Fraser and Charity Perry; Vique Mora; Michelle Banks; Nancy Ramirez; Monica Baltazar, Fawaz and Grace Al-Malood; Shahin and Negin Sahut; Ron and Cecilia Tate; Aurora Guzman; Margo Fell; John and Faye Waidley; Maher and Jen Salhani; Lamont Hartman; and Debra Chavira.

Fred Lipscomb has been a trusted friend, and I have treasured the friendship of Truc Mai; Greg Nixon; Dan and Poldi Rathbone; Jacek Zdzienicki; Pernell Wilder; Jeff Webb; and Cornel Hunter.

To the talented people at Sunbury Press who worked with me in developing *Dream Warrior*, I am grateful and appreciative of your skills and patience: Anaiah Davis, Crystal Devine; Victoria Mitchell, and Lawrence Knorr.

Finally, I'm grateful to the five accomplished and supportive friends who read early portions of my manuscript and provided their comments for the back cover: Luis Rodriguez; Reyna Grande; Ben Guillory; Jim Henderson; and David Massey.

# Introduction

In the spring of 2000, I was invited to read my fiction at the annual meeting of the African American Literature and Culture Society (AALCS). I felt honored. For years, I had been a member of this society within the larger American Literature Association, a national organization of scholars from dozens of universities and colleges. When introduced by a colleague who read aloud my publications—both scholarly and popular—a loud snickering emerged from the audience when my publication in a national martial arts magazine was recognized. For those who dismissed that popular publication, I recognized their condescension as the chuckling contempt swirled around the room. Within the Scholar's world, a particular elitism has existed that dismisses expressions avoiding a high-theory methodology. However, I was as proud of that published martial arts article as I was of the poetry, short story, short film, film scripts, and African American literature anthology I worked on—all published and/or completed within four years leading up to that particular reading.

The word "Creative" can be a noun or an adjective. As a noun, it is one of those peculiar words that uses a part of itself to define itself. For example, a Creative is a person *marked by the ability or power to create*. Importantly, there's no one way to become a Creative, as that identity includes numerous forms of expression. Whether it be through poetry, short stories, creative nonfiction, novels, plays, or screenplays, the opportunities to immerse in any or all of those genres are only limited by interests, skills, and hard work.

For me, my identity as a Creative was planted within my Southern roots by the various Black people intersecting my childhood, especially my parents. My mother hummed and sang aloud the melodies connected to a popular song or a solo she performed in the church choir. Her vocal expressions were joyful and soothing, falling pleasantly on my ears. My mother, Dorothy, was a remarkable personality. Raised by her grandmother, early photos displayed her physical beauty. More importantly, she was vibrant and smart when she met my father in high school, and following their teenage marriage, the two courageously left the familiar world in Bainbridge, Georgia, and moved to Fort Pierce, Florida, to pursue better opportunities in the segregated South. My mother's voice filled a room with warmth and infused her church choir solos with a clear, touching reverence. For me, she was that earliest voice that connected praise to my elementary school poems. She read aloud and had me recite those awkwardly written verses into rhythms that brought a distinct delight to her face. She hugged me with love and showered me with approval that rendered excellence to my words scribbled in pencil across a page.

At the same time, my father's bedtime readings from the Bible to me and my sister prompted images that swirled inside my head. On some occasions, he also read or recited stories and folktales. I first learned about Br'er Rabbit from my father, coming to understand that "Br'er" was a contraction of "Brother," giving a racial significance to the many animal tales. Some stories emanated from tales my father heard as he grew up, but there was one story that planted an early attitude inside me—an important perspective that sustained my personal resilience in my later years. My father told the story this way, but not in these exact words because the story was never written down:

*An old man, a young boy, and their donkey set off to leave their country farm to travel to the big city many miles away to buy some seeds for planting. Because he loved the young boy, the old man told him to ride the donkey while he walked. After a day of walking in the sun, they reached a small town, passing a main street and looking at all the people looking at them. The old man and the boy heard the people talking: "Look at that selfish boy. He rides the donkey while making that old man walk in this heat." The old man and the boy heard what the people said, so the boy got down from the donkey. Then, they came to a larger town with stores along the main street. Remembering what happened in the small city, the old man rode the donkey while the young boy walked because they knew the people were looking at them. The old man and the boy heard the people whispering: "Look at that heartless old man! He's riding the donkey and making that child walk behind in all of this heat!" The old man and the boy heard what the people said, so the old man got down from the donkey. Then, they finally reached the big city with wide streets busy with people. The old man and the boy remembered what was said in the first two towns, so they decided to both walk as they led the donkey behind them. Then, the old man and the boy heard the people shouting: "Look at those two stupid, country people. They're walking when they could be riding the donkey!"* My father explained, "Just goes to show you. You can't please all of the people all of the time!"

If I had to identify the origin of "The Old Man, the Young Boy, and the Donkey," I couldn't do it. Yet, that particular story came back to me repeatedly, resurfacing decades later at that reading when my fellow scholars snickered at my publication in a popular magazine. Of the many colleagues, agents, and publishers I've interacted with over the years, I've been able to survive the rejections and pejorative comments by remembering my father's words: "You can't please all of the people all of the time!"

The voices of my mother and father entered my ears with such positivity that my earliest perceptions of creative words were synonymous with pleasure—to the ear and to the spirit. Although I didn't comprehend it during my youth, I was already equating language, rhythms, and images to creations that would in later decades be identified as "Art" and "Popular Culture." Significantly, parents—and grandmothers, uncles, aunts, and cousins—were my foundation of personal growth and belonging, but there was another notable community in Bethel Baptist Church. This Black church, which was inextricable from our lives in Fort Pierce, was the repository of spiritual, community, and cultural meanings within my boyhood. On the one hand, the church influenced my creativity primarily through the "theater" of the sermon and the vocal responses of the congregation.

My participation in the church pageantry was through my Christmas and Easter speeches, which were assigned Bible verses that young people in the church recited during those holiday services. With my heart beating quickly as I walked forward and took the steps to the pulpit, various voices called out encouraging phrases. Upon ending my recitation, the collective "hallelujahs" and applause emphasized my success as a speaker.

However, the Black church in the late 1950s carried another significance for me and my peers: the confirmation of a community that collectively regarded its children as the future. The foundation of that future was rooted in education. Although the term "Scholar" was never articulated to me in the late 1950s, the expectations were that my baby boomer generation would fulfill the aspirations of the Civil Rights Movement, which were intricately connected to the Black church.

From my parents, my extended family, my teachers, and my church, I was consistently told that I was "smart," which was a powerful descriptor during that time. Adults concluded that my speaking skills, obedient behavior, and respect for elders signified an intelligence that resided deep within my chubby body. That early Southern identity gave me a confirmation of belonging to and representing someone and something beyond myself. At ten years old, that identity became a crucial source of survival when my parents decided to leave Florida and its racism to create a new life in Massachusetts.

Being "smart" was a general acknowledgement of my earned grades and respectful behavior toward adults. However, decades later, the term Scholar possessed a more narrow meaning. The term identified someone who was a dedicated specialist in a specific area of academic study. The task of a Scholar was to weigh and analyze a given topic to reach a comprehensive understanding or theory about that particular subject. As a Scholar during my career as a college and university professor, I researched, presented scholarly papers at conferences, delivered lectures, and published critical essays and books.

The Scholar label followed me over decades of working as a professor on five different campuses. Was I intellectual enough to be allowed into the society of deep thinkers? Could I demonstrate my identity as an academic by publishing pages of erudite analysis that argued or confirmed the same topic published by another Scholar in the same field of study? Most Tier 1 institutions required their professors to accrue a list of scholarly publications in academic journals and books, a way to boast the brain trust on that particular campus *and* award tenure to a professor. This issue received national attention in 2002 when the Harvard University president questioned Black Scholar Cornel West about the scholarship value of a rap CD that Dr. West performed on and released. From the perspective of the university president, a Scholar wrestled with the burden of qualifying the value of certain topics in a language deemed appropriate for academic discourse, considering the urban-generated hip hop and rap genres not worthy modes of expression for Scholars on an elite, Ivy League campus.

Often, the concepts of the Creative and the Scholar have been seen as oppositional, with the latter elevated as a label of outstanding intelligence and achievement. For me, these identities are not incompatible, as their fusion in my life has shaped my personal identity. I've written poetry, short stories, novels, screenplays, analytical essays, and critical books. I've written, produced, and directed short fictional films and stage productions. Do these accomplishments make me unique? Absolutely not. However, completing these various projects have required a devotion to both the beauty and emotional power of Fine Art and Popular Art *and* the analytical and theoretical framework of Academia. Over the decades, these diverse expressions—along with the demon of racism—have challenged my efforts to be included in the literary, entertainment, and academic worlds.

I'm certain that other Creatives have weighed the particular routes that gained them public recognition and/or private fulfillment. They have assessed those individuals who sparked and encouraged them in their pursuits. I, too, have benefitted from numerous people who gave hours to influence the days of my growth. There are many who I've named here in this autobiography, but there are many others who I've never met personally, though they inspired my imagination in ways they'll never know—through their written works, music, radio, films, and television programs. At the same time, I've identified those Scholars who suspended their professional sprints toward scholarly publications to walk me along a path that respects but doesn't deify academia.

For my own survival, I followed a pathway that integrated my identities as both a Creative and a Scholar. This dedicated approach provided a survival technique against the challenges to narrow my identity. For me, merging the Creative and the Scholar has been my pathway to recognizing and affirming my personal and professional identities.

When considering the challenge of writing an autobiography that covers decades, I was hesitant to even attempt the task of deciding what to include and/or omit. To what extent could I trust my memory to clearly recall decades of people and experiences?

So, I leaned on sources that could serve as frameworks to reconstruct my past. As early as the spring of 1972, I began journaling while participating in my college study abroad program. Importantly, I continued writing in journal pages until April 1998. My confessions, secrets, plans, frustrations, and celebrations took form as phrases and paragraphs across dated pages. These journals covered the emotions, longings, religious reflections, friendships, loves, and losses during decades of desire and discovery. The journals waivered in their details; some were partially filled, while others were more complete. Additionally, I had spiral-bound monthly planners with annual calendars that covered from 2015 through 2022. Those pages contained personal notes, appointments, and events attended. At the same time, with my collection of photos—black-and-white from the 1950s and 1960s and an assortment of colored depictions through 2022—I captured images of family, friends, and places over the years. Additionally, the collected programs from special dinners, film festivals, anniversaries, and funerals supplied details that underscored those milestone celebrations and commemorations, filling in the blanks created by aging.

Similar to scenes in a movie, I've structured *Dream Warrior* in vignettes, focusing on people, experiences, and events that were crucial to each episode while interconnecting that episode with others. Like many in my generation, movies were cultural teaching tools that entertained and informed all at once. I was a movie addict by the age of six, hooked and dependent upon that mesmerizing union of dialogue, sounds, music, and giant images across a seventy-foot screen. The interplay of those elements influenced the vividness of my imagination and written expression.

When all the notes, dates, and incidents flowed together—the common and exotic places, the campuses and degrees, the students and colleagues, the books read and written, the music heard and danced to, the hours of viewing movies and immersing myself in visual landscapes—I recognized that I feasted on a variety of emotional, cultural, and spiritual ingredients that sustained my life. I've been fortunate in my experiences as a Black American man who has absorbed life through the privilege of being loved by many. I've observed death, but tasted life in so many ways. I've walked blindly through the daylight, but received direction in the darkness. I'm innocent of very little, but guilty of guzzling down experiences in my selfish thirst. My hope is that my journey will provide readers with an understanding and appreciation of selfhood while assessing and loving the people, places, and experiences that have sustained their lives.

# CHAPTER ONE

## The Colored Section

I was drowning.

My body twisted and sank deeper into the murkiness, a space measured not by time but by movement. It wasn't fear that I felt. As a young child, I had no understanding of death. There was nothing to reference as I watched the shadows, movements of faint light that swirled like elusive ribbons. Confusion. Mystery. A gloomy wonderment that was tangible and alluring. In my four-year-old condition, my world was just a connection of senses relaying direct and unfiltered feelings. I could see through the heaviness of the water. I could taste the fluidity across my tongue. There was no speaking or hearing, just suffocating, elongated moments.

No time. No air. Merely the weightlessness of floating, pulled forward by a current I couldn't comprehend. The force that pulled me upward was more disturbing than the watery place that I was leaving. The sunlight was harsh against my eyes.

And I heard her voice. My mother's voice. Somewhere between desperation and a prayer, calling my name over and over. It was a dizzying series of moments where I felt her grasp my body, which was now sensing pain. Air fought its way into my lungs as the water rushed through my mouth and nose, my body falling into coughing spasms. I feared the place where I was, which seemed harsh compared to the peaceful place that I had been.

I saw my mother's inner thigh, blood trickling down her light brown leg. My eyes flowed to her waist where the water-drenched clothes clung tightly to the bump that would become my sister. I lay on my back, staring into her wet face, the water mixing with her sweat, her eyes expressing such a mix of pain and hope. Pain and hope—the polarities that would lace my life in the same way they collided on my mother's face.

Years later, those minutes of desperation at that canal when my mother snatched me from drowning fell into place. I would hear the story many times, told in different ways, as stories were often embellished in the South. I would hear the nuances of fear in her voice, coupled sometimes with exaggerated humor to please her listeners. She would weave in the silliness of my childhood fascination with minnows at the water's edge. Maybe mention the heaviness of my big head that made me topple forward, my little limbs not thrashing but giving in to the water's currents that pulled me deeper and away from her. Relay that my sister seemed to move in her abdomen to help her leap forward. It became a story of entertainment, and my mother's voice commented on the craziness that cradled life. In the many times that she told the story, there were variations in her reflections—ranging from disbelief to comical abandon, to affirmations of her religious faith. But mostly I heard fear. The horror understood only by a parent facing the loss of a child. On some occasions, she would show the mark on her inner thigh, a ridged scar that hardened like a dark souvenir over the years.

The documents state that I was born in Bainbridge, Georgia, on January 31, 1952, and if it reads that way on the page, it holds a certain kind of truth. But for me, I came alive in Fort Pierce, Florida, when I was four-years-old, on that day that my pregnant mother dropped her homemade fishing pole and jumped into waist-high canal water to save her firstborn.

And that wouldn't be the last time my mother saved me, nor the last time she would reach out to me with a strength I've never had. But over the years, it would come back to me how abruptly and quickly things happen in life. That moment at the canal would remind me of the particular bond that she and I shared. Nothing psychic or unexplainable. Just a pure and unfettered connection of woman and child, mother and son. It was a connection that would be tested on many occasions, but remain tangible and incorporeal at the same time. It would always be present and real, and my life was, at the very least, a living testimony of her unquestioned and remarkable love.

*\*\**

The first time I met Tarzan was at the Lincoln Theater on Avenue D in Fort Pierce. It was perhaps 1958 when Uncle Buster first took me to the picture show.

My favorite uncle was Buster, and when I was six, he would come late Saturday mornings and take me with him to the movies in his Buick. It was a singular experience for me because it didn't include my younger sister, Paulette, or my play-brother and play-sister, Charles and Stephanie.

Once inside his Buick, Uncle Buster joked and laughed and sang a favorite song. Along the way, he would pick up one or two male friends, who would all talk at once at a breath-taking speed, a cloud of laughter floating as they sipped from and passed around a small paper bag. They whistled and whooped at girls, sometimes speaking to one or two who would edge up to Uncle Buster's lowered window. The conversation would undulate, the girl's soft voice moving into laughter and back to a flirtatious flow. The girl would see me watching from the back seat and shift to her cutesy voice to address my shyness. I would peer over Uncle Buster's seat and smile at the pretty face.

That prelude of girl chasing quickly faded upon arriving at Avenue D. After he parked the Buick, I followed Uncle Buster and his buddies into the Lincoln Theater, where popcorn aromas drifted over the sound of the machine crushing ice to be scooped into snowballs in paper cones, colored syrup sprayed over the icy mound. For its "Colored" audience, the Lincoln Theater played a combination of older movies and Hollywood's "B" movies. Inside was a great hall that engaged my eyes—the darkened interior where ornate walls with light posts and colorful, scalloped curtains hung. The house was full, as Black people drifted back and forth, or leaned into conversations, the level of talking as high as the sound coming from the screen. And on the screen, a looming world of images that hypnotized and overwhelmed me. The slanted aisles carried us to a row where we stepped over hugging couples and plunged ourselves into seats to watch the movie that had already begun, which was all right because we would sit through the next feature and into the next. Once the first movie began, it was a continuous showing of two feature films with previews and cartoons spaced between.

But it was the big screen that captivated me, that kept me excited to return every Saturday for the next fix. And over the two years of my early movie addiction, I was eventually allowed to walk to the theater by myself and sit all day and into the evening to watch each main feature twice. The first movie was usually a science fiction or horror picture—*The Mole People* (1956), *The Black Scorpion* (1957), *The Cosmic Monsters* (1958), or *The Crawling Eye* (1958)—with white heroes such as Richard Denning, John Agar, and Forrest Tucker. The second movie would be a cowboy picture, which inspired my playtime with Charles and Stephanie. James Stewart, Randolph Scott, Joel McCrea, Audie Murphy, John Wayne, Gary Cooper, and Robert Mitchum starred in movies such as *Winchester '73* (1950), *High Noon* (1952), *Tall Man Riding* (1955), and *The Man from Laramie* (1955).

The Lincoln Theater, being in a "Colored" neighborhood, didn't show high-profile, first-run movies like the "White" theater on the other side of town. I never attended that movie house; however, Uncle Buster told me that Black people could go, but they had to sit in the balcony. So, my earliest interaction with White people was via the big-screen images, and I picked up differences in language, use of words, and accents that were not a part of my neighborhood. Additionally, White people wore clothes much different than mine and lived in houses much larger than mine. It was a curious world where music played over the lives and actions of White people and where happiness reigned over everyone at the movie's end.

And then there was Tarzan, usually played by Johnny Weissmuller. I was first struck by Tarzan not wearing pants and a shirt like most of the White men in the science fiction pictures. Instead, he spoke broken English and had this wild, yodeling yell he used to call to animals, to call Jane and Boy, and to scare the Black jungle natives. The many Black jungle natives looked like me, yet they were different still. They resembled no one in my family or anyone living in my neighborhood. They belonged to the scary, black-and-white jungle of a place shown on the big screen map as "Africa" before the opening scene. That's where Tarzan lived—in that frightening place called Africa, filled with jungle natives, elephants, lions, crocodiles, and killer rhinos.

I couldn't understand how inextricable the cinema would become to my life—intellectually, emotionally, and psychologically. It gave me so many messages about race and gender, right and wrong, nobility and courage, love and hate. I was simultaneously entertained and shaped by the product made for a marketplace—a product made specifically for me. Forming my imagination and enjoyment, movies immersed me into a variety of environments that were different from my own, yet reflected in small ways the world that was mine alone.

\*\*\*

In the "Colored" section of Fort Pierce, the streets were named after letters from the alphabet. A collection of wrinkled black-and-white photos proclaimed that my early years as a toddler were on Avenue D, one of the major streets that permitted commercial vehicles to speed across the pathways of Black people moving in many directions. When my family moved to Avenue F, I was five. Our front and back yards were peppered with numerous trees. There was a palm tree bearing dates and a rubber tree in front. An avocado tree on the side shaded our flat-roof, stucco house. The wooden back porch steps led down to Daddy's vegetable garden, and yards beyond it, was a large, imposing mulberry tree. Sharing the outside, there were fire ants, salamanders, black snakes, green grass snakes, and occasional scorpions that wandered onto the screened, cement porch. The screen's primary purpose was to discourage mosquitoes from making their way inside the house. The interior space was small, but sufficient for our family of four. The other indoor inhabitants were brown mice that squeaked when caught within the snapping traps throughout the week. It was a common occurrence to see Daddy taking the trap outside in the morning, dropping a dead mouse into the garbage without ceremony.

Life extended out onto the dirt road of my block. The Akins family next door stopped by to share a piece of sweet bread or a story about someone "filled with the devil." Mrs. Purvis was diagonal from us, and she filled my parents in on the health issues of the neighbors. And then there was the house on the corner that belonged to people we seldom saw, but whose front yard offered up a large mango tree that served as the springtime expedition for me, Charles, and Stephanie when its branches sagged with ripe fruit.

For me, happiness became flesh through Charles and Stephanie Gifford, who lived with their grandparents across the street from us. For four years, the sum total of all things meaningful was being in their presence. Charles was two years older, while his sister, Stephanie, was one year older than me, and life was rooted within the seasons of games that we played—cowboys, dodgeball, kickball, hide-and-seek, marbles, and, of course, Tarzan.

Much later in life, I would read of anthropologists theorizing about the value of "play," reflecting on the connections between class, race, and disenfranchisement; postcolonial treatises critiquing the socialization of oppressed children as seen in their preference for being the "cowboy" instead of the "Indian"; and Black cultural theorists celebrating the presence of the oral tradition in the interactions between Black children. The language and expressions we used, seemingly created in the moment, would decades later be seen as examples of signifying or playing the dozens. But from my young eyes, it was simply my world in the "Colored" section of the segregated Florida town we lived in.

\* \* \*

I was a good student, based upon the adult rules of "minding" and "respecting grown folks." Mrs. Purvis was a kindergarten teacher, and she had a small school room situated at the rear of her house. Carrying my own paper bag lunch after receiving my Mama's goodbye kiss, I hurried along the dusty driveway to the rear of Mrs. Purvis' house. There were about fifteen students, and Mrs. Purvis moved us from one activity to the next. Reading, singing, creating art work, writing the alphabet, and playing together peacefully. With Daddy's nightly Bible readings and Mrs. Purvis's instructions, I learned to recognize words and to read. She engaged students with her patient, yet demanding teaching style, making certain we knew basic numbers, the spelling of our city and state, the names of plants and flowers, and parts of the human body.

During that year, there were two body-related experiences that revealed my confusing relationship to girls. The first incident made as little sense to me then as it does now, but it happened. I was staying at my Grandma Ella Mae's house on Avenue K, a short but dusty walk from our home. Grandma Ella Mae's house was a one story, box-like stucco building like ours.

Grandma Ella Mae was a gentle, funny woman to my childish eyes. It wasn't until I became an adult that I learned about the complications of her personal life in Georgia—and my mother's. But at that time, I was one of many grandchildren who sometimes spent a night with Grandma Ella Mae, often when Granddaddy Jesse was "away."

It turned out that Grandma Ella Mae's oldest son of six children, Junior, had a fondness for single women with children. On one occasion, I was staying overnight at Grandma's house when the oldest of Junior's brood, Darlene—a girl who was about eight—asked me if I wanted to play a game since we were forced to stay inside while Grandma napped. Just the mention of "playing" had me hooked, and I was always eager to experience any new game that I could rush back to share with Charles and Stephanie.

Darlene began the game by placing her forefinger over her lips to signal my silence as she sneaked over to peek into Grandma's room. Assured that Grandma was asleep, Darlene tipped back over and led me to the lumpy couch. She began tugging my pants down, and I instantly grabbed her hand. She responded with her forefinger placed against her lips again, this time a marker of a secret activity she was about to launch. I was curious about Darlene's game, but I didn't want my clothes off, and I certainly didn't want my pee-pee hanging out before this girl. But she was older and seemed to know what she was doing, an indication that she had played the game before.

With my pants and underwear to my ankles, Darlene pushed me face down onto the couch. I strained my vision over my shoulder to see what she was doing when I felt her weight over my legs. In a moment, I felt Darlene's mouth on my booty—kissing, biting gently, her lips moving up and down and from one cheek to the other. Then, she placed her nose between my cheeks, breathing deeply and grabbing my booty cheeks with both of her hands. I was confused and uncomfortable. I didn't understand the game, and I knew that I wouldn't be able to explain the game to Charles and Stephanie because I didn't know the rules. Besides, it was an indoor game, and we always preferred being outside. To be indoors meant that you were either sick or being punished. I tried to endure Darlene's game because she seemed to be so intent on playing it, but I squirmed when she kissed and touched and grabbed.

"Okay, now you do like that to me," she ordered. She shifted her body and pulled down her pants and panties, but I looked away. In my mind, I heard

Charles's voice speaking of the "nasty" between a girl's legs. And if Charles said it was "nasty," that set the limitations of what I was allowed to look at.

Darlene laid on her stomach and guided me with her hands to get on her back. But she had completely removed her pants and panties, and she opened her legs so I could fit between. And as I looked at her booty, I saw how round and chocolate it looked, the flesh curving from her waist to her thighs, connecting to long skinny legs.

"C'mon . . . like I did you," she repeated. I wasn't sure what to do because I still had no comprehension of what she had done to me. I mimicked her actions—kissing and lightly nibbling her fleshy bottom, and after a moment she opened her legs wider, one leg now off the couch. I placed my nose between her cheeks and breathed deeply as she had done. I detected an odor, not unpleasant, but certainly not the sweet fragrance I associated with mangoes.

"What y'all doing?" Grandma yelled, entering the living room.

I looked up and saw Grandma's angry face. And in the remainder of that day, a series of faces and questions were strung together. Grandma's tone established that Darlene and I did something wrong. Later in the day, under Grandma's watchful gaze, Daddy asked again what I was doing with Darlene.

I answered honestly: "Just playing."

But I had no name for the game or information on how the winner would be determined. I defended myself with tears and an innocent hunching of my shoulders as adult voices rolled over me. I don't remember if I got a whooping or not, or exactly how long I was surrounded by the whispering voices. I just knew that Darlene was to blame for my inquisition, and I never wanted to see her again. I vowed to myself that, thereafter, the only girl I would ever play with would be Stephanie.

However, at seven-years-old, when I was playing hide-and-seek with Charles and Stephanie at their house, another confusing incident occurred. The Gifford house, with its deep backyard with bushes and a garage, always offered possibilities for hiding. As Charles counted at the front fence before the house, Stephanie and I took off running, concealing ourselves in the garage. I made my way through the back door and to a far corner, hiding behind an old door that leaned against the wall, leaving enough space for me to remain hidden. I heard the back door creak, the light footsteps, and I knew immediately it was Stephanie.

"Find your own place," I told her. "You can't hide here!"

"Yes, I can," she stated. She covered her lips with her forefinger as the back door creaked again. We held our breaths and waited. The door groaned once more, but this time we knew Charles's radar had not detected our presence, as he'd left the garage.

"How long should we wait?" I asked Stephanie.

She lifted her forefinger again to silence me and leaned closer.

"What?" I asked.

She never responded. Instead, she grabbed the front of my pants and crammed her hand inside my underwear. I felt her grab my pee-pee, squeezing hard and fast. I was confused, and Stephanie's forceful grabbing became painful. As I tried to disengage her hand from my pants, she pushed forward and I fell backwards, her weight falling on top of me, her hand continuing to squeeze and pull. I didn't understand what she was doing or why, but I heard her chuckling, and I heard my voice, whispering at first, but eventually yelling, "Stop it!"

And then she rolled to the side, grabbed my hand, and forced it inside her panties. I didn't know exactly what I expected. My fingers became lost within a warm crease of flesh, a set of long lips that wrapped around my fingers. Yes, I had shared bathwater in the tin tub with my sister, Paulette, and I'm certain I wondered why she didn't have a pee-pee. But I never had to touch her as Stephanie was forcing me to. And then Stephanie grabbed me once more, pulling and tugging, sending a pain through my body. My suffering made her laughter increase until the garage door opened, and Charles rushed in.

"I know y'all in here!" he announced. "Ahn-hunh, I see your leg, Stephanie!"

Stephanie jumped up, running around him and out the open door. Charles saw me struggling to get to my feet, and he punched me hard in the shoulder.

"You're it!" he proclaimed, running out toward the front fence.

I slowly found my feet, my little pee-pee throbbing in pain. Tears filled my eyes, and I returned to the front yard. Charles laughed as he pointed. Stephanie laughed even louder. I cut a hateful look at her and kept walking out of the yard, headed for home. I heard Charles calling me back, confused as to why I was leaving. But in my tears, I couldn't talk, and I knew Stephanie was still laughing.

At the time, I hated both Darlene and Stephanie in those moments, telling myself that I didn't understand girls and that I wouldn't trust them—ever. Since then, I've wondered what Darlene and Stephanie had witnessed as kids. Which adults in their lives had carelessly, or deliberately, carried out their sexual fantasies without concern for their watchful, younger eyes?

\*\*\*

My Daddy existed in various personas for me when I was a kid. He was the man who disappeared early in the morning, responding to the honking car horn from his friend, Shorty, who drove Daddy and other men to work at the Indian River Packing House. He was also the man who would appear just before dark, his work clothes ill-fitting above the heavy work boots he took off at the door. This man, the disciplinarian, was the one who would "whoop" me if he found out I had committed some transgression during the day; the one who would say grace before dinner began; and the man who was quiet on most occasions. At the same time, there was my Daddy who sat on the edge of my bed at night, providing his own fashion of "tucking in" by reading Bible scriptures to me and Paulette in our twin beds. Daddy's calm voice delivered the Old Testament that held scary readings about killings and destruction. Another side of Daddy was the stories that he read from a book with no covers—folktales that led to some final, confounding observation such as "Every shut eye ain't sleep" or "It's a poor frog that won't praise its own pond." I looked forward to those bedtime readings, as frightening or confusing as some were. I looked forward to watching Daddy's stern face as he led us in our prayers.

On Sundays, I saw that stern expression return as he led my mother, sister, and me into Bethel Baptist Church. Sunday school, morning service, and sometimes Sunday evening service were all conducted in the large white building where scores of Black people gathered in their best clothes, shoes, and hats, all seemingly moving in one accord—from their greetings to their singing, and their prayers to their "amens."

Reverend Byrd, the short energetic pastor, commanded the pulpit once he began his sermon. He waved his white handkerchief in the air—not as a surrender to the devil, but as a flag to stir the emotions of the hungry congregation feasting on each staccato phrasing of words. Punctuated by the stomping and marching back and forth, his head tilted upward, looking to heaven for permission to take his brothers and sisters deeper into the rapture of spiritual revelations. One predictable response always came from Sister McAllister, the plump, hat-wearing woman who "shouted" when the sermon reached a crescendo. Sister McAllister would clear out the church members sitting nearby who avoided her wild movements—allowing for two, sometimes three, deacons to rush in, subdue her, and fan her sweating face.

Daddy and Mama both sang in the choir, and on occasion, they would each have a solo. My mother's soprano was familiar to me, as I often heard it around the house, but my father's deeper solo always fascinated me. His eyes would look straight ahead over the congregation as if envisioning some place that only he could see. His eyes sometimes closed slightly as he moved with the swaying choir members, side to side, riding the melody that ignited loud eruptions of "Yes, Jesus" or "My Lord," coupled with waving hands and possessed bodies squirming uncontrollably. I often wondered who that man really was—that part of my father that I only saw on Sundays.

Even then, I was learning lessons by experiencing our family dynamics and the connection to a Black world beyond our small stucco house. I didn't understand what most of it meant, didn't question why things were as they were. But I never feared the world that comprised my life, mostly due to the way in which my parents shaped that world—the boundaries placed upon it and the responsibilities taught. For me, life was a wonderful intersection of positivity, with an extended family who supported each other. It was my only concept of a normal life that held a steady security and warmth. Other than the weekly rides to the Lincoln Theater with Uncle Buster and to Bethel Baptist Church in our noisy Chevy, life was centered on that one block of Avenue F, where there was never any doubt that the next day would bring the same fulfillment.

\*\*\*

Living in the segregated South in the 1950s was a condition that couldn't be fully understood through my child's mind. Looking around and seeing my all-Black neighborhood, all-Black school, all-Black church, and all-Black movie theater was just normal. I was a blessed Black child—one who had two parents who lived a particular brand of Christianity. They held their racially conscious ideas on a back burner, keeping their bitterness and anger in check and hiding any fears they shared in the darkness. Frequently, when Uncle Buster came by, he would share phrases about "those damn crackers" or "dirty, filthy White folks" or say how "they treat dogs better'n Colored folks." And from time to time, when our neighbor, Mr. Akins, dropped in, he'd comment with a bit of head-shaking, that "them white folks sho' some crazy people." Yet, there were no direct lessons or doctrines about hating and deploring White people.

My world was all about seeing Black men and women along the dirt road of my block. Seeing them at church each Sunday. Seeing them at school as teachers, administrators, janitors, and peers. Within the Black world was my inner circle of family from my mother's side—her brothers (Junior, Buster) and sisters (Regina, Betty) who had their own families. There were also those close friends of my parents, like the Akins family next door. From Bainbridge, Georgia, they all trekked to Florida to find better job opportunities.

However, the first step outside of that community of family, friends, and Avenue F neighborhood was my schooling. Mrs. Purvis thought I was smart enough to leave kindergarten and go into the first grade. But since my sixth birthday was in January, the middle of the school year, public schools wouldn't take me in the fall of 1957 when I was five, except for one place: a Catholic school.

I don't know how Mama found the large, one-story building with a small reception area and one large instruction room filled with wooden desks. Beyond that instruction area, there was a back area with offices. It was a Catholic school planted on the edge of the Colored section of town that taught Black youngsters in grades first through third. My first problem was that I didn't know what a Catholic was. Second, the school administrator and teachers were White nuns whose black-and-white habits frightened me. I only saw their faces and hands, and their habits billowed while their long rosaries hung from their waists and clacked when they walked. I was particularly afraid of the long ruler that Sister Mary used on me and the other students when taken into the rear office area. Yes, my parents often "whooped" me with yard switches and belts, but these White nuns struck me with extreme force and silent power—a peculiar kind of execution. Sister Mary was not like the White women in the movies; she was more like the alien monsters in the science fiction pictures that threatened my very existence.

By the fourth grade and fifth grades, I was back into a segregated, public school not far from our Avenue F house. The kids were talkative and playful, and the Black teachers were smart adults who gave hours of instruction and hawkish stares during recess. Those Black men and women demanded respect and obedience in listening, reading, and writing, but offered quick and generous smiles and winks to confirm good grades and appropriate behavior.

My fourth-grade teacher, Mr. Russell, was a chocolate-skinned man who wore glasses. I believed that those glasses allowed him to see everything within the room, whether a subtle shifting of students' eyes, a shared joke, or a hasty note. He was stern, disciplined, and demanding, and his barber's razor strap was prominent on his desk, a visual reminder of the seat of power. There were occasional whoopings where the entire class received a strapping for any one student's indiscretion. But Mr. Russell was quiet, and he made us read aloud each day.

Mrs. Butler was my fifth-grade teacher, and my crush on her was undeniable. She was the prettiest woman I'd ever seen—even prettier than the White women in the movies. Her hair, her clothes, her smile—which I felt always widened when she looked at me. I knew I was her favorite student because she called on me to read out loud in class, and on those occasions when the entire class received a whooping, her paddling on my booty was always lighter than on the other kids.

And it was Mrs. Butler who introduced me to poetry. In class, she had me read selections from our coverless books, but she also had us write poems. In particular, I felt pride watching Mrs. Butler and Mama's reactions when they read my poem about President George Washington. I'm sure that poem was filled with the most nonsensical, bland, and silly phrases ever, but the responses from those two women showed me the connection between writing, reading, and delight.

\*\*\*

The movie *The Help* came to movie screens in 2011, but it displayed a version of the segregated South in which I was raised. On rare occasions, I joined my mother when she drove across the bridge to work at Mrs. Doyle's house. Mrs. Doyle was a short, thin White woman whose stringy hair always seemed to be in her face. She was pleasant enough, yet distant. Mama cleaned the house, which took several hours, and sometimes she hung up wet clothes outside on the clothesline strung across the yard between two leaning posts. I stayed outside, playing cowboys by straddling a long broom handle as my horse, hopping around and mimicking the hoofing noises as I rounded up crooks near the shed. The back of the shed was where I would also have to urinate if necessary during the day. However, one of the benefits of Mama working at Mrs. Doyle's house was that Mama always brought home a bag of food.

Daddy worked at the Indian River fruit-packing house just across the bridge on the White side of town. Several times a year, I would go with him to work, excited to travel in the car with him and his work pals—Shorty and Willie James being the two I remember most. They were loud talking men with endless streams of stories about people. They laughed generously, their overlapping voices folding into one another before crashing into louder decibels of enjoyment. At the packing house, Daddy planted me on a stool where I watched the large moving conveyor belts carry oranges that rolled forward like colorful circles. The bruised and damaged fruits were removed by Black hands as the selected oranges were deposited into wooden crates bearing the company's logo. Then, the grapefruits would take the same journey. But the best part was the sliced oranges that Daddy delivered when he checked in on me. The smells and sounds—both human and mechanical—were captivating.

Back at home, our daily meals revolved around buttered rice topped with stewed tomatoes and homemade biscuits. On a few occasions, we had the luxury of bacon on the plate. There were grits and fish—usually freshly caught and delivered by Uncle Buster or Mr. Akins from next door. On Sundays, fried chicken legs and wings were complemented with collard greens and cornbread, iced tea, and a homemade sweetbread or lemon pie. Although pork chops would be fried on occasion, beef and lamb were foreign concepts to our menu.

My childhood was filled with family, friends, church, and Saturday matinees. The stark change to my life occurred in the spring of my fifth-grade year, when my family relocated from Fort Pierce to Hyannis, Massachusetts—a move that submerged my family into "integration."

\*\*\*

## Uncle Buster
### (a saturday afternoon in 1958)

Anticipation held a sweet smell
on saturday afternoons,
morning cartoons passing the time until noon,
the sacred hour, when he skidded along the dirt road,
his Buick waxed and clean to cruise for girls.

Before the girls,
before he met his buddies from school,
or the ones that left school to work the tomato fields,
or the ones who sometimes needed a lift to their
cousin's house to borrow money,
Uncle Buster came for me.

his handsome face, black and shining with a smile,
his voice sailing across the patchy yard,
calling my name, floating like a warm whisper,
lifting towards the florida clouds in ripples of tenderness.

along the sun-slicked avenue, black people
criss-crossed and merged, unmindful of the segregation
of their southern town on a day without aggravation,
a saturday afternoon, a moment in time, filled
with their streets, their people, their day,
filling the alleys, barber shops, and favorite cafes

and in the midst of this dark paradise,
Uncle Buster, his hand on mine, took me to the matinee.
And when we reached the picture show,
neon signs and colored posters nestled
like jewels beneath the smell of popcorn and cones of snow,
inside, we saw the world of lights and dreams,
where people, white and black, loomed like tall angels
to fight the monsters, to save the weak, to do the good,
Uncle Buster and me, together laughed, like kings of hollywood.

# CHAPTER TWO

## Years That Ask, Years That Answer

In the novel *Their Eyes Were Watching God* by Black author Zora Neale Hurston, the narrator opens the third chapter with the observation, "There are years that ask questions and years that answer."[1] By my adolescent years, I began to understand that there would be an abundance of questions in life and fewer satisfying answers.

Living in the South, vigilance to the legal segregated system was the norm and expected path to follow. But after the journeys back and forth over several years, perhaps the customs became too much for my parents. On one occasion near Fayetteville, North Carolina, we were quite hungry. Mama had been looking for a grocery store, but nothing appeared on our stretch of the road. So, we finally stopped at a roadside diner, but there was no side opening marked "Colored." Never leaving us alone in the car, Daddy led us inside to be greeted by clusters of angry White faces. We huddled against the wall, watching the White waitress move back and forth, ignoring us. Then, her voice drifting loudly across the room, we heard the waitress' declaration to the chef across the order counter: "I ain't taking orders from no niggers."

"Wilbert, let's just go," Mama said, her voice weary.

Daddy breathed hard. He knew better, but he was tired from driving ten hours. And he was hungry. I saw the fat-faced White chef waddle from the kitchen and into the small dining area. Maybe the chef didn't want the situation to escalate. Maybe he didn't want police coming to cause a scene that would scare away customers. He approached us, his greasy apron stained and tight around his generous midsection.

"Y'all got money?" the chef asked Daddy.

"Yes, sir," Daddy assured him. "Just wanna get something t'eat for my wife and children."

"I can only make y'all some sausage sandwiches."

"That would do."

---

1. Zora Neale Hurston, *Their Eyes Were Watching God*, p. 20.

"Okay, y'all g'on back outside, and I'll bring 'em to you."

The chef disappeared into the kitchen, and the waitress demanded he cook her orders first. Eventually, he came outside to meet us, the greasy sandwiches already staining a brown paper bag. He told Daddy the cost, and Mama counted out the coins.

"Thank you kindly," Daddy said.

But the chef had already retreated into the restaurant without responding. Back in the car, Mama delivered the sandwiches to me and Paulette as Daddy drove back onto the road, eating his sandwich while driving. He kept looking into the rearview mirror until we were miles along the road. The car was quiet as we ate, and I fell asleep with a full stomach. When Mama shook me, we were at a Colored motel somewhere in the woods of North Carolina.

However, the most intense situation happened just outside of Valdosta, Georgia, the following year when we were traveling north. We stopped for gas. We all knew the plan; we only stopped for gas when it was absolutely necessary and that stop would be the only place to use a bathroom.

"What you want, boy?" a wiry White teen in overalls asked at the gas station. He was unkempt and years younger than my father.

"Fill up, please. And we want to use your bathroom."

"Colored bathroom out back," the teen stated.

Daddy, as usual, assigned himself to watch the White boy insert the gas nozzle and then go beneath the hood to check the oil and water—to ensure that the White hands would only touch the dipstick and not sabotage any engine wiring. Daddy nodded to my mother, and she led me and my sister around the side of the small building, past the men's and women's bathroom doors, and to the back where the "Colored" sign hung on an opened door. There was a tiny sink and toilet, but the room was stuffed with rusted barrels, boxes stacked atop a dirty floor, oily rags piled beneath the sink, and walls with layers of grunge—a testimony to spilled oil and intentional neglect. The only way to navigate the toilet was by executing a painful, pretzel-twisting maneuver. I could balance my weight on one leg and pee into the brown, crusted bowl of the toilet, but there was no way my mother and sister could negotiate the space. Mumbling under her breath, Mama stormed back to the front, pulling us with her, relaying to my father the pigsty conditions.

"Stop!" my father told the White boy. "Take the hose out! You ain't got a bathroom we can use!"

"Told you out back!"

"I ain't letting my wife use the place you got!"

"It's filthy!" my mother emphasized.

"Well, listen here! I ain't gotta—"

And that was the last thing I heard clearly before Mama pushed me and my sister into the back seat. I strained to hear the angry tones through the glass. I watched my father pointing at the car for the White boy to remove the gas hose. Watched the White boy's angry red face.

"Wilbert! Wilbert, let's go!" Mama urged, touching my father's arm. I heard the gas hose being yanked out by the White boy. Saw him snatching the money from Daddy's hand. Finally hearing Mama's urging voice, Daddy slid behind the wheel, slamming the car door. Daddy's anger burned the car's interior as he accelerated and steered out onto the highway. A rare moment of my mother cussing under her breath pricked my ears. Daddy was silent, his temper propelling the car forward.

"Slow down, Wilbert!" Mama warned, touching his arm. "Slow down!"

Paulette and I were silent, wrapped in the tension of the moment. I wanted my Daddy to turn around and go back and punch the White boy, like Joel McCrea and John Wayne did in the cowboy movies. I wanted him to grab that White boy by the shirt and toss him over the hood of the car. That's what Humphrey Bogart and James Cagney would've done! Why did Daddy run away? I was furious from the back seat, expecting my Daddy to stand his ground. But I was only left with disappointment, a confusion about what *didn't* happen, even as I understood what *did* happen.

That night, when we reached a Colored motel and were all unpacked in our one, small room, Mama sent me out to bring in the small wooden box of silverware from underneath the passenger seat. Following her orders, I felt nothing beneath the passenger seat. When I went around and reached beneath the driver's seat, I felt the box pushed back toward the rear, but as I pulled out a folded rag, unwrapped its heaviness, and looked inside—I saw a handgun. I touched it gingerly, wondering why Daddy didn't use it earlier at the gas station.

Years later, when reflecting on that day, I understood the context and larger picture of what happened. Yes, Daddy could have beaten that wiry White boy into a lifeless heap. He could have bloodied his face and broken his bones. But that same redneck could've crawled inside the station, phoned his buddies, described our car, and launched a mob of White Klansmen to catch us, gang-beat my father and me, gang-rape my mother and sister, and leave us all for dead. My father's control of his anger went beyond the Bible he read and recited, far beyond any fear that he may have had.

In that legally segregated world, his command of his anger was one of the most unselfish acts I'd ever seen—a sacrifice of his primal need to defend what was right. Daddy held back his anger, a monster that had been waiting for years, no doubt, to be released. He controlled that natural instinct to strike back and destroy the threat that stood before him. He chose first to protect the family he loved with the only effective weapon he had: swallowing his pride and rage.

\* \* \*

The film *Home of the Brave* (1949) frightened me. It was the first World War II film that convinced me that I never wanted to be in combat, disturbing me with the indiscriminate manner in which pain, suffering, and death found a soldier. When I first viewed the film, I was struck by the sequences of fighting and off-screen torture, and then there was the unforgettable presence of James Edwards, the Black actor who played the lead character, Moss. Moss was burdened by a number of concerns: being the only Black man in a squad of Whites; discovering his high school buddy and squad member, Finch—played by Lloyd Bridges—could actually call him "a yellow-bellied nigger"; and dealing with his physical paralysis in the aftermath of Finch's death.

The complexity of the characters and issues were thought-provoking, as *Home of the Brave* was categorized as one of four "Negro Problem" films that appeared in 1949. The other productions included *Pinky*, *Lost Boundaries*, and *Intruder in the Dust*. On the heels of the "Jewish Problem" movies of 1947—*Crossfire* and *Gentleman's Agreement*—"Negro Problem" films were dramas that explored the various ways in which being Black and/or biracial in American society posed serious, life-changing obstacles.

But in the summer of 1961, *Home of the Brave* was memorable for a different reason: I met Lloyd Bridges. Daddy worked as a short order cook at Luigi's Restaurant, while Mama was the housekeeper at the Yachtsman Hotel. The establishment was a popular venue, nestled next to Veterans Park Beach—the combined public picnic area and beach site—and the Hyannis Yacht Club, a private social club that boasted numerous sailboats in and around its short pier. Paulette and I took care of one another during the day—taking swimming lessons, eating homemade lunches, and playing on the swings. Then, in the late afternoon, we wandered back over to the Yachtsman to meet our mother.

The hotel was owned by Mr. Clifton, a jovial White man who was always kind, extending the use of the pool to me and Paulette. Although we accepted the invitation on a few occasions, swimming in the ocean was always our preference. The hotel pool and lounge area were too crowded with White people, and many stared at me and Paulette to remind us that we were outsiders. One day, when we followed Mama from the housekeeping office to the pool area, Mr. Clifton signaled us over.

"Melvin, Paulette . . . I want you to meet Mr. Sea Hunt," Mr. Clifton said, smiling.

I knew Mr. Bridges at once, with his blonde hair and angling eyebrows. His television show, *Sea Hunt*, was a popular series on the air at the time. I shook Mr. Bridges' offered hand, but I had no control over my voice. I became the silent nodder to his questions and genuine effort to welcome me and Paulette. He took several minutes to engage me in a discussion, but my nervous, chubby body became a mute pile of chocolate.

Somehow, I made it through the visit—overwhelming and satisfying all at once—excited that I had met a movie star. I relived the moment all through the night, hearing the voice in my head asking all of those things that I wanted to know. In particular, I wanted to ask if Mr. Bridges went into an actual jungle to make *Home of the Brave*. And if so, I'd ask if Mr. Bridges ever saw Tarzan.

In my boyish visions, the real world and the movie world were often inextricable. On one level, I knew they were different, but at times I wanted them to be the same. I knew that the White people on the big screen were different from me, but I liked them when I watched movies. The cinematic worlds were the places where I felt most comfortable. People, beautiful and handsome, always said the right things during music-cushioned emotional moments, and the endings were positive. That was the world that fed my dreams and imagination.

*\*\*\**

Before finally settling on Cape Cod, our seasonal trips back and forth created a rather interesting five-vehicle caravan of five families. Black people trekking north, making our exodus to the promised land, a new home to escape the Southern pharaohs of racism. We didn't need Moses, but we journeyed with faith in God and in one another. Nomads in our own country, our five cars completed a five-day parting of the Mason-Dixon line by driving ten hours a day. Five cars of prayer-believing Black people sharing food, fears, and faith while pressing forward. Our efforts exemplified what Martin Luther King, Jr., affirmed in the 1960s: "We must accept finite disappointment, but never lose infinite hope."[2]

When the decision was made to remain in Hyannis, my transition from a segregated South carried an additional personal trauma. I went from settings of all-Black kids who looked and spoke like me to spaces where I was the only dark face in a sea of Whites. To me, White kids were peculiar creatures who smelled like salt water, with their cornsilk hair, pink and pasty faces, and words spoken

---

2. Quoted in Holly Lebowitz Rossi, "Martin Luther King, Jr. on 'Infinite Hope'." (Https://guideposts. org/ inspiring-stories/stories-of-faith-and-hope/martin-luther-king-jr-on-infinite-hope/

with a quick-tempo and elongated vowels. Boston became "Bah-ston." Coffee was pronounced "cah-fee." Their last names were just as perplexing—Shaunessy, Papadopolous, Rossi, Brezeski, Zimmerman. These Irish, Greek, Italian, Polish, and Jewish people were all aliens to me. White people were suddenly not one amorphous entity, but ethnic groups crisscrossing my life as teachers, store clerks, ministers, auto mechanics, dentists, and doctors.

However, the most puzzling development at the time was the way in which Black people were divided on Cape Cod. In the South, a Negro was a Negro, and a sense of connection could be recognized in a nod of the head, a whispered greeting, or a wave of the hand. To my confusion, on Cape Cod, there were Portuguese, Cape Verdeans, and then . . . Negroes like me. Throughout my junior- and-senior high years, I was consistently reminded of that difference. My skin was darker, my nose was broader, my lips were thicker, and my hair—too nappy and unacceptable. Yet, to me the fair-skinned Portuguese and Cape Verdeans were no lighter in complexion than many of the Black people I knew in Florida, on my mother's side of the family in particular. Perhaps, it was the connection that my mother's side of the family had to Cherokee and Black intermixing—as did many coming out of Georgia and Florida—that made fair-skinned Black folk quite common in my life. But in Hyannis, the Portuguese or Cape Verdean differences were confirmed by particular surnames—Pena, Gonsalves, Gomes, Barrows, Santos, Monteiro, and Andrade. Their names became reminders of how different and separate I was, as my Southern Negro roots were beneath their acceptance.

So, between the ever-present Whites and the pervasive Cape Verdeans and Portuguese folks, I was an outsider, seeking connections like the ones I had with Charles and Stephanie. And there were occasions when I ached to be back in Florida, in the comfort of my true friends on Avenue F.

However, by the summer of 1963, when I was eleven and we had planted permanent roots on Cape Cod, my parents faced a bigger challenge when they discovered that the liberal veneer of Hyannis covered a reticence to rent property to Negroes, particularly those with children. My parents spent their post-work evenings searching for a home for us. That searching led to the local NAACP, which worked devotedly to help Black folks find permanent housing and employment. It was through that organization that my parents made their connection to those enlightened folks who were, collectively, Colored people.

Through that NAACP network, we eventually found a rental home that was actually a Quonset hut, a property owned by Julian Whitted, a Black man, and his White wife, Vi, who lived next door in their more traditionally styled house. Although our dome-shaped, one-story, two-bedroom, one-bathroom house looked strange in comparison to other shingled, picture-windowed homes in the area, it was a playtime treasure for me and Paulette to have a backyard that was a shrubb-filled, pine and birch tree landscape.

Mr. Whitted, our landlord, was a grumpy, Black man in his sixties who watched us with critical eyes. The attribute that softened this haunting presence was his wife—the short, talkative White woman who insisted we call her A'nt Vi. Although hidden inside her house most days, she sometimes appeared in her yard, offering a smile while chain-smoking cigarettes and carrying a glass of vodka and orange juice. Her remarks usually ended with the word "darling," a kind of coda of endearment. When I asked Mama why Mr. Whitted was married to a White woman, she didn't answer directly, but she shared that A'nt Vi once worked in New York as an assistant to an actress named Tallulah Bankhead. I didn't know anything about Tallulah Bankhead at the time, but years later on television, I saw her performance in Alfred Hitchcock's *Lifeboat* (1944). Soon, our life on Strawberry Hill Road became the new normal, and Mr. Whitted slowly became Uncle Julian.

\*\*\*

Out of the various churches we attended when we first arrived in Hyannis, my parents chose Calvary Baptist Church, a humble building with a modest steeple, resting in solitude along West Main Street. The choice of church was odd to me, considering that our relatives joined the Black congregation of the Zion Union Church on North Street. However, I came to understand that the decision was made deliberately by my parents—not with any disdain for our family members, but out of their effort to chisel out a distinct identity for me and Paulette from our extended families. Perhaps, it also their effort to bring me and Paulette into a closer proximity to White people to curb any discomfort about being around them.

So, following Sunday morning visitations at a couple of churches, my parents decided on Calvary Baptist, with its overwhelmingly White membership, where worshiping was quite different from Bethel Baptist Church in Florida. There was no large, robed choir singing emotionally, clapping excitedly, and lifting hands and spirits to the Lord. Instead, Mrs. Rounds, a quiet White woman who smiled generously at us, played the piano while several women—including my mother at times—would share a rather reserved rendition of a selection from the church's hymnal. There was no shouting in the congregation, and either Daddy or Deacon Williams would usher any new visitors to the many available seats along the padded pews.

When we first attended Calvary Baptist, the lead pastor was a man named Paul Cranston. He was a tall White man, and his wife and daughters were friendly and sincere. Pastor Cranston attracted school kids—from elementary to high school—to attend the church, forming a youth group that met regularly. Going to church was enjoyable, and though Pastor Cranston's messages sometimes made my eyes heavy, the welcoming friendship of him and his family made the long Sunday mornings bearable.

Calvary Baptist became a significant part of my life, and as I moved toward turning twelve, my family and Pastor Cranston's family shared a closeness. As lead pastor, he welcomed youngsters of all races and backgrounds into the church.

\*\*\*

On one occasion, Daddy and Mama allowed us to miss our church services at Calvary Baptist to travel to Sea Street and park along the side of the road. Joining many others who congregated in the early morning, when the cheers erupted, I saw the police officers motorcycles leading several dark-colored sedans.

"There he is," Daddy announced, pointing.

President John F. Kennedy's pale face glowed inside the tinted windows, his waving hand blessing those who applauded and shouted. His route was a familiar one to Hyannis residents, one that would lead to Saint Francis Xavier Church—the small, ornate Catholic church on South Street. On a later occasion, we bypassed the parade route, drove to the Catholic church, and stood in line to gain admission to the eight a.m. mass. My parents, long standing Baptists, led us inside, sharing their thoughts about Jesus and their admiration for President Kennedy. Inside the church, Jesus and Mary were visible—the crucifixes with Jesus's tortured White body and the paintings of a young, White Mary looking blissfully toward the blue heaven speckled with clouds and chubby angels.

Stand up. Kneel. Stand up. Repeat the Latin words. Make the sign of the cross. Cling to your rosary. Kneel. Pray. Listen. Mass was a ritual of exercise, where the hour-long setting was crammed with body movements and a Latin liturgy of indecipherable words.

But there in front, I saw the back of his head—President John F. Kennedy. A White man who held such respect among my parents and other family members. He was a "precious Lord" in a time of trouble. A friend to the Negro. His name remained such a sacred one within our home. "Jack" Kennedy and his brothers represented a world of possibilities. The promise of a country that understood that its greatness depended upon those people who had the least power, but showed the most faith and commitment as a passionate army of citizens. Christian soldiers—both Protestant and Catholic—standing at the dawn of a new day in America.

As I watched my parents' enthusiasm for glimpsing President Kennedy, and as I listened to their conversations at home, I understood at an early age how important politics were. I grasped the importance of what a leader stood for and how it resonated to them personally, but also to the Negro community. I also understood that White men were not automatically approved because they were White. For all the praise my parents assigned to Jack Kennedy, there were extensive criticisms of Strom Thurmond, George Wallace, and Barry Goldwater.

At home, my mother read the newspaper aloud, sharing political content with Daddy. When she watched television news, she recapped the crucial points when Daddy got in from work. When she listened to the radio broadcast, she told us about the local developments and the national events that affected Black folks. My sister and I listened and learned.

Although my parents remained vigilant about local politics, they knew the significance of Medgar Evers; the March on Washington; Dr. King; Swerner, Goodman, and Cheney; Selma; and the Edmund Pettis Bridge. They discussed what was important to Black people and their Christian faith, and I became aware of the myriad ways in which people who never met us—senators, representatives, ambassadors, presidents—were constantly making decisions that affected our lives. My parents articulated that those people in power had to be watched, questioned, and held accountable for what they said *and* did.

\*\*\*

My seventh grade English class was taught by Mr. Moore, who had been an actor in New York, but was now teaching composition and literature in a way that captured my attention. Edgar Allan Poe, Emily Dickinson, Ambrose Bierce, Stephen Crane, e.e. cummings, and Robert Frost were White writers I never heard of before, but I was pulled into their poetry and fiction. And then, there was Black writer Langston Hughes, who became my favorite author! Hughes wrote pieces in every genre: poetry, fiction, drama, essays, and, as I learned years later, scripts for movies with all-Black casts.

The other love I had at the time entered my life during an auditorium assembly—the alto saxophone. The gathering was a strategy for introducing students to musical instruments by allowing them to look, listen, and touch. But there was no rival to the brassy, woodwind, sultry, hypnotic sound of the saxophone. I hurried home that day and told my parents about the beautiful thing I saw and heard. I confessed that I wanted to take lessons and play the instrument, begging with my eyes and my excited attitude. When I received their "yes," I was the happiest, chubbiest Black kid on Cape Cod.

\*\*\*

The biggest disturbance to that happy world of food, movies, and music were those unexpected occasions when I clashed with the Cape Verdean and Portuguese kids. They attacked me with their looks of disdain and shared laughter as I walked by or deliberately snubbed me by turning away and not seeing me at all. Most times, it was name-calling and critical comments about my appearance, and Daddy listened quietly to my comments one evening at dinner. He paused with his forkful of food in the air and looked at me.

"Don't let nobody mistreat you, Melvin. Stand up for yourself."

I nodded, knowing in general what he meant but not knowing the specifics. But Daddy's words reverberated during those instances when loud talking and name-calling led to the brink of a physical fight at the school bus stop, in the school hallway, or during gym class. My fists were up and ready as I danced around in my Cassius Clay-fashion to confront some wavy-haired, fair-complexioned Cape Verdean kid who peppered me with verbal attacks of "fatso," "beady haired," "big lips," "Blackie." When the insults heightened to attacks on each other's mothers, profane cussing erupted. Fortunately, at those moments, the school bus would appear, or when at school, a teacher would approach, ending any real exchange of fisticuffs, often to the disappointment of the vampire-like onlookers who were thirsty for a bloody fight.

I was glad no punches ever landed on my face in those confrontations, but more importantly, I was proud that I stood up for myself like Daddy instructed.

\*\*\*

By my first year of high school, my parents were able to build our house on Mitchell's Way in Hyannis. Built from the basement up, we had this wonderful three-bedroom home with a back patio and ample space for Daddy's vegetable garden. I knew nothing about the complexities of home ownership, but I saw their pride. I understood that something remarkable had happened for my family.

However, even with the new home, I maintained my selfish teen focus of not fitting in with my peers. So, I turned to three places where I could find acceptance and some semblance of recognition. First, I placed my energy into the saxophone my parents rented and my participation in the high school's music groups. The woodwind section became my family away from home, where the rhythmic sounds merged in a wonderful network of parade marches and show tunes. It was in the concert band, marching band, orchestra, and jazz band where I learned that some White kids were outsiders like I was. I came to understand that even White kids struggled to exist within the unwritten policies of popularity.

Another part of my life became my participation in the Troop 55 Boy Scouts. My scout troop met weekly in the basement hall of a church on Main Street, which had permanent basketball backboards and nets. I met a number of White guys from that troop—Greek, Irish, Italian—but there was one other Black boy who looked like me named Reggie McDowell. Reggie was tall and reserved, and he loved playing basketball. I discovered that he didn't live too far from my house—close enough that I could ride my Schwinn 3-Speed to visit him. He and his family lived on Straightway Road, and his father was a stern, quiet, ex-military man. For all the warmth Mr. McDowell lacked, Mrs. McDowell made up for it. So, too, did Reggie's two brothers, Gary and Darren, and his sister, Claire. At that time, I couldn't have known that Reggie would continue to be a friend and force in my life throughout our fifty-plus years of friendship.

However, the person who saved me from the cave of my shy, awkward personality was a Black boy whose name suggested he was Portuguese, but he had a personality that confirmed an openness and kindness. I first met James Tobey as he walked along Mitchell's Way, passing our new house before disappearing toward homes in the distance. One day, for no particular reason, he nodded as he passed and said "hello." Eventually, the greetings became conversations, and we found the primary cornerstone for bonding: music. James was a drummer. And in his head, there must've been a tsunami of beats and rhythms that moved him as he walked from one side of town to the other. He and his mother lived in a small apartment on North Street, closer to the town's center. His older sister lived in the apartment beneath them. Being in a small, two-bedroom apartment on the second floor, James had no space to permanently set up the drums, so rubber drum pads attached to thin boards served as his instrument for practice.

In James' room, we'd sit for hours as he placed a succession of vinyl albums on his turntable, positioning his drum pad before him to play along to the music. He would describe the rhythmic streams, choruses, hooks, and back beats, showing how the percussionist provided a foundation to the song. He was a guru of rhythms, his head constantly moving as he narrated the rhythms of drummers like Gene Krupa, Jack DeJohnette, Buddy Rich, and Elvin Jones. But in the 1960s and into the 1970s, he was down for a wide range of rock as well, whether we listened to The Young Rascals, The Who, Three Dog Night, or Grand Funk Railroad. He was no stranger to R&B, as his turntable hosted the Temptations, Marvin Gaye and Tammi Terrell, The Four Tops, Smokey Robinson and the Miracles, and Stevie Wonder. He was a musicologist without a degree, and those hours spent in James' room were marvelous moments of connection and liberation. James nicknamed me "Kool," an affectionate way of adopting me into his musical brotherhood. Our weekly visits to the music store on Main Street was a ritual of gathering the latest *Downbeat* and *Circus* magazines in order to keep up with the musicians, bands, and successes in jazz and popular music. It was the genesis of decades of friendship and brotherhood.

James and his mother lived in a second floor, back apartment, but in the upstairs, front apartment lived another Black kid, Mark Fernandes. Mark was fair-complexioned and the coolest, best dressed, most articulate Black kid I ever met. He could talk to girls and knew all the new dance moves. He was a social bee who floated from one group of kids to another—White, Black, didn't matter. With blood connections to numerous Cape Verdean and Portuguese families, Mark was the personality who moved in and around circles that James and I didn't. Mark was our contact and often the translator for the world of the cool Black kids who always seemed to be going somewhere fun. Sometimes, Mark joined us in James' room, but the three of us usually hung out at the movies and along Main Street at the Signor Pizza parlor or the Dragon Lite Restaurant, where I secretly gazed at people who were called Chinese. Other than the restaurant, the only places I saw Chinese people were in movies or on the *Bonanza* television series.

James and Mark were no strangers to my house, as they frequently dropped by to visit, talking to Mama while sitting at the dining room table. Throughout our high school years—James and Mark were one year behind me at Barnstable High School—we were a trio that became a visible trinity of friendship. When the NAACP Youth Group was formed, the three of us were the young leaders that the adults confidently praised. To adults, we were "good kids" who were respectful and concerned with our education and futures. James had a part-time job at a car wash and then the Candle Factory. Mark worked at a fast-food restaurant on Main Street. And I worked part-time with Daddy's self-owned business, Donalson Cleaning Service.

Throughout high school, James and Mark were my disciples of deliverance, their acceptance of me without question or qualification. That's why, during my senior year, I was surprised by Mama's serious, carefully shaped inquiry in our living room. Her eyes studied me closely as she leaned forward.

"Melvin, there's something I want to talk to you about," she began.

"Yes, M'am."

"You're going out with Mark and James tonight?"

"M-hmm," I murmured, confirming the obvious.

"I know Mark is your friend, but . . . I was wondering. Has he ever *said* anything to you? I mean, what do y'all do when you go out together?"

I was lost. I searched for some semblance of what her question was about. Even more difficult, I attempted to put into words, for an adult, the significance of "hanging out." Hanging out, just being together—that's what we did. It was something "to do," but more so, it was somewhere and someone "to be."

"Well, we just, you know, drive around. Sometimes we go to James' place and listen to music. We walk Main Street . . . go to a movie. Why?"

"You see," she began. "Some people been talking . . . about Mark. That he's a little on the . . . sweet side."

I searched every possible meaning of "sweet" in my limited vocabulary.

"Mark has his *ways*," she added. "But I know he's a good boy. I just want to make certain that nothing's been happening."

"I don't know what you mean, Mama."

"Okay. I just want to make sure you're okay. And if there's anything you want to talk about, me and your Daddy are here."

"Yes, M'am."

She smiled and moved away, leaving me examining what had just transpired. And then, weeks later, it hit me—the winds of cruel words swirling along the high school hallways, the bus stop, the band room. *Fairy, Queer, Light in the Pants, Homo, Faggot.* Mark's image floated before me, and I searched my limited mind to fit the Mark I knew into the suspicious realm of words that identified him as "one of those." Thereafter, I became conscious of what Mark said and did, but I never said anything to him. I wouldn't do or say something that would hurt him. He was my friend, a friend for life that I didn't want to lose.

\*\*\*

In the early summer of 1967, like other fifteen-year-old boys, I was anxious to get a job and have my own money. I found a dishwasher's position at a restaurant, but it left me too hot and sweaty as I stood over steaming water and food-crusted pots. I moved on to a gardener's position, and I weeded, watered, and cut lawns, but the constant bending over and humidity made me nauseous.

So, during that summer, Daddy helped me get a job with his former boss, a Black man who owned a custodial business. I was teamed with Benny, a tall Cape Verdean boy, but we never spoke much to one another. Dropped off daily at the small but busy Hyannis Airport in the morning, Benny and I cleaned bathrooms, swept floors, and polished and dusted furniture in the wide lounge area.

One day, Mr. Washington—the elderly, Black man who served as a uniformed porter and information specialist—came to me. Benny and I didn't pay him much attention because he always berated us for being a part of a younger, disrespectful generation. He was the worst part of the job, and the one part we couldn't escape as he hawked us while we completed our tasks. As I collected full trash bags from their metal containers, he edged up to me.

"Hey, Melvin," he smiled wryly. "Come here."

"I can hear you while I work, Mr. Washington."

"Boy, I said c'mere!" he replied angrily.

I sighed, lowered the bag, and stepped within spit drops of him. Then, he gave me his I-know-more-than-you smile.

"Guess who just got off the plane."

"I don't know, Mr. Washington."

"Guess, boy! Your favorite movie star."

Performers were consistently arriving by air throughout the summer, mostly older singers and actors performing at the Melody Tent, the popular Hyannis entertainment venue. I figured it was just another old White singer who sometimes surfaced on *The Ed Sullivan Show* to belt out a show tune.

"Mr. Washington, I don't have time—"

"—See, that's what's wrong with you kids!" he insisted. "You're too impatient, but don't know nothing! I'm trying to tell you that Sidney Poitier is inside!"

Hearing that name, I was deaf to Mr. Washington and the world around me. I was suddenly within a dream, my legs churning away, my body floating toward the front doors. Breathing hard and sweating, I sucked the humid air, scanning the doors that opened to the outside tarmac. I searched the lounge area. No Sidney Poitier. As I turned to exit again, I glanced at the wall where three wooden phone booths were all closed with customers using the pay phones. I focused on the middle booth and clearly saw him—the phone against his ear, his eyes fixed directly on me. He smiled and waved! I was mindless, incapable of controlling any part of my body. I sensed my mouth was open and my eyes stared in a daze reminiscent of Stepin Fetchit, the Black American comedian who embodied the plantation stereotypes. Suddenly, my body was running, not stopping until I was outside at the end of the front walkway, sucking deeply for breath that wouldn't come.

After finding my senses again, I felt my heart racing. An inner voice urged me back inside. "Tell him you saw him in all his movies, fool! *To Sir, With Love* at the beginning of the summer—four times in one weekend! At that point, I hadn't seen some of his earliest movies, and *In the Heat of the Night* and *Guess Who's Coming to Dinner* wouldn't come out until later in the year. I felt my body heading back inside, the airport sounds rising around me. I tipped to the phone booth again. But he was gone! I moved briskly into the building, searched quickly in all directions. No Sidney Poitier. I saw Benny emerging from the men's restroom, pushing a dustmop.

"Benny, did you see him? Sidney Poitier?"

"What're you talking about? I ain't seen no Sidney Poitier."

I moved with more urgency, through the building and out to the back entrance. I saw a plane with people stepping out, descending the mobile stairway, and moving toward the single gate where I stood. No Sidney Poitier. Back inside. Out the front doors again. Looking into taxis. Watching moving vehicles creeping from the curbside. I rushed back toward the front doors. My disappointment in myself left me hollow inside. I had missed a once-in-a-lifetime opportunity. I crumbled into a sad lump of sorrow. I sat on the curbside near the garbage container and cried.

\* \* \*

James and Mark were my brothers during high school, but in February 1967, I was caught off-guard by the birth of my biological brother, Brian. Fifteen years younger than me, I was unsure how to interact with a baby. Since the house had belonged to me and Paulette for so long, it took time for me to comprehend this stranger. Yet, as he grew older, my responsibility to him increased. In many ways, I felt more of a father than a brother to Brian, particularly as he was becoming a toddler when I left for college.

The house's interior was re-organized for him to navigate without danger threatening at each table edge. And the house became a relay station where neighbors and friends stopped to touch, smile, and purr over the smallest person in the home. The house took on different dimensions of family—baby clothes, diapers, toys, bassinet.

I saw my parents responding to the new infant with gushing words and lingering smiles. Admittedly, I was jealous of the time and attention that Brian received that summer and over the following years from my father. My brother's ice hockey games, in particular, began in his elementary school days and continued through high school, and he was excellent in varsity football, ice hockey, and baseball. Daddy made the time to attend my brother's practices and games, despite his demanding work schedule. I was glad for Brian, but in my teenage mind, I was envious in ways I never expected to be.

\* \* \*

Rita Mendes. At sixteen, in the fall of my senior year, just as my world of friends and school were shaping me in many positive ways, there was the world of girls that never quite found synchronicity for me. Ever since my experiences with Darlene and Stephanie in Fort Pierce, I wasn't quite certain what to make of girls. I looked from a distance and imagined what would happen when I was alone with a girl. Would it be like the movies where music would swell as we sat snuggling on the beach or running hand in hand along the surf? Or would it be more like looking into each other's eyes and dancing closely as the kids did on *American Bandstand*?

Rita and her family lived on Pinewood Avenue, a five-minute walk down the street from my house. I was a paperboy at the time, delivering the daily *Cape Cod Standard Times* on my 3-Speed Schwinn with my full saddle baskets arching over the rear tire. When I first saw her, we both smiled. The second time, we waved. By the third occasion, I knew at what time she was usually sitting on her front steps, so I made sure I stopped at her house first so I was fresh and lotioned up—as opposed to the sweaty mass of chubbiness I became after my twenty or so deliveries. I thought I would be dead after "hello"—which was the extent of my conversation—but to my surprise, she carried the discussion. She asked *me* about my family, my classes, and my interest in movies. When she mentioned movies, I knew I was in love. Not long after that, she suggested we take a walk across Mitchell Way into the field behind the trees where we could "talk."

Rita was in her senior year. She was Black Portuguese, but she never emphasized her background. More importantly, she never seemed to mind my chubbiness. Her hair was a collection of soft brownish curls teased out around her face, not the tight nappy hair that plastered my head. And her voice was softly hypnotic. At that time, my crushes were on two White actresses in particular: Hayley Mills in movies and Patty Duke from television. Rita was the first *Black* girl that excited me. And I was very interested in going for walks in the field with her, where we talked about all that she did during the day and all that she planned for the weekend.

"So, what's your favorite drink?" she asked me one day.

"Coca-Cola."

"No, Melvin . . . I mean, well, I like vodka and orange juice."

"Oh," I said. My mind raced with what to say. And I thought of the bottles I saw at my parents' parties in the basement. "Rum."

"Mm, yes, I had that once. So, where do you think you're going to college?"

"College? I don't know. You?"

"Four C's. Cape Cod Community College."

"Oh, the new school."

Then, she looked at me and smiled.

"You have a girlfriend?"

"Me? No."

She stepped closer to me. Placed her arms around me and pulled me into a kiss. A light meeting of the lips. I wasn't sure of what I was supposed to do, so I peeked to watch her expression. She came up for air and pulled me into her kiss again—harder, her tongue plunging into my mouth. I pulled away quickly, confused.

"What's wrong?" she asked.

"I have to be home . . . s'pose to be home now."

"Okay."

She grabbed my hand, and we walked across the field, through the trees, and onto Mitchell's Way. The remainder of the night was pure joy as I relived the kiss in my head. And we met several times after that, walking over into the field, sitting in a clearing, holding hands, talking . . . and kissing.

I told James about Rita, and he was happy for me. I hoped he could help me with a bigger challenge—where to go for a date. I didn't have a car. There was no public transportation in Hyannis. And my weekly cash flow was more of a trickle. The only possible date that came to mind was walking to the movies. James thought that was a good idea, and he would spot me some extra money if I needed it.

Soon after that pact with James, my mother said she wanted to talk with me. Nothing new. We often talked as I flowed to and fro. But her attitude was serious as we sat in the corner of the living room.

"You know the Mendes girl down the street?"

"Yes, m'am."

"Someone told me she saw you walking with her on Mitchell's Way."

"Yes, ma'm," I said, beginning to sweat. "Just walking."

"Is there anything you want to tell me?"

"No."

"You sure?"

I was quiet beneath her stare, wondering why she was asking questions. I chose silence as my defense.

"Okay. Melvin, do you know that Rita is pregnant?"

Pregnant? As in having a baby? The air rushed from my chest. A heavy pressure crushed my lungs. I searched the movie archives in my head for what made sense. Kissing and babies? Sean Connery kissed Claudine Auger in *Thunderball* (1965), and Dean Martin kissed Ann-Margret in *Murderers' Row* (1966), but no one became pregnant. And how did my mother know about Rita's condition?

"No," I said in a low voice. "I didn't know she was pregnant."

"Okay," Mama continued. "I needed to ask."

"Yes, ma'm."

I stumbled to my room and collapsed on the bed. My mind exploded in a cacophony of sounds, and eventually I realized it was my tears I heard. A few weeks later, Mama told me she heard that Rita had "been with" Bobby Jones. Bobby, a Black man in his late twenties, worked at the Colonial Candle Factory and, according to Mama, he had a "reputation." *He* was the father of Rita's baby, and though I never heard from Rita again after that, I figured that Mama's version was the truth.

I don't know if Rita ever made it to college. But I was left with a deep scar along my heart with the sudden omission of Rita from my life. And once again, a girl was the origin of the pain I experienced and couldn't erase. Even as I felt pulled to girls as my body changed, I didn't know if I could ever trust a girl. Whenever I got close, it left me suffering. So, I found solace in my imagination and fictions I could create and control in my head, where girls were pretty and forgiving of my chubbiness. Where they talked to and kissed only me.

\* \* \*

I'm not certain when our basement became the nexus for Mama and Daddy's parties. Perhaps, it was their renovations—carpeting the cement floor and stairway; placing wood paneling on the wall; creating a separate bedroom with twin beds; and fashioning the small living room area with furniture and new lamps. The Saturday night occasions came along in frequent waves as family and friends showed up with potluck dishes and bottles in brown paper bags. They were enjoyable gatherings that me and Paulette watched from the stairway, as the grown folks dismissed the weekly dramas at work or personal problems already shared with Mama during a phone call. In the basement, the joyous dance steps and the laughter-filled air was thick, as the stack of 45s dropped in rigid consistency. Martha Reeves and the Vandellas, Wilson Pickett, Sam and Dave, Otis Redding, Jackie Wilson, The Supremes, Percy Sledge, The Temptations, Aretha Franklin, The Four Tops, James Brown, Gladys Knight and the Pips, Stevie Wonder. And in the middle of the stack was Ruby and the Romantics' "Our Day Will Come." I discovered it was my parents' favorite song . . . *their* song. Everyone expressed themselves in their party outfits and jokes—no arguments, no drunken staggering, and no drugs heavier than the alcohol sitting on the small table. For me, it was a chance to see my parents possessed by happiness while enjoying people they cared for.

However, no matter how late the festivities ended the night before, Sunday morning always meant Sunday school and church services. Whether I wanted the church in my life or not, there was an expectation that it would be a cornerstone of my life. So, I remained at Calvary Baptist Church primarily to please my parents. In spite of my commitment as I approached high school I discovered another layer of politics inherent within organized religion.

At one point, Pastor Cranston had to respond to another higher power that loomed over him—the Baptist Association. He was reassigned to another church out of state, and in his absence, the Association sent temporary preachers to helm Calvary Baptist. Eventually, the permanent position was bestowed on Pastor Drabkin, a minister with a rather icy personality.

My resentment crystallized when Pastor Drabkin targeted two of my friends at church, Henry and Melanie. Henry was an outgoing kid who had a mellow way about him, but his personality merged with Melanie's vivaciousness and energy. Henry's father was Black and his mother White, while Melanie's parents were both White. This racial distinction prompted Pastor Drabkin to commit himself to terminating their pronounced boyfriend-girlfriend relationship. Pastor Drabkin reached into his Old Testament bag and pulled out the dusty, worn interpretation of Genesis 6:19-20: *"You are to bring into the ark two of all living creatures, male and female, to keep them alive with you. Two of every kind of bird, of every kind of creature that moves along the ground will come to you to be kept alive."* And he pronounced that people of different races were not the "same kind." Eventually, Melanie and her parents acquiesced to Pastor Cranston's reduction of that Genesis passage, and Henry moved away from the church. Melanie, soon afterward, left the church as well. Then, during a short period, other young people also drifted away.

If Pastor Drabkin had only taken the time to read a few verses further as I later did, he would have confronted Genesis 7:2-3: *"Take you seven of every kind of clean animal, a male and its mate, and two of every kind of unclean animal, a male and its mate, and seven of every kind of bird, male and female, to keep their various kinds alive throughout the earth."*

Eventually, Pastor Cranston was recalled, and until the Baptist Association sent a replacement, the church leadership fell upon two of its deacons—my father and Deacon Williams. Deacon Williams was a kind White man, always ready with a smile while consistently fingering the middle of his balding head. Due to the church's loss of high school age students who were Pied-Pipered away by Pastor Drabkin, I became the sole high schooler in church by my senior year. By default, I was sent to Deacon Williams' adult class, and I had numerous questions regarding the Bible:

"Adam and Eve had two children—Cain and Abel—and Cain murdered Abel and was sent away to the land east of Eden. The scriptures say he had two wives.

*But where did the wives come from if Adam and Eve had only two boys at that point?"*

"*In the book of Job, the scriptures suggest that God and the Devil had an agreement to test Job's faith by destroying his worldly possessions. But since God knows all, He already knew that Job would remain faithful, so why go through the experiment in the first place?*"

Deacon Williams stammered through my inquiries through a frozen smile, receiving little help from the other adults in the class as they were attempting to understand the questions. On one Sunday as the class was ending, I posed another question to Deacon Williams:

"*Since God knows all and is the Alpha and Omega, then God already knows who will be saved and who will go to hell. Therefore, what is the need for human beings to live in a world of pain, disease, and death? God already knows who will be saved and who will not, right?*"

Mercifully, the central bell ending classes pinged, and Deacon Williams was saved. He dismissed class and rushed from the room. The various episodes at Calvary Baptist Church opened my eyes to a number of issues. It was then that I lost my religion, even though years later in Germany, I would experience my *Faith*. That distinction between "religion" and "faith" has shaped my life to the present, urging me to stop seeking answers in ministers and deacons who retreat to their problematic interpretations.

\* \* \*

The summer of 1968, before my high school senior year, I took a full-time position working a job at Smuggler's Beach Motor Lodge. The hotel was situated north of Hyannis, just beyond the small towns of Bass River and South Yarmouth, on South Shore Drive at Rum Runner's Lane. The name of the beach resulted from the history of it being part of the illegal rum smuggling that occurred during Prohibition, and the local lore was that Hyannis Port's most famous family had its wealth rooted within that illegal alcohol trafficking.

The two-story hotel was an eye-catching establishment that stretched from the roadside to its rear swimming pool that overlooked its private beach on the south end. My mother, in her position as the head housekeeper, got me the job there, just as she had arranged maid positions for other family members and friends. As the housekeeper's assistant, I spent the day collecting used bed linen and towels from the guest rooms and delivering fresh laundry to the maids. Doubling as the pool boy/beach boy, I routinely hurried to the pool to make sure that fresh towels were plentiful on lounge chairs that had to be clean. Trash, empty beverage containers, forgotten robes, sandals, and toys were all my responsibility. At the same time, I was a bell boy who rushed to the main office when I was called to assist arriving guests who were too tired or lazy to carry their own luggage. The latter duty held the benefit of receiving generous tips.

My mother obtained her position due to her experience at the Yachtsman Hotel and after interviews with the owner of the Smuggler's Beach Hotel, Mr. David Adelman. Mr. Adelman, a short, wiry man with a curled mustache, sported a long cigarette holder with a burning cigarette constantly present. He usually wore a sport jacket, an open shirt collar, Bermuda shorts, and topsiders with socks. He was an articulate, business-oriented man, and he was kind and giving to me and my family. Mr. Adelman was the first millionaire that I ever met, his money coming from his New York-based business that made imitation diamonds and jewels placed into various settings. Despite having a wife and adult children, Mr. Adelman resided at the hotel by himself. He had the ability to make the workers feel that we were doing him a favor by working at the hotel, and when he heard that I was a movie and television fan, he smiled cryptically.

His smile materialized in a specific manner about midsummer when I was summoned to the front office. I saw Mr. Adelman at the front desk speaking with a man whose voice immediately caught my attention. It was actor Lee J. Cobb from *The Virginian* television series (1962-1971), but he had been more recently known for his roles in the *Our Man Flint* movies with James Coburn. Meeting him, I stuttered, stringing elliptical phrases together while staring uncontrollably. I finally heard the request to carry his bags, which I did by floating before him to his room. He was vacationing and appearing in a local summer theater production, and throughout his stay, I made certain I was the one who answered the call to run errands and carry out requests, giving me a chance to stare again.

On many occasions, Mr. Adelman would have me accompany him to the hotel's private beach area. When he walked quickly and talked in clipped phrases, I knew we were heading to catch pool jumpers—local kids invading the hotel's private beach and sneaking up the stairway to the swimming pool. It wasn't that the pool contained magical waters; it was simply because the local boys enjoyed creating havoc and annoying Mr. Adelman. We were a motley pair—him in his Bermuda shorts and sport jacket and me in my coordinated husky pants and T-shirt, running along the sand attempting to catch and tackle pool jumpers. The whole melodrama of rushing to the pool and onto the beach entertained the guests, but it often became a Keystone Cops sequence with me and Mr. Adelman chasing the scattering rule breakers.

Much more memorable and significant was the day when Mr. Adelman asked me to join him in a walk along the beach. He began by mumbling some words about his son and daughter that weren't very flattering, but he made a seamless transition into questions about me.

"So, Melvin, you enjoyed meeting 'The Virginian'?"

"Yeah, that was cool," I told him.

"He's a good man. Regardless of that un-American bullshit he got caught up in!"

I had no idea what he was talking about. It would be another few years as a college history major that the McCarthy era and the Communist hunt meant anything to me. It was then that I would understand that Lee J. Cobb testified before the inquisition, naming other people to secure his patriotic label.

"Is he coming back before the summer's over?" I asked.

"No, not this summer," Mr. Adelman said. "Now, tell me . . . do you have any Jewish friends at school?"

"I don't think so. I mean, I don't know."

At that point in my life, I associated Jews with the Bible—they complained a lot in the Old Testament, and some were the early Christians in the New Testament.

"I have a book I want you to read. You like reading?"

"Yes, sir."

"Okay, I'll have it for you tomorrow."

True to his word, Mr. Adelman brought me a copy of Viktor Frankl's *Man's Search for Meaning*. I wasn't sure what kind of book I was reading. It told of the author's experiences in a concentration camp, but it wasn't *Hogan's Heroes* (1965-1971). It also contained his long, philosophical reflections that forced me to repeatedly reread some sentences. But after completing the book, I knew I had read something that was unforgettable and challenging. Mr. Adelman then told me to read another book called *Night* by Elie Wiesel. I didn't read it that summer, but instead read Mr. Adelman's other recommendation, *Go Tell It on the Mountain* by James Baldwin. Baldwin immediately became a favorite writer of mine. And he was Black! He won a place on my personal shelf of favorite authors along with my Langston Hughes collection.

Years later, I would be teaching Hughes and Baldwin's various works, along with Elie Wiesel's *Night*, a book that haunted me with the combined poetic language and cruel reality of the author's life. These three authors served as cornerstones to years of teaching ethnicity and culture, and the full spectrum from evil to human resilience.

\* \* \*

At the beginning of my senior year at Barnstable High, I made a change. I left the sax in its case for the fall and went out for the varsity football team. I always loved football, joining in neighborhood pickup games on the elementary school field or the vacant lot near my neighborhood. The pickup games were often tackle-based, not so much to demonstrate how tough we were, but because that's how the pros did it on television. In those late 1960s seasons, I was a lover of the old AFL teams, especially the Boston Patriots who played in Fenway Park. But my absolute favorite AFL team was the Jets with Joe Namath, Jim Nance, and George Sauer, Jr. I truly longed to be a receiver like George Sauer, Jr., Lance Alworth, Paul Warfield, or Charlie Taylor. However, for the high school team, I was placed into a third string fullback position on offense and earned a cornerback spot on defense.

The varsity football team, coached by Tom Daubney, took me into the world of team sports, and tough behavior and tough talk were the essential wardrobe to being a well-dressed senior male. Individually, most guys were decent kids, but there was a group personality that existed, coercing teenage boys into outrageous behavior and salacious comments. It was different from the bonding among the musicians in the band and orchestra, which emanated from a grateful sense of belonging to a creative community. The football players were a more aggressive cohort where displaying physical skills and bombastic language was required to fit in.

My self-confidence grew in that one year of football. Adding to the verbal confrontations with Cape Verdean kids, the physical and mental development from football urged a new sense of personal pride. Varsity football gave me one more block to place into the foundation of my self-identity. I came to realize that I possessed several strengths; I was someone who loved movies, poetry, and music *and* someone who was tough enough to compete physically.

But the meteoric senior athletes still inhabited a world that was distant from my own. They always knew much more than I did about life and had gone to places I hadn't seen. And the talk about girls went beyond teasing and timid notions of romance. They talked about sex in various ways. For many of the varsity stars, their Saturday game triumphs led to Saturday night "scoring," according to their narrated versions of events at Monday practices.

I didn't know if their sexual adventures were true, but in my virginal condition, I often wanted to believe they were. It provided some type of assurance that if they were "scoring" with girls, then perhaps that possibility awaited someone like me who felt so awkward and nervous around girls.

\* \* \*

The fall of my senior year brought on new anxieties—preparing for college, the complexities of college catalogs, applications, statement letters, SAT scores, and decisions about my future direction. According to the adults in my life, I was about to take the next step toward a future "full of opportunities."

Alice Owens, my favorite English teacher, encouraged me to attend college, promising that I would excel. She identified schools in the state that would welcome someone with my potential. One day, Coach Daubney located me in the band room, and though I wasn't one of his outstanding players, he encouraged me to consider a small school in Maine called Bates College, a place for a "smart kid" like me. As a Division III school that offered no athletic scholarships, he felt Bates would allow me to continue to play football.

Mama and Daddy emphasized the need for college, and they encouraged me to participate in a program that was co-organized by the NAACP and the B'Nai B'rith of Hyannis. In those days the word "mentor" was not in vogue; instead, the term "big brother" was the label given to this program of cultural interchange and support. So, being the leaders of the NAACP Youth Group, James, Mark, and I were chosen to meet with a group of Jewish leaders, who were randomly matched up with each of us. Both James and Mark eventually drifted away from their Big Brother relationships. As for me, I was the fortunate one—I met a man who became my mentor and friend for over thirty-three years until his death in 2005.

Harold Perkins was a businessman who owned and managed the Old Harbor Candle Company in Hyannis, and he was an articulate, warm, and intelligent person. I was both comfortable and nervous when we had our initial meeting, as he impressed me with his range of knowledge about people and politics. When he invited me to his home for dinner, I met his wife, three sons, and daughter. They were vivacious kids, watching me intently, smiling at me as I offered a quick smile in return. His wife, Elaine, was very pretty, like Anne Bancroft in *The Graduate* (1967).

Harold urged me to see college as the next logical step in my life, identifying all the possibilities that would be associated with continuing my education and submerging myself into the wealth of knowledge that awaited me. He praised my intelligence, and he was aware of the need to apply in the fall of 1968 to enter college in the fall of 1969. I didn't understand that calendar, nor the need to take SAT exams and fill out what seemed to be the endless applications forms and financial aid papers. More so than the teachers and guidance counselors at school, Harold's voice connected with me. His easy manner and his unwavering belief in me were new things in my life. Daddy and Mama always provided their love and encouragement, but Harold wasn't a family member nor a paid educator. He was a sincere and loving man who became a strong influence in my decisions.

Harold did one other significant thing for me: he encouraged me to write creatively. I knew how much I enjoyed reading and rereading my favorites, but I wasn't sure what *writing* was all about, other than a poem that I would occasionally scribble. But Harold encouraged me not to limit myself by what I didn't know, but to keep reading and writing to see what would develop. The first step, he insisted, was going to college.

I felt I couldn't fail Mama, Daddy, Harold, and my favorite teachers. The more they pronounced their belief in me, the more I believed in myself. Despite the anxiety about the unknown territory of education ahead of me, I knew I wasn't alone. That realization gave me courage and direction, even though I was uncertain where it all would lead.

\*\*\*

I was the oldest of sixteen grandkids, as Grandma Ella Mae often reminded me. As the oldest, she insisted that I lead the way for all my cousins who looked up to me. Mama stated a similar acknowledgment of my status, and I was given the mantle of leadership to carry. When I was accepted into Bates College, my family members were happy and congratulatory, as I became the first in my immediate family, and the first among the grandkids, to reach that respected goal.

Somewhere between receiving the Bates College acceptance letter and packing for football camp in August 1969, I was sobered by a realization that had long been present: my going to college was not just about me. I represented my family, and just as important to many—my race. The notion of being the symbolic Black student resonated years earlier when James, Mark, and I led the NAACP Youth Group. My parents' generation saw me as the culmination of the decades that had preceded me, where all kinds of battles—the small personal ones to the larger group marches—were hard fought.

During my four years of high school, the racial and political climate in the country had been transformed from a patient supplication from Negro communities to a loud, assertive stand from Afro-American communities and "Black Power" politics. This shift had a certain generational significance to it, as I witnessed the emergence of afro hairstyles, Black Power fist salutes, bell bottoms, and dashikis. The argot of young Black folks also transformed noticeably, as verbal exchanges were laced with expressions, such as "right on," "outa sight," "solid," or "brotherman." Politically-infused songs of social protest surfaced in pop music from performers as different as James Brown; Bob Dylan; Stephen Stills and the Buffalo Springfield; Creedence Clearwater; Crosby Stills, Nash, and Young; Jefferson Airplane; and Joan Baez. The lexicon and images of the times even reached the remote, bubbled environment of Cape Cod. Hyannis was not immune to the realities of a changing America, captured in references to the Black Panthers, the Vietnam War, counterculture, psychedelic trips, hippies, and "happenings."

Movies began to change as well, partly due to the times since studios needed a way to pull viewers from their color televisions and into movie theaters. Graphic violence and sex saturated the big screen, a strong lure to get people out of the house and into the theater seats. With those two new elements, a ratings system was established in 1968 to warn people about violence, sexuality, and adult language in films, such as *Bonnie and Clyde* (1967), *Night of the Living Dead* (1968), *Once Upon a Time in the West* (1968), *Rosemary's Baby* (1968), and *Midnight Cowboy* (1969), to name some.

As I ended my senior year, I exposed myself to as much big-screen violence, sexuality, and adult language as I could. At the same time, I also was glad to see more Black faces on the screen. I still loved my Sidney Poitier films—even a love story like *For Love of Ivy* (1968). But it was invigorating to see additional Black faces on the small television and big theatrical screen like Ivan Dixon, Abbey Lincoln, Yaphet Kotto, Roscoe Lee Browne, Diahann Carroll, Robert Hooks, Jim Brown, and Beah Richards. And by the 1970s, I was "blown away" by the number of screen actors who emerged during the Blaxploitation cycle of films. Although I couldn't articulate the manner in which all of these developments coincided with my physical, emotional, and political changes, there was a synthesis happening. And I believed that *something* better was waiting for me beyond Hyannis. The writing, movies, music, and college experience all existed beyond the Cape Cod peninsula, connecting me to the mainland that would lead me into a future that I craved, despite its elusive and undefined borders.

CHAPTER THREE

# Pieces of a Young Man

In the fall of 1969, Lewiston, Maine—about thirty-five miles north of Portland—was a small town in disintegration. A former mill center with large, empty buildings along the Androscoggin River, the landscape appeared to be a scorched rural area caught between its history as a shoe factory village and its ambition to be an emerging small city. There was a grey drabness in the mornings that accentuated the lingering stench from the river. With Maine's majority population of White people and its 1 percent of Black residents, Lewiston remained outside of the Black revolution that was canvassing the country.

Nestled in this environment, Bates College stood out like a diamond embedded into the complexion of a dying man. In my freshman year, this small liberal arts college of about 1,100 students had perhaps twenty Black students, including several African international students. The pathways that brought us all to Bates were varied, just as we Black students were diverse in our personalities and backgrounds. Massachusetts, Connecticut, New Jersey, Philadelphia, Chicago, Ethiopia, Cameroon. We were a motley group that learned quickly to find bonds that supported our collective survival, even as we tolerated our sometimes clashing personalities.

Reaching the campus in mid-August for football camp, Roscoe Lee and I were the only Black players on the initial roster of about fifty guys. Roscoe was from Newark, New Jersey, and having grown up in the inner city, he was always watchful, keeping his eye on the surroundings and everyone within a given area. Roscoe—at 5'11" and 175 pounds—had been a standout ball player at his high school, and he displayed a tough, confident demeanor. His small 'fro haloed his chocolate complexion, and out of the four Black brothers I would gain that first year at college, he had the strongest personality.

At the Bates campus, where there were no athletic scholarships or fraternities, we young men who braved that summer week of triple sessions possessed a gut-love for the game. Beginning with an early morning workout before breakfast; a late morning workout before lunch; and a two-hour mid-afternoon workout before dinner, the football camp pushed my physical limits in ways I hadn't expected. There were talented guys on the squad who could really play the game, and by the end of the week, it was clear that the plurality of the players were good and decent people, with a small sprinkling of White boys who didn't have much to say to me and Roscoe.

Off the field, Roscoe and I filled the time in the student commons, particularly in the pool room, where four tables offered up the beautiful green felt, shiny balls, and an assortment of cue sticks positioned in wooden racks bolted to the walls. It was all I needed, as I easily beat Roscoe with each visit. On those occasions when Roscoe and I walked off campus into the nearby streets, we were viewed as Black aliens who had disembarked from a spacecraft. On one day that first week, Roscoe and I wandered into a small sandwich shop several blocks from campus, ordering food before waiting at a jukebox. Roscoe returned to the counter to take his soft drink from a White woman with greying hair, who looked to be in her fifties. Roscoe returned to my side, and we settled on a Creedence Clearwater song before I edged to the counter to grab my drink.

"Excuse me, miss," I said looking at the empty counter. "Want to get my Coke."

"What?" she said, tilting her head in confusion. "I just gave you your drink."

"No, I just—"

"—Oh, oh, that was the *other* one," she chuckled, looking over at Roscoe.

"That's all right," I quipped. "All you White people look alike to me, too!"

I said it so quickly, I surprised myself. The woman looked confused, not comprehending both the aggressiveness and sarcasm within my statement. Her face cloudy, she stepped away to gather the sandwiches. Behind me, I heard Roscoe laughing. As we walked back to campus, I lingered on what I said—not the content as much as the quick defensiveness that came forth. I was conscious of my sarcastic personality that was emerging at that stage in my life. It blossomed with more political, racial statements, and over the next four years, my growing vocabulary, quick wit, and sardonic disposition became more formidable. I became aware that my words could make people laugh or give me the upper hand in a conversation.

During that week of football camp, Roscoe and I shared our backgrounds. He was from an inner-city environment, where a daily strength was required. His world was a segregated one of working-class Black people seeking dreams that many White people saw as their normal American lives. It was clear that Roscoe's background was quite different from my ethnically-integrated, middle-class Hyannis environment. Yes, there were those occasions when I wandered through an all-Black world when my family traveled to Boston to visit cousins living in the Black section called Roxbury, but that wasn't a daily experience for me.

I recognized that my Cape Cod world made me accustomed to White people, though it took years away from Fort Pierce and the segregated South for me to reach that comfort zone. My language was closer to the majority New England rhythms and expressions than to the Black-laced, inner-city expressions that flowed from Roscoe's upbringing. So, my interaction with Roscoe and the inner-city Black students who arrived the following week required me to do a bit of verbal shifting, forcing me to become a communicating chameleon. Yet, the other Black students and I shared an ethos, one that superseded our different class backgrounds. We understood that from White perspectives, Black people were the same, regardless of the distinctions that actually existed.

At the same time, I began to lose the chubbiness that had plagued my early teens. Perhaps, it was the football workouts that attacked the many calories I scoffed down daily at the team dinners, but I became slender and fit, with an afro and growing mustache. Soon, people suggested my resemblance to Jim Brown, which puffed up my modest pecs even more.

But I wasn't the only one taking notice of my body—so, too, were girls. I couldn't turn in any direction without bumping into White girls. Certainly, I was familiar with being around them throughout my high school years, but in college, they became attractive because of their late-teen shapely and defined bodies. And as my "hellos" to different girls flowed into conversations about movies and music, I utilized my quick wit as a way to keep conversations going. But my humor was important for masking one other reality: I was a seventeen-year-old virgin.

After freshman orientation, we moved into permanent dorms that were separated by gender and required curfew limitations. Through football practice, Roscoe and I still connected daily, but when classes began, we interacted with other Black students. In particular, I gravitated to Walt Toombs from Teaneck, New Jersey, a brother who was a poet at heart and a music aficionado. We hit it off right away. Walt and I took some of the same classes and professors and we were in the same dorm, so our late evenings usually ended in his room, debriefing about the day and listening to the Isley Brothers on his turntable.

There were two Black seniors who were beginning their last year at Bates College when we arrived. One student was Bryant Gumbel, a baseball player who hung out with his White friends. When I passed him on campus, he always shared a courteous and friendly greeting. Bryant went on to be one of Bates

College's best-known alumni. He spent years as a *Today Show* host and years anchoring one of television's best sports shows, *Real Sports*.

The other Black senior was Marjorie Dixon, who had a smooth, chocolate complexion and a very athletic body. Marjorie was the only Black girl on the cheerleading squad, and she extended herself to the Black freshmen. She became both a senior class leader and major Black leader on campus. Early in the fall semester, Marjorie was a key force in connecting Black students together for political purposes.

So, with less than twenty Black American students, we assessed the campus and knew the issues we wanted to address. We wanted to keep in step with other campuses across the country, seeking full-time Black professors since there were none. We wanted classes that explored and reflected Black people in history, literature, political science, and the arts. At the same time, we wanted our voices heard about particular social activities, concerts, and dance mixers at Bates. Black students pushed forward in establishing the structure and mission goals for a new organization—the Afro-American Society—that we hoped would stir changes on campus.

I initially wondered why the campus gave so little resistance in comparison to other colleges around the country where Black organizations and Black Studies were met with fear and hesitation. One answer was the active Black alumni who shaped the college's national visibility and commitment to Black inclusion. Dr. Benjamin E. Mays (1894-1984), class of 1920, earned a graduate degree at the University of Chicago and became a dean at Howard University; an outstanding civil rights leader; and a president of Morehouse College in Atlanta, where he mentored Martin Luther King, Jr. Just as significant, Peter Gomes (1942-2011), class of 1965, became a minister, professor, and author. After earning his degree from Harvard Divinity School, he was a professor at Tuskegee University. He later served as the professor of Christian Morals and minister at the Harvard Memorial Church and the acting director of Harvard's W.E.B. DuBois Institute for African and African American Research. At the same time, I heard a great deal about the importance of the Boone family. Nate Boone, class of 1952, had distinguished himself with his outstanding military career and attendance at Boston University Law School. Due to his participation as one of the first Black soldiers to train at the segregated Marine Corps' Camp Lejeune, he received the Congressional Medal of Honor in 2012. His brother, Dave, class of 1962, was a successful businessman who conducted an extensive amount of Black student recruitment for Bates College.

It became apparent that the college administration understood the benefits of bringing in Black students. An increase in the Black student population and

Black faculty would promote the college's "progressive" reputation during the political times and fundraising of the 1970s. To outshine its nearby liberal arts colleges—Bowdoin and Colby—Bates acquired Black students to build upon the civil rights and educational legacy of the institution's most distinguished and nationally-recognized Black alumni.

With Roscoe as our president, Marjorie as vice president, and me and Walt as officers, the Bates College Afro-American Society was launched. By the end of the fall semester, Dean James Carignan, a White scholar, announced that the college was going to pay for him and three Afro-American Society members—Marilyn, Walt, and myself—to attend a conference on Black Studies at Atlanta University. I was excited to be selected, and I looked forward to seeing Atlanta after years of knowing Georgia only as a segregated state.

The theme of the conference introduced me to an area of Black Studies that fed both my academic and cultural hunger—the Harlem Renaissance of the 1920s and 1930s. In attendance, Black literary scholar Houston A. Baker received praise for his extensive knowledge and forthcoming anthology, *Black Literature in America* (1971). The main speaker, Arna Bontemps, was one of the recognized contributors to the literary body of the Harlem Renaissance. He was hypnotic in his readings of his works and the personal stories about Langston Hughes, Countee Cullen, W.E.B. Du Bois, and others. I had never seen so many intelligent, creative, and articulate Black people in one location, and I was moved by the magnitude of the contemporary Black Arts Movement that treasured earlier Black expressions and talents while praising the present-day creative artists, scholars, and materials.

At the conference, Walt, Marjorie, and I dove into discussions with Black students from other campuses. We were impressed by the number of students who attended the conference—some from predominantly Black campuses as well as majority White campuses. There was a collective pride in articulating and acknowledging our common Black history. At the same time, we felt the possibilities of our future pursuits, wrapping ourselves in the Black achievements of the past and wearing our race and culture as suits of honor.

One night during the conference, I hung out in Marjorie's room after Walt had eased back to our shared room. She and I continued the conversation about the most memorable parts of the day, but it was clear that she was circling closer to me, until we leaned into a kiss. Deep and warm. And then, with no transition, she pulled me over to the bed. I was both excited and lost, but I rallied my plan by synchronizing the numerous football locker room stories and movies that didn't provide me any dialogue, but suggested what my hands should be doing. Touching and caressing. I was walking in the dark without a light of confidence. She continued to let me touch her body, but held my hand back as I reached beneath her waist. It suited me just as well, because I was unsure and rather afraid of exactly what I would find there.

As we both were drifting into sleep, I got up and went to my room with Walt. I was still a virgin, but I knew I had traveled to a galaxy where I'd never been before. And within Marjorie's body, as *Star Trek*'s Captain Kirk assured television viewers in 1969, there was a "final frontier."

\*\*\*

After an enjoyable trip home for Christmas and New Year's, I experienced my first winter in Maine. It was snowy, cold, and abrasive—the kind of cold that permeated the bones and pierced the marrow until thirty minutes of recovery in a heated room.

I never developed the love that many of my fellow White students had for the outdoor winter activities: ski trips to nearby lodges, cross-country skiing, ice skating, tobogganing, and skinny dipping in Lake Andrews, the campus's pond. Most of the Black kids thought the White kids had lost their minds in celebrating the harsh elements that shifted from fluffy snowbanks to early morning temperatures near zero degrees.

We Black kids found our own way of sheltering from the cold. The brothers used indoor intramural and pickup basketball games to pass the time. Some brothers and sisters took over the pool room, as some of the White students avoided a recreation room filled with Black students. We talked loudly, laughed just as loudly, and sang lines from our favorite R&B songs. On the weekends, we would have a "screech" party in someone's room, which was a way to create a crazy weekend evening with music and dancing. "Screech" was a code word for a punch consisting of Seven Up, a can of fruit juice, and a mix of various alcoholic beverages available—usually a combination of beer and cheap wines like Silver Satin and Boone's Farm. But the magic of the party revolved around the music—Sly and the Family Stone; Earth, Wind & Fire; James Brown; Curtis Mayfield; Roberta Flack; The Stylistics; the Jackson 5; and any Motown artists.

Bates College provided a top-tier formal education for Black students, but we developed our social, Black selves by fashioning so much out of so little. Yes, there were those of us who didn't always get along. And there were those who chose to avoid their "Blackness" in the midst of the overwhelming Whiteness of the student population, the faculty, the administrators, the staff, and the natural elements. Yet, there were sustaining friendships that carried most of us through the anxieties of being different in a place attempting to address and understand that difference.

\*\*\*

Weeks before my January 31 birthday, my seventeen-year-old mindset was as erratic as my hormonal body. Marjorie and I had been spending more time together; we shared cafeteria meals, walked playfully across campus to her dorm, and studied together before getting into long discussions about politics and music.

It was a weekend night when a movie screening occurred in the campus's Schaeffer Theater, projected onto a screen that was lowered from the rafters onto the stage. The movie was the 1933 classic *King Kong*, and it held enough humor that made it enjoyable to the packed audience. As Marjorie and I walked back to her dorm, I lingered on a thought about the movie: *What exactly was Kong going to do with Fay Wray if he actually won her? Just how big was Kong's dong, and how would the sex part work out with Fay?*

In Marjorie's single room, our kissing and touching unfolded as it had several times before. There was one exception, however. When I reached below her waist, she didn't brush my hand away. And that liberty took me to a place of trepidation. I didn't know *what* I was touching, nor did I know what it looked like. I was a lost man with no map to follow. I had no movie reference, no song lyrics for guidance, no locker room instructions to follow. But I heard Marjorie's voice soften, moaning slightly when I moved my hand. And as she moaned louder, I touched further.

"Do you have a rubber?" she whispered.

Oh, the next step. Yes, I remembered, but that brought me to a new fear. Although I had bought the condom at the beginning of the fall semester—as advised by my football buddies—and slipped it into my wallet whenever I was with her, I didn't have a clue about how to open it and place it on my body. As my fingers picked at the wrapper, my excitement reached out in the darkness, needing no encouragement from me.

"What's wrong?" she asked.

*Everything*, I thought.

I heard the wrapper rip, and I pulled out the moist rubber, trying to roll it one way without success. Reversed it—no, that didn't work. Tried it again the other way. Success, as it rolled over my skin. From there, Marjorie took control, pulling me on top of her, guiding me, hugging me tightly. I held on as best I could, and after the quickest minute ever recorded in Western civilization, a jolt of pleasure seized my body. I screamed like a madman.

"Are you okay?" she asked.

"Yeah, yeah, I think so," I said, breathless.

She kissed my forehead and snuggled closer. She began talking, but I didn't hear anything she said. Instead, my body floated in this strange, unknown place. I knew it was close to curfew, so I slipped into my clothes. Walking across campus back to my dorm, I was struck with a heaviness that would consume me for weeks: *Will she get pregnant now?*

Years of pulpit messages collected over my head like threatening clouds. If Marjorie became pregnant, what would I do? And then there were my parents—their disappointment and tears. I imagined pastors pointing their fingers at my sinful nature. Those thoughts stole the following days, as I went to Marjorie and asked her if she had her period yet. She seemed surprised by the question, and by the third time I asked her during the next two weeks, she became annoyed. I fell deeper into my guilt, as images of the blonde-haired Jesus filled my vision. In one nightmare, Jesus loomed large over my bed, his forefinger touching my forehead, sending me directly to hell without mercy. In that nightmare, hell was not a fiery pit, but an ice-covered island with no igloo in sight. Then, finally, after dinner one night, Marjorie said the four words that set me free: "I had my period." I was resurrected. I was free at last.

And on Marjorie's part, she freed herself of *me*, and soon after, she began dating Roscoe. They became the inseparable Black Power couple on campus—their afros trimmed at the same length, their Blackness palpable whenever they entered a room together. But I never blamed her for ending things with me. She found what she was looking for: a brother who could satisfy her womanhood *and* her Blackness. I took refuge in my inexperience and naïveté, knowing that my greatest fear at the time had been avoided.

As I met other girls that year, I was apprehensive about anything that went beyond kissing, touching, and getting drunk together. I believed I had a future only if I avoided being a father, even though I had no idea what that future would be. I only knew that being a teenage father would end any fulfilling future for me. So, above all, I was grateful that Marjorie and Roscoe were together, and that the blond-haired Jesus allowed me to sleep again at night. More importantly, I realized that I really didn't want to know what King Kong and Fay Wray might do in the dark.

\* \* \*

The dating scene at Bates was a peculiar obstacle course. First, Lewiston, with little public transportation, had few venues for off-campus socializing. Being a student without a car added to the limitations. So, with very little money to spend, no car, no off-campus destination, and dormitory curfews, a date night was usually reduced to meeting a girl at her dorm and walking to the student commons and chatting in "The Den," the campus's version of a social cafe. A really daring date was to convince a girl to walk back to my boy's dorm where we would have wine or beer. The understanding was that I would have to escort the girl back to her dorm by the midnight curfew. Second, the number of Black girls on campus was miniscule, and some claimed to have boyfriends back home or enrolled at another college, so they optioned to be nuns. I attempted to reach out and try other girls of color, as we would currently say, and found that I was confronted with cultural differences.

In one case, there was Esther, an international student from Ethiopia. She was very quiet, lovely, and smart, and we sat in her dorm lounge discussing classes and her educational plans in America. We didn't even make it to the Den for a conversation over coffee or a soft drink, as my references to American music and movies didn't connect with her. It was a short night. Then, there was Hanam, a beautiful, smart girl from Tehran who had some very strict rules about holding hands and kissing. Her lack of interest in cheap wine also made visits to my dorm room unlikely. American music and movies were of interest to her, but not essential to her enjoyment of life. Her affection for Persian music was educational, but I was too lazy to explore unknown cultural expressions. The truth was—I was a horny Black American kid who wanted to rush into physical intimacy before developing any intellectual and emotional connection with a girl.

My dating options and immaturity led me to the familiar majority, and White girls became a collection of interesting personalities. Some were curious, while others were distant. Many had attended private schools in New England and had little association with Black people beyond those on television or movie screens. But some of the White girls were aggressive in their own coy way, and it was easy to schedule a Saturday night connection with a White girl who offered a lingering smile in class or during a meal in the Commons. However, one particular date stood out—Sandy Brannigan. Sandy was in my biology class, which was the largest required lecture course in my schedule. After a couple of occasions of leaving the classroom at the same time, Sandy's generous smile and cuteness grabbed my attention. It didn't take much effort to convince her to join me for wine and music in my dorm room, as she had little else to do on a Saturday night.

Alone in my room with the lights off and flickering candles for atmosphere, I poured the Boone's Farm wine as I asked Sandy about her favorite music. She shared her favorites: Led Zeppelin, The Rolling Stones, The Zombies, and Tommy James and the Shondells. I confessed I liked some of the songs by the Stones, but I didn't have albums by the groups she mentioned. She deferred to my music choice, and I went for Isaac Hayes's *Hot Buttered Soul* album, which, when combined with the wine, might bring on the desired effects.

By the time we completed our discussion about the biology class and the professor, the wine was doing its part as we began kissing—those long, sloppy, sweet wine kisses. And the more we kissed, the more handsy *she* became. Then, like a wrestler making a calculated move, she rolled me on the twin bed, my body at an awkward angle on top of her. I liked her take-charge attitude. Then, it happened. She began rubbing both her hands across my booty—up and down, side to side, harder and harder.

"Sandy, what . . . what are you doing?"

"Hunh?"

"What are you doing?"

"I'm . . . looking for your tail?" she explained.

"My what?"

"Your . . . well, I was told that Black men had tails."

Silence. I waited for the punchline to the joke. My cheap wine buzz dissolved. I can't remember what I said, but I quickly and silently walked her back to her dorm. When I returned to my dorm room, I emptied the wine bottle in one long swallow. I went to bed with no plans of waking up the next morning.

During the next few years, I still went out occasionally with White girls who shared a curious gaze with me, but I remained guarded. Additionally, in two, sickening situations, I had to deal with visiting parents. One girl—a dancer—invited me to join her and her parents for dinner after a campus theater performance, but at the restaurant, the parents never spoke directly to me for over two hours or even acknowledged my presence. I was Ralph Ellison's *Invisible Man*. With another White girl, I met her parents in the theater lobby after her acting performance. The next day, she told me tearfully that her parents would stop paying for her Bates College education if she continued dating me.

It *was* what it was. I adjusted my expectations while leading with my self-preservation. I was friendly and sociable, but with limitations. I knew that my Bates College years had an expiration date, and my future waited beyond the limited dimensions of the campus.

\*\*\*

On May 4, 1970, the impact of the foreign war blazed into our vision. At Kent State University in Ohio, four students were shot down by National Guardsmen while protesting the Vietnam War. I never imagined I would see the images and facts of that day. In particular, the photo of Mary Ann Vecchio kneeling over the dead body of Jeffrey Miller sent me into a peculiar haze, where I was numb and furious at the same time. The other kids killed were Allison Krause, Sandra Scheuer, and William Schroeder. And in the aftermath of national tears and solemn White faces, one realization made its way to the forefront of my thoughts: *If White people were willing to shoot down White kids to maintain their power, what would those White people do to a Black kid like me?* Eleven days later, as an eerie response to my question, at Jackson State College in Jackson, Mississippi, two young Black men—Phillip Gibbs, a pre-law student, and James Earl Green, a high school student—were shot and killed in a confrontation between students and the police, and a dozen more Black people were wounded.

When the shootings happened in May at the end of the spring semester, I wasn't on campus. I was back in Hyannis, working with my father in his cleaning business. But that summer I couldn't escape the song "Ohio"—the Crosby, Stills, Nash, and Young tribute to the Kent State victims. It took me a few years before I could find my personal way of responding to those murders. Whenever attending a public event, I refused to stand during the national anthem, an act of defiance that drew its share of accusatory stares and mumbled comments. It didn't matter. It was the least I could do, and to this day, it remains my personal action to remember May 1970 and to honor the six young people who were killed.

\* \* \*

An unexpected revelation occurred at the end of my freshman year. I earned a D average, a 1.66 GPA, and was placed on academic probation. How was that possible since I went to classes and read *most* of the required assignments? Besides, I had been a B+ student in high school, so I expected the same results at Bates. It became clear that simply sitting in class in college and frequently reading assigned pages was not sufficient. The exams, quizzes, papers, detailed lecture notes, and discussions were essential parts of the process. Somewhere in my late-teenage brain, I expected that my excellence at playing pool and chasing girls would be calculated into my grade point average.

When my grades arrived in the mail, my parents expressed their surprise and disappointment. With finality, my father gave me a choice: *"Go back to school in September and raise your grades where they should be, or you'll come and work for me."* I knew what he meant. Washing windows, cleaning bathrooms, mopping and waxing floors, and cutting and weeding lawns for eight to ten hours a day, six days a week was *not* what I wanted for the remainder of my life. Working in that fashion for a three-month summer job was torture enough.

I was young, but I wasn't a young fool!

\*\*\*

At the beginning of my sophomore year, someone life-changing appeared. He was loud, voracious, and charismatic—John Jenkins. John knew Roscoe from Newark, and John arrived at football camp in a gray suit, sprinkling his greetings with *"A-Salam-Alakim!"* He knew a great deal about Black Muslims, and he was constantly talking, like a man afraid he would lose his voice if he didn't constantly speak. He never knew when to shut up, and I disliked him immensely. His short height mirrored my 5'8" frame, but when he ran, he flew. On the field, his muscled physique drew stares from all the players, and he was the fastest guy on the team. At his high school, he played the backfield with Greg Latta, who later played in the NFL for the Chicago Bears. But at Bates College, a Division III school, John couldn't get the nod to start on offense. Basically, the coach seemed to dislike him as much as I did. As the season began, John lived in my dorm, and night after night, he burst into my room, disturbing me and my roommate, Joe. Shirtless and in only his underwear, he crooned a verse of jazz musician Les McCann's "Compared to What." John would sing and yodel until Joe and I kicked him out of the room, and then he would return the next night and start all over again.

It took me a semester of conversations—listening and speaking with John—for me to know the young man beneath the surface. He survived the late 1960s inner-city Newark streets, an absent father, and a drug-abusing brother. John's world was strikingly different from my privileged Cape Cod background, and he helped me to appreciate that fact and to cherish my parents for all they had done and were doing. John was negotiating a new universe, transitioning from an all-Black urban environment to the White rural territory of Bates College and Lewiston, Maine. He had been plucked from an inner-city concrete field and planted in an alien terrain, surrounded by White kids from prep schools and the suburbs of Massachusetts, Rhode Island, and Connecticut.

John and I talked endlessly. We laughed until our sides cramped—at other students, professors, coaches, and politics. I hadn't been that close to anyone since my years with James Tobey and Mark Fernandes in Hyannis. And like them, John Jenkins became my brother.

John got to know my family as well, particularly when my parents visited the campus, bringing large boxes of treats from the Dunkin' Donuts in Hyannis that was maintained by Donalson Cleaning Service. On those days of their arrival, John raced to my room, waiting enthusiastically for "Papa D" and "Mama D," as he affectionately called my parents. Surprisingly, those nicknames stuck, and they were christened and identified as such thereafter.

Forty-nine years later, John was still one of my closest friends. John's brother-love helped shape my life in college and the decades that followed. He urged me to believe in myself, and he emphasized how blessed I was to have family and friends who loved me unconditionally. He urged me to appreciate the people and things in front of me that I often took for granted. He encouraged me to push forward with my talents that he identified, but would criticize me when I stepped backward into self-pity.

Sometimes, the hidden rhythms in life are vibrant enough to tear through the dissonance of chaos and confusion that fill each day. In my life, John Jenkins was that rhythm, that melody, that riff that settled my soul and offered moments of joy that transcended the social, political, and religious nonsense that surrounded me.

\*\*\*

After taking two history classes, I began to consider that area of studies as my possible major. European History was taught by Professor Christine Holden, who was the only full-time female faculty member in the department. She was extremely knowledgeable, and her class initiated my interest in traveling to countries outside of the United States. The other class was Colonial History, taught by Dr. James Leamon. He was a slim man with dark hair, glasses, and a penetrating voice. He often dressed in casual wear that appeared to be khakis, so Walt and I gave him the nickname of "Jungle Jim," inspired by the White protagonist from the "White man tames Africa" television series. Jungle Jim was essentially a televised, reimagined version of Tarzan with khakis, a pith hat, and better English grammar.

Dr. Leamon was a specialist in Colonial History, and so his knowledge and pride in the period was obvious from his lectures. In one class while lecturing about the value of one of his favorite Founding Fathers—Thomas Jefferson—I became upset with the golden halo he placed around Jefferson's head. My understanding of Thomas Jefferson had widened with the various writings coming out of the Black Power and Black Aesthetic perspectives. So, in a burst of youthful anger and my submergence into Black history, I raised my hand and pronounced in my loud voice: "Thomas Jefferson was a bullshitter! He wrote about freedom, but he was a slave owner!"

There was a thick hush that choked the room. Every student knew that I had trespassed on the sacred ground of Dr. Leamon's garden of heroes. With a stern look and a firm tone, his eyes pierced my chest as he ordered: "Donalson, I'll see you in my office after class!"

All eyes fell upon me—a condemned man awaiting execution. I sat through the remainder of the class, deep into the apprehension of what awaited me and how painful the ordeal would be. As expected, when I reached his office door some thirty minutes later, Dr. Leamon sat behind his desk, his anger floating like a storm cloud overhead.

"Donalson, there are some things I will not tolerate ever in my class! You cannot curse and swear like some drunken sailor! You will respect me, my class, and every student in the class! Is that clear?"

"Yes, Dr. Leamon, I just—"

"That's all!"

He adjusted his chair and turned his attention to the open book on the desk. I was dismissed and ushered out by his silence. Truth was, I really admired Dr. Leamon. I thought he was an immensely intelligent and eloquent man. Although I only earned a C in his Colonial History class and wasn't fortunate enough to take another course with him, he went on to be a major influence in my future decisions. Following the semester's end, I stopped by his office, talking casually and listening to the ways in which his research and teaching about Colonial America fascinated him. I asked about his process of becoming an American history major, the requirements for becoming a college professor, his graduate study at Brown University, and the rewards and challenges he faced on the road to completing his academic journey. In the peculiar way that life sometimes bends in on itself, it would be years later that I had one more remarkable interaction with Dr. Leamon, the man who first sparked my interest in becoming a college professor.

\* \* \*

Although I was a starting cornerback and lettered during my second year of football at Bates College, I knew my gridiron experience was finished. I disagreed with the plays and choices made by the head coach, and though I loved football, playing at Bates wasn't satisfying anymore. After I finished my sophomore season, I went with Walt to visit the campus radio station. Walt was already in the station's cycle as a weekly deejay, and knowing my love for music, he told me to check it out. As he promised, the world of the radio station was another kind of home. With shelves of vinyl albums—rock, soul, folk, jazz, classical—the music library was impressive for a small 10-watt station that could only broadcast several blocks beyond the campus.

I began first as the sports commentator on the early evening newscast, gathering information from the station's teletype. Then, gaining my third-class radio license, I won a four-hour spot as a deejay in the evening rotation once a week. With two turntables and several pots (control knobs) across the console, I became skilled at cueing up the vinyl track at the beginning of a song's intro.

As one song ended on the turntable on my left, I'd punch in the next song from the album on the right turntable. I enjoyed sitting in the deejay's chair and sharing music that I loved. I called myself "Marvelous Mel the Music Man." I played an eclectic mix of tunes, including my favorite Jazz-Rock groups: Blood Sweat & Tears; Chicago; If; and Chase. Miles Davis's *Bitches Brew* led the way for the jazz fusion of Donald Byrd; Herbie Hancock; Freddie Hubbard; Flora Purim; and Weather Report on my turntables. Every so often, I gave airtime to popular White groups like Deep Purple; Cream; Grand Funk Railroad; Steve Winwood & Traffic; Crosby Stills, Nash, and Young; Joe Cocker; and Creedence Clearwater Revival. When it was time to jump into the funk there was Sly and the Family Stone and Parliament-Funkadelic. When a reflective mood was needed, I slipped in a track from Carole King's *Tapestry* and Marvin Gaye's *What's Going On*. When there was a need for great guitar work, I played Jimi Hendrix and Santana. And there was always time given to cuts from my favorite, Gil Scott-Heron's *Pieces of a Man*.

With the transition to the radio station, my creative side developed further. A flame was lit again, but I wasn't certain how that flame would illuminate a future direction for me. Although I placed my saxophone in its case the year before, my immersion into the radio station and deejaying unleashed an invigorating satisfaction. The musical calling was strong again, but my college didn't offer deejaying as a major to fulfill my BA degree. I reflected on how much my parents and extended family back in Hyannis saw me as the role model for my cousins and for my hometown community. I remembered how my D average disappointed my parents after all their efforts to support my passage through college. I felt compelled to pursue an academic major that provoked and informed me, namely American history.

With the political times and cultural renaissance of the late 1960s and early 1970s, American History was an intellectual and visceral experience. Looking back at America through Black perspectives was a thrilling pursuit. It shaped conversations among the Black and White students, both in and outside of classes. In the classrooms and the library, I kept copious notes, but in my dorm room and at the radio station, I kept the turntables spinning with music.

\* \* \*

The great achievement of any guy living in my dorm was to obtain a single room, the major liberation from the initial doubles accommodations that were imposed. My chances looked great, given that my roommate announced at the beginning of my sophomore year that he was going to study abroad at the University of Beirut during the spring semester. As I saw it, that would transform our double room into a single for me. My euphoria was tangible as I looked forward to the privacy.

However, the Bates College universe had other plans. Dean James Carignan called me into his office, and I thought his request was related to the Afro-American Society that had grown stronger with additional Black students that year. Our cordial conversation was truncated by his announcement: "Mel, you'll have someone sharing your room while your roommate is away." I was in shock, stuttering incoherently. Although apologtic, Dean Carignan affirmed the growth of the student body, announcing that I would be sharing the room with Ray Hunter. Ray was talkative. Thin and energetic. A chain smoker. A talented piano player and stage enthusiast. And Ray was gay . . . and I was a hypocrite.

Despite my lingering friendship with my close friend, Mark Fernandes in Hyannis, I was as guilty as others with my biases and prejudices. Mark was one of my oldest friends, and he was my brother. However, in Ray's case, I was insensitive and more critical—but why? Simply, I aligned myself to the dominant perspectives of discrimination. In high school, Mark exhibited the approved displays of masculinity; on the other hand, at Bates College, Ray Hunter conveyed the limp wrist, high-pitched voice, swishing—effeminate traits that were assumed to be contagious. Certainly, I suspected that Ray was on the prowl for a cute guy like me.

All of those thoughts went through my head as I sat in front of Dean Carignan. I pleaded and begged to be placed in another double with someone else. Dean Carignan listened to my closing arguments and rendered his verdict: "If there's a problem, let me know." Yes, there was a problem! On campus, I was doomed to be laughed at, pointed at, and whispered about. I feared I would know the true meaning of purgatory during that upcoming semester.

In those first few weeks that we shared the room, I made certain I kept different schedules than Ray. I avoided walking to the student commons cafeteria together. I shunned walking across the street to Ernie's Market together. I didn't want to be seen with him, on or off campus. I undressed and dressed in the hallway bathroom in the morning and at night. And I always, always, slept with my back and booty against the wall, facing the room in case Ray ever attempted to pounce on me and do whatever.

But the first few weeks went by, and Ray never pounced. He never attempted to touch me, look at me, smile at me in any "queer" kind of way. Most nights, he didn't come back to the room at all, and when he did it was often after midnight. On the weekends, I would seldom see him. So, in my curiosity about what he did elsewhere, I began to talk to him. And I listened.

Ray was into the theater and was involved with a Spring Variety Show production that kept him late most nights. On the weekends, he played the piano at a local church to earn money. Often his weekends were also spent with his "boyfriend" who lived in town—an older White man who was recently divorced. The boyfriend gave Ray money when he needed it and allowed Ray to use his car when necessary.

As I learned more about Ray, I was slightly disappointed. Ray wasn't interested in me at all. He had no plans to convert me to his side of the sexual line. I wasn't his type—he preferred older men. Soon, I learned that Ray was not a threat to me, but a very fascinating person who had a different background—that is, the little that he told me about his personal life. As my fears dissipated, I discovered that with Ray as my roommate, I became the beneficiary of something I never expected: girls! Since he was into theater, Ray knew the actresses, singers, and dancers who participated in various productions. And that semester, due to the most effeminate man on campus, I met more girls than during the previous year. I looked forward to girls dropping by our dorm room to study and rehearse performances. In turn, I would often drop by the theater and watch rehearsals, observing another world on campus that I knew little about.

Through Ray, I met Barbara, a White girl from a Boston suburb with shoulder-length, auburn hair and a passion for the guitar and tennis. She was a senior, and I was in love, which led to both pain and glory—more of the former than the latter. After she graduated, she remained for a while in Lewiston, singing in a rock band and living with the lead singer, a guy who looked like a skinny Gregg Allman with shoulder-length black hair. Through Barbara I learned a truth: when the heart breaks, the pain persists like a ravenous monster feeding through the flesh, bones, and soul—a slow torture that leads into an emotional abyss.

And just as I had misread Barbara, I was absolutely wrong in my apprehensions about Ray Hunter. As he and I became friends, I was immune to what others said. I became acquainted with the good person that Ray was, learning that he aspired to have a happy and fulfilled life—just like everyone else. Hopefully, he did so, despite people like me who were quick to judge and dismiss.

*  *  *

In the fall of 1971, fear haunted me. It stole my sleeping hours, leaving me in a tortured state of anxiety. A Vietnam War draft lottery occurred to determine which young men would be called to active duty in 1972. To employ fairness as to who would serve, birthdates were pulled at random from a cylinder cage.

If one's birth date was pulled within the first 195 selections, the odds were that person would face induction.

Given airtime on radio and television, the tension of the event was suffocating. At the point when I heard my birthdate called, I breathed again. January 31 was selection number 239 out of the 365 birthdates in the year. I prayed thanks. I lived again. I found my breath and inhaled again, alive with the possibilities of pursuing my dreams. Of surviving away from the bloody jungles of a foreign land. To own my life. To live! In all, there were three Vietnam War lotteries, and the average age of those who served was nineteen.

CHAPTER FOUR

# Wanderlust

I was twenty years old at the end of my junior year at Bates College. Out of curiosity, my interest was caught by an off-campus, short-term course to study the German language and culture while living in Germany. The ten-week course would include group excursions through the historic cities of Trier, Cologne, Nuremberg, Munich, and Vienna, Austria. After three years of demanding college studies, I hungered to experience something "different" before beginning my senior year of an academic routine.

In the initial meeting, about twenty-five students showed up to hear Professor Karl Arndt pitch his course. Tall and blonde, Professor Arndt described an intriguing itinerary: flying from New York to Luxembourg City, and once in Germany, we would travel for two weeks through the country before settling in the small town of Murnau for two months of classes in Goethe Institute's language school.

When I announced my intentions to Mama D and Papa D, I'm sure they thought I had lost my mind in the snowbanks of Maine. But as they had always done, they saw the course as an educational experience that would add to my knowledge of people and the world. With their blessings and financial support, I registered for the course that would end up with sixteen students traipsing behind Professor Arndt through numerous cityscapes. I immediately connected with two easy-going guys: Teddy, who was at an intermediate level in the German language, and an advanced-level student named Humberto, who we nicknamed "Hum." Most of the other students were women, including Brenda, a pretty, dark-haired woman with green eyes. Of course, I was the *only* Black student to join the academic and cultural hejira, but I was accustomed to that status. Someone in the group suggested that we all should keep a journal as we traveled. It seemed a good suggestion, so I purchased a hard-bound diary, placing it inside the shoulder bag I bought.

We flew out of Kennedy Airport in New York on Icelandic Airways, with a stop in Reykjavik, Iceland, and then on to the international airport in

Luxembourg City. During the first week, we traveled through and by train to Trier, our first German city; Cologne; Nuremberg; and Berlin. To reach Berlin, we traveled through the Communist country of East Germany to reach our destination. Crossing the border into East Germany was sobering when the train stopped and armed military walked through checking passports. Once we reached Berlin, the political division was evident, as one area belonged to the West (a replica of capitalism and the connection among American, British, and French allies) and the other area belonged to the East (Russian Communist).

Professor Arndt had carefully organized our schedule, and on that first day, he took us to the Berlin Wall. Huddled beneath our umbrellas in the dreary mist, we reached a platform where a middle-aged White man in a black overcoat and black hat paced in a tight circle. Mumbling and muttering, his voice cracked when repeating the same phrases aloud in German.

"What's he saying?" someone asked Professor Arndt.

"It's about the wall . . . they shouldn't have let it happen . . . his family lost, gone . . . they shouldn't have let it happen."

"Who's they?" another student asked.

"*They* is us!" Herr Arndt stated.

The next day, after an early breakfast, Professor Arndt arranged for us to walk over into East Berlin with our student status. Once there, we met a young East German woman who was a college student as well, and she served as our guide for the day. She and Herr Arndt conversed in German, and she was kind and patient with us students, but not warm. Following her along various streets, we saw some buildings that were similar in architecture to those in West Berlin, but other buildings displayed bullet holes and small, crater-like dimples from bombs that had fallen thirty years earlier. Our guide provided explanations of the contradictory landscape and buildings, but I was caught by the contrasting expressions of the people we passed. Some seemed like people you might see in an American city, bustling toward busy obligations. Other people carried sad, dour faces like people caught within a maze of confusion.

The day of our visit to East Berlin was May Day, which made me recall my childhood in Florida with festive games, carnival-like music, and kids dancing around and braiding poles with colorful strands of rope. But in East Berlin, May 1, 1972, the celebration was all about the military parade. Lines of uniformed soldiers marched before and after displays of rolling tanks and flatbed trailers carrying mounted missiles.

As it grew dark, Herr Arndt hustled us to the checkpoint to cross back over into West Berlin. At dinner that night, everyone was eager to share their impressions of the day, and when I spoke, I commented on the uniformed soldiers with stony faces and shouldered rifles. The thick crowds of people with sad White faces. I observed few smiles, heard no pop music, and saw no Black faces like mine. I was a foreigner in a strange land of wounded people.

*\*\*\**

It was a five-hour train ride from West Berlin to Munich, where we spent the afternoon. Munich was the capital city in Bavaria, the largest region in the southeastern area of Germany. Herr Arndt explained that the Bavaria region stretched from the historical city of Nuremberg in the north to the German border that touched Austria.

From Munich, we had a sixty-minute train ride south to our destination—Murnau, a small town that offered cobblestone *strasses*, a village-like environment, and a view of the Alps in the distance. Adding to the character of the town, some of the older local citizens wore the traditional *lederhosen* and *dirndls* associated with Bavaria.

My group had spent two weeks together traveling, inhaling, tasting, absorbing, and reflecting. For the next two months, we would be on our own, living at host homes and attending the Goethe Institute's language classes where people of various backgrounds came to learn German. They were learning the language to conduct business, for academic research, to secure employment, and to enjoy learning about the country.

Our group would continue to see one another at the two-story school, but having different skill levels with the German language, we were assigned to different classes. This allowed us to meet new people, explore our individual interests, and travel at our discretion. It was at this point that Herr Arndt announced that he was leaving, and that we were on our own. He promised he would return in a month to take us on a group excursion.

My primary-level class was taught by Frau Sturtzenhoffecker, and she was an excellent, patient instructor. She only spoke in German, as the immersion education was about listening, repeating, and questioning. The class population was comprised of various backgrounds: Turkish, Greek, Japanese, Korean, West African, Australian, and Mexican. Five Americans, including me, rounded out the class of twenty. One of the Americans was Patty Endicott, a White girl from Florida with a heavy Southern accent. Her twang endeared her to the men in class, and she sat beside me, often whispering about Frau Sturtzenhoffecker: "What she say? I don't get it!"

Similar to my elementary class, the intermediate and advanced sections were composed of international students. During the first few days at the Institute, it was apparent that many of the male students were aspiring engineers or businessmen seeking careers in Germany. The women were generally college students from various locales, as well as a few wives of American servicemen stationed in the area. The town of Garmisch-Partenkirchen, where a United States base was located, was thirty minutes south of Murnau.

I was assigned to live in the house of the Koglmayr family, where a second floor was divided into two bedroom areas, each on either side of the stairway. My roommate was from Malaysia, but I never got his full name. Upon meeting, he smiled and told me, "Just call me Charlie." Charlie was short with a faint mustache, and he had straight dark hair and clear bronze skin. It didn't take us long to relax with each other. He was fascinated with America—its anti-war politics, Black American history, and popular foods. Charlie's plan was to finish his intermediate class at the Goethe Institute and then move to Stuttgart where an electrician's job waited for him. His devotion to studying was also fed by his shy nature, and he was a sensitive man. There was a recognizable tenderness in his eyes, voice, and patient manner.

Moving into the second week, I fell into a routine. Arriving at the Institute an hour before class, I met my Bates group for *Frühstück*, consisting of *Brotchen* and coffee at the Institute's tiny café. I didn't understand how a hard roll and a hot drink could be considered breakfast, but as the days rolled by, I looked forward to the meager meal and catching up with my fellow travelers.

Classes were held for two hours before a fifteen-minute break. The next ninety minutes of class were followed by a two-hour break in the afternoon, before the day ended with another ninety minutes of class. On most days, my collective of friends would spend that two-hour afternoon break at the Staffelsee.

The Staffelsee was a large lake about a twenty-minute walk from the school. I was told that the lake, with its clear, inviting surface, was an impressive two square miles. During those warm days, the locals—some families, some couples—would picnic at the lake. And it was not unusual to see both children and adults angling toward nearby bushes, turning their backs to us, and changing into their swimwear in the open. It was surprising to me at first, but soon, like everyone else, seeing moments of nudity was not alarming or worthy of comment.

My love of the lake was enhanced by the time I spent with my new friends: Patty (from Florida), Eva (from South Africa), Bill (from Arizona), Jorge (from Mexico City), and Jade (from Australia). We shared a late lunch of wine, bread and cheese, and conversation. According to Eva, who spoke both French and German, our Staffelsee excursion was our *fête champêtre*, and our rationale for sometimes skipping the late afternoon class to speak only German to each other provided us the benefits of class. But, inevitably, as we drank the second bottle of wine, we slipped into English, and then, into a warm oblivion.

\*\*\*

Eva Benjamin was in her late twenties, but she seemed older. With an alluring physique and energetic personality that the men at the Institute couldn't resist, she was quite popular. During the morning break on the patio, I watched her butterfly from one conversation to the next, each man waiting his turn to stand close to her. She was in the advanced class, and I could hear her speaking fluid German, which meant I had no chance of having a conversation with her. But toward the end of the first week, she walked over to me.

"You're American, aren't you?" Eva began in what sounded like a British accent.

"Yeah. You're British? I thought you were German."

She lit a cigarette, smiling at me.

"I'm from Johannesburg . . . South Africa. It's the Afrikaans that confused you. Dutch in origin, but some people here in Germany do speak it."

"How many languages do you speak?"

"Well, let's see," she said, exhaling the smoke to the side. "I also speak French, Italian, and English, of course."

"Five languages! I can barely speak one."

Following an instructor's urging voice calling from the doors, the students began moving back inside.

"I'm Eva."

"Mel."

"So, join us tonight," she stated, "at the disco . . . bring some friends. It's just before you reach the Staffelsee. Just follow the music. See you then."

When I returned to class, I asked Patty and Jorge if they wanted to go dancing that night. They said "Ja!" and Bill invited himself to stay close to Patty.

That evening when I reached the small club, I was surprised that a rural town would have a club that played American music. I saw Eva waving as she crossed the room to meet us at the door.

"I'm glad you're here," she said, smiling at me. "I feel like dancing tonight!" At the door, there wasn't an admission fee, but the tall German security guard looked me over.

"You with military?" he asked me in his accented English.

"No, I'm a student at the Goethe Institute," I responded.

As Patty, Jorge, and Bill followed me inside, the security man merely nodded, but he didn't question them.

"What the hell was that all about?" Patty twanged. "I don't git it."

"They've been having some problems with the American soldiers from the Garmisch base," Eva explained. "Misunderstandings . . . fights. It's that damn Vietnam War!"

We followed Eva to the table where a thin, dark-haired man smoked a cigarette. He was Italian, wearing a stylish sports jacket and open collar shirt. His name was Matteo Ricci, with the chiseled facial features of a male model, and his demeanor was smooth and polished. He understood English, but he didn't speak it fluently. But by the end of the evening, I was able to understand that he was an Italian businessman who traveled back and forth between Italy and Bavaria representing a company selling Italian wines.

There wasn't a deejay, but the speakers blasted American songs back to back. Oddly, some of the songs I heard while in Germany were not released in the states until after I returned home; other tunes played at the club had been hits in the states years before. But the small club cranked out tunes such as Stevie Wonder's "Superstition"; The O'Jays' "Back Stabber"; The Temptations' "Papa Was a Rolling Stone"; and Billy Paul's "Me and Mrs. Jones." The speakers also mixed in popular rock from Elton John, Rod Stewart, Carly Simon, and Neal Young.

On the main floor, Eva danced from one song to the next. The colorful, interior lights brushed her face into a soft loveliness. As she took a break from the dance floor, she sat next to me. Her face suggested innocence, though that possibility was betrayed whenever I looked into her experienced eyes.

"So, Eva, tell me more about yourself," I said.

She responded slowly in German to my question, the words rolling across the table.

"Whoa, whoa!" I pleaded. "I can't understand anything you're saying. In English, *bitte*."

"You can't learn the language, Mel, if you don't speak it."

I responded with a begging expression.

"Okay . . . well," she said, lighting still another cigarette, "I'm Jewish . . . my father's a doctor . . . and I think that what's happened in South Africa is a tragedy."

"Are you studying medicine, too?"

"No, my father's rich, and I'm living off his money. I travel and study . . . and travel some more."

"Sounds like you're running away from home."

"Exactly. There's going to be a bloody race war there before any lasting peace."

The head-nodding dance tunes stopped, and Neal Young's "Heart of Gold" flowed across the floor.

"Come on, Mel, let's dance," she said, standing and reaching back for my hand.

Eva pulled me to the middle of the floor, and she swayed, rolling her hips in a rhythm that could only be translated as a woman stricken with heat. She moved closer, and I hung with her as she grooved.

"So, whenever you hear this song," she said, "I want you to always think of me!"

She spun around and backed into my body, grabbing my arms with each of her hands, pulling me closer. The song was definitely over much too soon.

Back at the table, Eva announced, "Tomorrow *fur unser mittagessen*, let's go to the Staffelsee." There were no objections, and that's how we began spending our afternoon breaks with wine, cheese, bread, conversations, and laughter. But it was obvious that first night at the club that Eva Benjamin was running away from more than the politics of her country, and whoever or whatever was haunting her had purposely been left on the dance floor.

\* \* \*

Minkah Kuwarte, from Ghana, was in his thirties, and he spoke in slow, deliberate statements, often snapping his thumb and middle finger together to emphasize his point. He had a discernible accent, and he was lean with deep ebony skin. It was really his voice that confirmed his age and the loneliness of missing his wife and friends back home.

Whenever we crossed a *strasse* together, he held my hand, which disturbed me the first time it happened. Holding another man's hand. I wasn't prepared for such a quick closeness, such caring expressed in a physical way. It was a gesture I would never see in Lewiston or Hyannis. But as he took my hand, the grasp expressed a sign of brotherhood. He was free enough, secure enough to share himself and be physical—not in some sexual manner, but in a sincere display of friendship.

"You see, dese mahn," he began while sitting at the bistro, "who t'inks he cahn leave his past has no future. *Wir sind alle Schwarze Leute* . . . we're all Black people."

I looked over my beer and watched his eyes dazzle.

"Back home in Accra, we do not have dese problem. We know . . . no, we have lived our ancestry. We are our ancestry! We do not need to raise this consciousness as you Black Ah-mare-rekahns."

I began to respond, but he stopped me with a lifted forefinger and a smile. Leaning forward in his chair, he continued his thoughts aloud.

"You see, when I studied in the university in Ah-mare-rekah, dese Black students talk about Black dormitories and Afro hair and dese handshakes and dashikis. But they never associate themselves with Black African students. They laugh at us... too Black, too ugly. *Das ist richtig!* We were Black, we were Africa! We were all those t'ings they protested to be! *Verstehst du?* Do you understand what I am speaking?"

"I think so. But I'm at a small college, and we don't have that problem. We have maybe thirty Black students... only a few Black African students."

We both laughed. Then, he continued his observations, shifting into a praise of Black American struggles representing the very ideals of democracy. He weighed the manner in which the United States was built on Black sweat.

He stated, *"deine Kultur und dein Leben*—your culture and your family—is what your life is about."

I nodded my understanding of the point he was making. We continued our cultural and political points until we finished our beers, with me attempting to keep up with his intermediate-level German. Our discussions were usually heavy with such matters, though peppered with frequent laughs, both of us pleased to have another Black person to share time and thoughts.

Minkah was in Germany to study engineering, and with his grasp of the language, he was moving steadily toward his goals. His plan after leaving the Institute was to remain in Munich for three years more to study, work, and send money home. He saw the privilege in his life to be able to do so, but he also acknowledged his responsibility to return home and help his family.

Minkah always humbled me. He was much more knowledgeable and mature than the other folks I met at the Institute. Sometimes, I felt I was robbing him by taking so much of his time. What he thought, planned, and spoke seemed so much more important than my adventures. Most times, my thoughts drifted from one beautiful woman to another, but his thoughts were rooted in politics, economics, and ideologies that came easily to him. I sat in the shadows of how little I knew, but he never held it against me. He merely looked at me, smiling, as if to say, "Your time will soon come."

\* \* \*

One of the advantages of living in Bavaria with its prevalent Catholicism were the Monday holidays that came along during our two-month study at the Institute. On one of those weekends, Jorge and I caught a ride to Italy with Matteo Ricci from the Advanced German class. On those holiday weekends, Matteo would drive home to Bologna to visit his wife and three children. He was pleased to have Jorge and me join him for the five-hour drive, and Jorge believed his Spanish would help us meet Italian girls. The rapid-speed autobahn ride with Matteo took me to the threshold of a heart attack, and Jorge's faith in the power of his Spanish in Italy fell short during the first day in the city.

On the second day in Bologna, we finally met two girls who were patient enough to have a glass of wine with us at a café. There was no effective communication with the girls despite Jorge's desperate attempts, and though cute, neither girl had shaved their underarms. And one neglected to shave the slight mustache above her top lip. In Bologna, the food was great, the architecture was impressive, and the girls were hairy.

On the second holiday weekend, Herr Arndt appeared again in Murnau to take our Bates group on a scheduled train trip to Vienna. I looked forward to seeing Vienna, the capital of Austria, which was a huge canvas of culture when compared to small-town life in Murnau. There were numerous sites that we squeezed into that weekend: the historical architecture; the incredible gardens; the Spanish Riding School with the Lipizzaner horses; the 1,400 rooms in the Schönbrunn Palace; the impatient Viennese waitresses; and the obnoxious American tourists. As we did before, the group stayed in a Vienna *Jugendherberge*, a youth hostel which had been a bomb shelter during World War II.

One of the personal highlights for me was the evening at Ludwig Hall to take in the symphony. Herr Arndt had reserved tickets for our group, but we had to stand in line to collect them at the ticket booth. While in line, I was chatting with Teddy and Hum when an elderly Austrian woman approached us. She looked at Teddy and Hum and then me. She reached into her purse.

"*Guten abend*," she smiled at me. "*Entschuldigen sie mich. Ich muss jetzt gehen. Hier,*" she continued, handing me a ticket. "*Sie konnen meine karten haben.*" She added, "*Sie habenein stark Gesicht.*"

I was puzzled. Teddy fingered the ticket.

"Of all the luck," Teddy said. "The ticket for the orchestra section . . . main floor. Our student seats are in the balcony."

"Why me?"

"She said you have . . . a trustful face," Hum stated.

"But, Hum, you know more about this kind of music than I do! Here, you take the ticket!"

"No way! She gave that ticket to you!"

I was speechless. Dressed in my casual attire, I headed through the main doors and immediately noticed that the patrons surrounding me were in formal wear. They smiled and greeted me before returning to their conversations. Once seated, I examined the program and read it as best I could. It was Gustav Mahler's *Titan Symphony No. 1* in four movements, performed by the Vienna

Philharmonic Orchestra. The music was beautiful, melancholy, forceful, haunting, burning! When the symphony was over, I was exhausted. Afterward, walking back to the hostel, Teddy and Hum continued to tease me about my luck and the woman's comments about my face. I heard them, but my senses were filled with Vienna and Mahler.

Months later, after returning to the United States, I researched composer Gustav Mahler (1860–1911) and discovered he was an Austrian Jew who rejected his Jewish identity and faith. Some saw him as a tormented man who conceded his cultural roots and family for his German nationality, even to the point of marrying a woman who was anti-Semitic. After his death and despite his musical accomplishments in Austria, Nazi Germany labeled his work as inferior, allowing it to be performed by only Jewish musicians.

Upon learning some aspects of Mahler's life, I thought about Minkah Kuwarte's statement that one's culture and family was what a person's life was all about. I comprehended with more clarity the significance of Minkah's observation and the tragedy of Mahler's choices about who he was. I was blessed to have the family I did while growing up in the racist South, and I was fortunate enough to embrace the political climate and Black cultural renaissance of the time in which I lived. To deny my roots and heritage for acceptance by mainstream American standards would only reward me with a cultural and spiritual death.

*  *  *

It was a sunny weekend morning when I decided to walk alone through Murnau village. The familiar *strasses* were empty. So, I made my way to the Staffelsee, walking in a different direction, away from the area where I usually had lunch with my Institute *Freunde*. I reached a small clearing where several wooden picnic tables were empty. I chose a table and sat on the tabletop with my feet resting on the bench. In the quiet warmth, I watched the lake's calm loveliness. In the calm and quiet, I had a distinctive experience. The sounds, both distant and nearby, faded out. The sunshine grew brighter, and I was *not* alone. No singing birds or rustling leaves overhead. No swimmers in the water or families enjoying a picnic. I looked over my shoulder and scanned the woods. No one. I looked back over the lake. Nothing. Yet, there was *something*, an abrupt warmth in the silence that caused me to look up. The sky was a clear blue with no clouds.

And I felt it again, stronger. A *Presence*. There was no deep voice. No burning bush. Just a silence and *Presence* that made me feel . . . peaceful. Exhilarated, but peaceful. No fear. No anxiety. Just calm. Time was suspended. I couldn't speak, because I didn't want to speak, afraid that my voice would break the tranquility. I wasn't alone. The calm embraced me, and I *knew* that I wasn't alone. I *knew* there was God.

I don't know how long I sat there. At some point, slowly, like a wave pulling me back from the shore by an unseen current, the *Presence* ebbed. The serenity lifted. My senses crept back over my body, and I heard birds, the rustling woods, and the lapping of the water. I looked around again and saw no one. Eventually, when I was able to move physically, I hesitated to leave.

At some point in my life, I knew I would attempt to write about that encounter, to use the limitation of words to capture and transform that experience into a language that others might understand. But at that place and time, the experience was solely mine.

\* \* \*

Charlie had been shy and reclusive, so it surprised me when he announced that he had a date. His high spirits bubbled over as he moved briskly around the room, humming to himself.

About a week before that happy mood, Charlie had requested, "Tell me about American girls."

"What do you mean?" I asked.

"Are the American girls at the Institute . . . average American girls?"

"I guess," I answered, thinking over his question. "Well . . . in a way, yeah. They're examples of White American girls."

"Mmm, I see. So, are they different—White American girls?"

"Depends, man . . . where they're from . . . their social background and income . . . just depends."

"I see . . . so will you write a letter for me in English?"

"Yeah, sure."

The following week, Charlie underwent a metamorphosis. He was seldom reading and studying in the room. He even borrowed money from me—which was surprising because on one occasion, he went without eating for a day rather than borrow one *Deutsche Mark*. But suddenly, he wore new clothes and requested that I teach him to dance.

Finally, I saw her. She was talking to Charlie during the morning break at the Institute. He stood close to her, drinking in her every word like pure, spring water. He never stopped smiling. I didn't know the thin girl with blonde hair, but I knew she was in the advanced class with Eva. I asked Eva about her, and Eva returned an equivocal smile without really telling me much.

Days later, I was at the disco with Eva, Patty, Bill, Jorge, and Minkah. Jorge and Minkah discussed politics while Patty and Bill discussed, well—Patty. Eva and I danced, squeezing through and around the crowd as we improvised. It was there on the dance floor that I saw Charlie's American woman. She was dancing with one of the Turkish men from my class. I looked around for Charlie, but he wasn't there.

When Eva and I returned to the table with the others, I kept my eyes on Charlie's woman. Eventually, she got up and left the disco with the Turkish guy, his arm wrapped around her waist. Later that night when I reached my host house, Charlie sat at the desk with an open book.

"*Grusse Gott*, Charlie!"

"*Guten abend, mein freund, vie gehts?*"

"Had a good time tonight. Eva and I danced like Gene Kelly and Cyd Charisse . . . on second thought, make that Bill Robinson and Shirley Temple," I joked.

I chuckled a bit, attempting to ignite a smile from him.

"And you, Charlie . . . a good night?"

"Yes, but for only a short time."

I undressed quietly, not wanting my high spirits to depress him. I noticed a sweet fragrance in the room, and glancing around, I saw the flowers filling the trash can. From my bed, I watched him close his book, turn off the light, and fall across his bed fully clothed.

"Mel," he said softly, "I cannot soon repay you the borrowed money. But before you leave Murnau, I will have it. I am expecting money from home soon. *Es tut mir leid!*"

"Nothing to be sorry about. Get it back to me when you can," I told him.

"*Danke, mein freund.*"

"Sure thing."

I heard him roll over in bed, and I was uncertain whether I should talk or not. Then, drifting toward me, I heard the faint sound of his crying.

\* \* \*

I wanted to see Switzerland. It was one of those places that stuck in my mind as being unique. It was the last long weekend due to a religious holiday, and I studied the maps to find the best route for hitchhiking to Zurich. Confident in my plan, I knew that hitching would save me money.

A few days before leaving, Eva approached me during the break and introduced me to Hinata, a young Japanese woman she knew from Advanced German, who spoke no English. Hinata was short and cute with round cheeks. Eva knew about my Zurich plan, but Hinata was traveling to Innsbruck, Austria, in another direction. For some unshared reason, Eva didn't want Hinata to travel alone, and she found us a ride on Friday afternoon to Innsbruck. From there, I could take the four-hour train ride from Innsbruck to Zurich, giving me more time in the city. On Sunday, I could hitch rides back from Switzerland to Murnau. It sounded like a plan that might get me to Zurich more quickly, but it also meant reaching into my pocket for the train fare.

"So, Eva, out of all the people at the school, why did you ask me to do this?"

"Because I can trust you, Mel," she said, smiling.

I looked at Hinata who smiled and bowed. I returned the bow before Eva pulled her away to secure our car ride to Innsbruck. Back at my host house, I returned to my maps and shaped the altered plan for hitching back from Zurich to Murnau.

At the end of classes on Friday, carrying my shoulder bag, I met Hinata at the Institute. We smiled and bowed, and she gestured for me to follow her to the back of the school to an older White man waiting in his small car. He was Austrian, and he said his name so quickly that I couldn't understand. I wasn't sure if he was a student at the Institute or someone in town that Eva knew. I slid in the back of the car, while he and Hinata sat in front, fluently flowing in their German conversation. For the next ninety minutes, they talked and laughed, often looking back at me to see if I was smiling.

When we finally flowed around the winding roadway that took us down into Innsbruck, I soaked in the natural beauty of the city that rested at the base of the mountain range. When the car stopped and Hinata gave her final bows to our driver, I added my smile as the man drove away. Hinata looked at me and smiled, waiting. I wasn't sure if she was waiting for a handshake or a hug, but I tried in my elementary German.

"Hinata . . . *Ich gehe Banhof*," I told her. "*Wo gehen sie?*"

She nodded and pulled out a sheet of paper which had an address written in German. I hunched my shoulders. Reached inside my shoulder bag and pulled out my map, but there were no details of the city of Innsbruck.

"*Scheisse*," I mumbled, pointing. "Okay . . . *diese strasse*."

My plan was to stop someone on the street who looked approachable. We walked a lengthy street until we saw two women dressed in business attire. I prompted Hinata, who explained in German as she showed the paper with the address. The women didn't know. Nor did the next two people. We finally lucked out with a young guy who shared a smile with Hinata. She nodded as they chatted, and we followed his directions that led us to an apartment building.

"*Herr Mel, hier*," she smiled, pointing.

She pushed the button at the Japanese name on the directory. Moments later, a thin Japanese woman opened the door, and I stood there observing the mini-reunion between her and Hinata, their Japanese words overlapping. Hinata introduced me, and I said, "*Banhof.*"

"*Links..drei strasses . . . und folgen den Zeichen,*" the tall woman stated.

"*Zeichen,*" I repeated, thinking back to class. "Signs."

I smiled at them both, and Hinata gave me a hug before they disappeared inside. I hurried to the end of the block and turned left, noticing that it was getting dark. I walked to the third street and saw the sign with the image indicating the direction to the train station. In another twenty minutes I stood in line for my ticket before reaching the platform, where I had to wait another hour. Once on the train, I knew I had four hours to go, so I allowed myself to nap. When there was the long stop at the Austrian-Swiss border where the conductor walked through and checked passports, I figured I had another hour before reaching Zurich, so I eased back into sleep.

Abruptly, in about thirty minutes, the train stopped at a station. I looked out the window into the darkness for a sign indicating the name of the town, but I saw nothing except people stepping off the train. So, I waited, and when the conductor entered the car, he stood over me.

"*Sie mussen hier aussteigen,*" he said.

"Zurich?"

"*Nein, aber sie mussen hier austeigen!*"

The man stared at me for a long, silent moment. A second conductor entered the car from the opposite direction, and the two men had a brief discussion.

"*Ihre Fahrschein, bitte,*" the second conductor said to me.

I retrieved my ticket from my shoulder bag and showed it. The man nodded.

"*Dieser Zug endet hier,*" the second conductor explained slowly. Then, he pointed out the window at the next track. "Zurich . . . *diese Strecke . . . in einer Stunde.*"

I finally understood. Somehow, I purchased a ticket that had an hour layover. I had to get off the train, and then catch another train to get into Zurich. I thanked the conductors and gathered my shoulder bag to step out onto the platform. The train reversed its direction and moved slowly into the darkness.

I glanced at the clock that indicated it was after ten—behind the time frame I had planned. I found a bench and pulled my jacket tightly as the chilly air crept in. In the distance along the platform, I saw several Turkish men in conversation, the strong smell from their cigarettes wafting to me. My empty stomach growled slightly, asking for attention, but I held fast, opting to wait until I got into Zurich to grab something to eat.

When I looked up, two women were standing over me. The older woman appeared to be in her forties, though the moonlight might have softened her actual years. But there was no mistake about the younger woman. She was maybe twenty, her face alluring by a mix of moonlight and platform lights. She reminded me of someone I'd seen before.

"*Sind sie American, ja?*" the older woman asked.

"*Ja*," I answered.

"*Gut*. I speak English . . . some."

"Oh, really? Great . . ."

"Where go you?" she asked slowly.

"Zurich."

"Ahh, Zurich," she repeated. "*Sehr schoen* . . . beautiful."

She nodded and rummaged through her bag. She muttered a string of harsh words and placed her bag on the bench.

"Cigarette?" she asked.

"No, sorry, I don't smoke."

The elderly woman stood up and nudged the girl, pointing to the space beside me. When the girl sat beside me, she offered me a smile. Then, it came to me. She resembled a young Ingrid Bergman from the movie *Casablanca*. Her hair was styled the same, brushed back, allowing her smooth complexion to glow.

"You look like Ingrid Bergman," I told her.

"Bergman," she repeated.

"Yeah . . . Bogart and Bergman . . . here's looking at you, kid."

"Bergman . . . Ingmar Bergman?"

"No, no, Ingrid Bergman! *Sprechen sie Englisch?*"

"*Nein, Ich kann nicht* . . ."

Her smile broadened. She moved closer until her body touched mine. She spoke slowly, loudly, as if the volume would help me understand. I shook my head, hunched my shoulders to indicate my ignorance. But she kept talking in a sad tone, almost desperate. I wanted to understand her, her speech quickening in her halted phrasing. Then, she placed her hand on my knee. Effortlessly. The touch was deliberate, her fingers moving up to my thigh.

At that moment, the elderly woman returned, smoking a cigarette that smelled of Turkish tobacco. The girl and woman exchanged several quick phrases.

"My friend . . . likes you," the elderly woman stated.

"Oh, well . . . I like her, too."

"But she likes you much. *Verstehen sie?* Must go to Zurich? *Konnen Sie hier bleiben?*"

"*Bleiben* . . . stay?" I said, understanding. "*Nein* . . . *nein*."

The older woman sighed. Threw her cigarette to the platform. She spoke hurriedly to the girl, pulling her arm as they both walked away. I strained to see the girl's face for as long as I could. I debated changing my mind, to take a chance. Zurich would still be there tomorrow. I looked over my shoulder to catch one last look. The girl stood alone in the doorway looking terribly lovely. At that moment, the older woman stepped into the doorway with two Turkish men at her side. She moved her arms in conversation before the four disappeared.

I turned my attention back to the track. It seemed colder as I folded my arms across my chest, my stomach growling again. During the next fifteen minutes, my inner voices argued about my decision, deliberating back and forth until I heard the train's whistle growing louder, the clickety rhythm along the tracks as it edged to the platform. I focused back on my destination, joining other people entering the nearest car.

As I settled into my window seat, I slipped into a light sleep as the train gathered speed. An hour later, I felt the train's speed slowing, the city's lights shimmering in the distance. I took the map from the side pocket of my shoulder bag, studying the best route from the station to the youth hostel. The map suggested that the station was on one side of a peninsula, so I needed to take the underground walkway, a tunnel stretching in various directions, to reach the *rues* leading to the hostel. But when I took the stairway to the street level, the signs were more difficult to read with tired eyes. Following a number of faulty turns, I finally arrived at the hostel. The front doors were locked, and after minutes of knocking at the heavy door, a man appeared to tell me in his accented English that the hostel was closed and would reopen at what sounded like seven a.m. A glance at my watch indicated I had six hours to wait. I cussed and tried to figure my next move, knowing that a hotel would cost me the entire allocated budget for the weekend.

So, I walked, hoping to find an open coffee shop, but all the businesses were closed. I drifted back toward the city's center and found a bench near the river. I could sleep there and use the distant trees as my bathroom. I was tired, and the bench's wooden slats grew harder as I tried to rest. No comfort. The chilly air was an irritating blanket over my body. Finally, I had to move. I thought I could return to the underground tunnel and escape the chilly air.

The lights in the tunnel were brighter than the streetlights, and I moved away from the drafty stairway, edging along the tiled wall to find a clean space on the cement floor. I tucked my knees close to my body, my eyelids heavy. Then, I heard the voice—singing, reverberating off the tiled walls. It was a man's voice, and I saw a tall Black man, dressed in a long, black, full-length coat with matching black pants, shirt, and hat. I thought I was dreaming.

"Brother!" the man greeted. His voice was shaped by a mixture of accents, but dominated by a Caribbean lilt. "Brother! I can't believe it! What you doing here in this place?"

"Hello," I said in a sleepy haze.

He stood over me for a few seconds smiling, and then he slid down the tiled wall to sit beside me.

"Good to meet you," he said, reaching out for a handshake. "I'm Devon, mahn."

"Mel . . ."

"I've been through this station many times, but never saw you!"

"Well, my first time here. Got a late train into Zurich, and the hostel was closed."

"Ah, the hostel . . . yes, yes, it closes early . . . too early for me. Good to see you, mahn!"

"Um . . . yeah. I was just going to sleep for a bit."

"No, no, can't sleep here, mahn. *Policier* come around."

Devon explained that he was a musician, originally from Grenada, and lived with his Italian girlfriend in Como, a small Italian city about three hours south of Zurich by train. Devon was a bass player and vocalist, filling in that night as a singer for a house band that covered American rock and R&B. After his music and girlfriend, he had a passion for American movies, particularly Black films. So, for the next few hours we talked about American movies and Black actors.

After the *Policier* passed by us the third time, tapping his nightstick against the tile walls, we had discussed numerous films. We slipped into the politics of America, and Devon went into a soliloquy about how confused and spoiled Americans were. And after he was mugged during a New York City visit, he also added how dangerous and violent Americans were. I listened as best as I could, fighting sleep and the rumbling in my empty stomach.

In the early morning, Devon offered to buy me breakfast at a small café he liked, and I happily followed him from the tunnel to the small business. I wolfed down the food and walked him back to the station to catch his train. He hugged me like I was a favorite relative, and as he boarded the train, he told me to make sure I kept in touch. However, he never gave me his address. But I understood. For him, it was a great night to just talk to another Black person.

Leaving the train station, I hurried to the hostel, checked in, and was told I would have to be out during certain hours. I took a quick shower and headed out to see the city under a sunny sky. With my passport tucked inside my pocket, I walked for hours, snapping pictures as I strolled the streets. To me, the city was extremely clean, almost too pristine for the number of people who crossed my path.

As I continued from the busy avenues of businesses to a lovely park area, I heard faint music in the distance. I walked the length of the park until I came to a plateau that overlooked the Swiss Motorway. Descending the stairway to take the footbridge over the highway, I stopped to watch the cars zooming below me. The overpass ended at the edge of a field that stretched for about fifty yards ahead of me. The landscape seemed incongruous—the city behind me, the countryside before me. But it was an alluring contrast, and I high-stepped across the unmowed field until I reached a two-lane roadway. The music grew louder now, and I moved quickly, trying to recognize the melody.

Opening up before me was another, much smaller field and contiguous to it was a narrow, placid stream of water. On the other side of the stream, a stage held musicians and instruments, a large striped canopy blocking out the sun. I couldn't distinguish the faces of the musicians, but I heard the steady rhythm of the percussion beneath the reverberating electrical instruments. There were dozens of people in front of the stage, dancing and clapping their hands to the music. I noticed a few people on my side of the stream, curiously watching as I was. The music ended with applause, and a hippie-looking guy stepped to the microphone, speaking in French and then in German. The crowd cheered in response.

Behind me, the sudden roaring of police cars and black-and-white vans grew louder. The vehicles sped by me before crossing a short bridge over the stream and angling near the crowd. Uniformed officers jumped out. One officer lifted a megaphone, shouting words to the crowd. A wave of jeers erupted, and chanting, the crowd now moved toward the vans. Simultaneously, the uniformed officers advanced, armed with night sticks and wearing helmets and masks. Abruptly, the police released smoking canisters that arched into the crowd. Screams and shouts erupted. The people surged. The officers wielded their sticks. People scurried in different directions. The steady flurry of sticks sliced through the smoky air.

It was never a matter of thinking. My body moved ahead of my mind, my feet plowing back across the field in short, rapid strides. I ran. Raced back across the large field and to the footbridge. My side ached as I sucked for air. I ran up the steps and raced to the other side, sweat rolling down my neck. At the first café I saw, I claimed an empty chair. Ordering a full meal and a glass of wine, I leaned into my thoughts. In my mind, Zurich was an idealized place of peace. However, in those moments, I altered my perspective to one basic truth: *Wherever you find human beings, there will be no ideal place.*

By early morning the next day, having skipped breakfast and with my map fixed in my hand, I began walking away from the city center. My first ride, the shortest of all that day, was with a quiet Zurich businessman who gave me a lift to the outskirts of the city. And as I walked and waited for the next vehicle to pass my way, my stomach ached in its emptiness. My shoulder bag grew heavy, and the late morning sun began to bake my forehead.

I wished I never accepted my second ride. The driver was a wild-eyed Turkish man in a red Volkswagen. He was quite horny. In the five minutes I was in the car, he kept his left hand on the steering wheel and his right hand grabbing my crotch. I repeatedly yelled, *"Nein, nein!"* Exasperated, he abruptly stopped the car and forcibly pushed me out, screaming at me as I held onto my shoulder bag. I rolled onto the asphalt and saw him make a U-turn, speeding back in the other direction.

The third lift appeared quickly. It was a young girl driving her visiting grandparents back to their home in St. Gallen. I sat in the rear with the grandfather who didn't speak English, but he showered me with a series of beatific smiles. The grandmother in the passenger seat glanced over her shoulder to greet me before returning her gaze to the passing scenery. The girl was young and cute with her blonde hair cut close. She was enthusiastic to practice her English with me, as she asked numerous questions about American politics. We both were disappointed when we reached St. Gallen.

I walked for more than forty minutes before my next ride with a bearded, heavy-set man driving a BMW. Flashing back to the Turkish driver, I slid cautiously into the car, holding onto my shoulder bag with both hands in case I needed a weapon. Hearing my accent, he proudly informed me that he had studied one year at a California university. He spoke English quite well, and we slipped into a discussion about his favorite sport: American football.

Reaching the Swiss-German border, he stopped the car and instructed me to walk through customs and meet him on the German side. Apparently, some Americans carried drugs, and if caught in his car, he would come under suspicion. I approached the gate and presented my passport to the Swiss guard. Silently, he checked my shoulder bag before returning my passport. Some meters further, the German guard, with a similar surly expression, duplicated the Swiss guard's search before permitting me into the country.

True to his promise, Mr. BMW was waiting for me on the German side. Once we reached Lindau, he stopped and telephoned a friend, inviting me to join them. My empty stomach gurgled at the thought of food, but I didn't want to spend hours away from the road. I thanked him, positioned my shoulder bag, and continued on.

Walking casually, I wondered if my Black American cynicism shaped my decisions. Despite the generous people I'd met during the past weeks, my suspicions about White people prompted my attitudes.

As my stomach knotted, I continued along, staying on the road and looking down at the next town in the distance. It had a picture-postcard allure, and I began rolling words through my head that might eventually resemble a poem. A string of phrases that could capture the glistening lake, meadows, and hillsides. At that moment, I ached to share what I saw with someone—the colors, sounds, smells, and textures that surrounded me. There was something sacred about all that I took in. Yes, I would have the photographs I took, and I would have the words swirling through my head, but that exact moment would never exist again. I removed my journal and jotted down only nouns and adjectives that captured what I saw. I was too hungry, thirsty, and tired to attempt writing a poem.

After another hour of walking, I got a ride with a group of six young people about my age. There was no comfortable space available in their small van, but they insisted I join them. Growing weary, I didn't reject the invitation. They were drinking beer, singing in German, and applauding themselves for their off-key rendition of the song they all knew. They had no food, but offered me beer, which I welcomed for my thirst, my head quickly spinning as I smiled my thanks. Their ride ended in Fussen, and they told me I was about *eine stunde* from Murnau.

I thanked them as I crawled out of the packed rear seat. I kept to the roadway and staggered for another thirty minutes or so before another car stopped for me. The driver was an elderly man wearing *lederhosen* and his elderly *frau* wore a *dirndl*. For my benefit, the old man spoke very slowly in German, criticizing Americans because they loved war. I understood some of his remarks about Vietnam, but his tirade intensified in a flurry of arm movements. His wife frequently turned, uttering one or two supportive words. The ride became an ordeal, and I was trapped in the back seat of a two-door Volkswagen. I was being verbally tortured for the sins of Washington warmongers.

Finally—Murnau!

It was dark, and I was elated to be back—home? My hunger over the past nine hours had rendered me dizzy. On my way through town, the cafés were closed. It was Sunday night, and Murnau was asleep. I knew I had nothing in the room to eat, and entering my host house, I called out for Frau Koglmayer. After a moment, she appeared from a back room, and I begged her for fruit or bread. She understood and moved into the kitchen, returning with a hard roll. I thanked her and made my trek upstairs, finding my room empty. I fell across the bed and devoured the bread. It was the greatest thing I had ever eaten!

\*\*\*

Suddenly, the last week at the Institute was before us. There were nightly visits to the Staffelsee club, and extended conversations during scheduled breaks at school. Addresses were exchanged, and gifts were shared with instructors and classmates. It was an exciting and sad week all at once. Herr Arndt appeared again, gathering the Bates group to determine who would be traveling back to Luxembourg City with him or taking their own excursions. Teddy planned to see more of Germany. Brenda planned to travel to France before returning to the States. Others were ready to journey back home directly. Based upon my meager funds, I was still undecided. Herr Arndt reminded everyone that we had standby tickets for our return flight out of the Luxembourg City Airport. He urged us to arrive several hours before departure to place our names on the waiting list.

So, I used the early portion of the week to say my goodbyes to Charlie and Minkah, and I connected with Patty, Bill, Jorge, and Eva during our afternoon Staffelsee gatherings. During our last afternoon together, Eva signaled me to follow her to the water's edge. I joined her, and we eased our bare feet into the water.

"Mel, I want you to come with me to Amsterdam," Eva said, lighting a cigarette.

"Amsterdam?" I repeated. "What's there?"

"Me and you . . . the Rembrandt museum . . . the paintings of the Dutch Masters . . . the Anne Frank house . . . the beautiful canals . . . they're building the Van Gogh Museum. The city is romantic, artistic, and sad all at once. It's a place for writers!"

"I . . . I don't know."

"Oh, don't think about it. Let's just do it! We'll take the train to Munich . . . fly into Paris . . . then take the train into the Netherlands."

"My funds are a bit—"

"I have money! Don't think about the money!"

"Give me a day to consider . . ."

"Ah, Mel, that means you'll say *no*."

"So, why me? You have these guys falling all over you at the school."

"It's because . . . I can trust you."

I stared at her. Smiled. Eva Benjamin excited me and scared me at the same time. It would take me months after returning to the States and reliving those days in Murnau to fully comprehend her. She was a woman who squeezed as much life into each minute as possible. Then, she rushed off to the next moment looking for more. If not more, then something fascinating. She was a woman of privilege who needed someone close by to take away the edgy guilt of getting anything she wanted. She was restless and addicted to impulses, knowing that there was no cure for her condition. She was a Jewish woman who knew the history of her people's oppression, but felt guilty about the oppression of Black people in her home country of South Africa. Perhaps my being Black eased some of her anxieties. Rather than actively involving herself in addressing and changing the oppression she witnessed, she used her wealth to escape that reality.

But I certainly couldn't judge her for who she was and what she did. After all, I stepped away for ten weeks to selfishly indulge myself in a different world while young men my age—many of them Black and Brown—were dying in Vietnam to allegedly establish a democracy rule, though democracy wasn't ruling for them at home in the States.

Eva read my face, sighed, and led me back to the others. She opened another bottle of wine and poured herself a cup before passing the bottle around. It wasn't the *last supper*, but it was the only remaining opportunity for us to share our reckless and irresponsible time together. Eva surprised me with a quick kiss on my lips before looking out over the Staffelsee.

\* \* \*

Brenda was asleep. I reached over and adjusted her shoulder bag that was slipping from her lap. It was her suggestion that we travel back to Luxembourg City together via Strasbourg, France, giving her time to practice her French. She had mapped out the trip and figured out the train schedules, but she didn't want to travel alone. I agreed to join her, yearning for a few more days of seeing Europe.

Brenda wore her hair long, the full strands falling along the contours of her face. She claimed her green eyes and olive complexion emanated from her French, German, and Italian heritage. I didn't ask her how she knew this family history. I was simply content to gaze as she slept. After Brenda stirred and stretched, she pulled out her itinerary. We had another three hours before reaching Strasbourg, and she gave me a preview of what we would squeeze into our one day in that city. She wanted to take pictures of the Strasbourg Cathedral and spend time at the Museum of Fine Arts. She insisted that we find the Ill River and walk one of the bridges to get a view of the city's varied architecture. I agreed to all of it, but I confessed I was most interested in tasting the French wines.

Reaching Strasbourg, France, we checked our suitcases into lockers at the station, taking out plastic bags with personal items and a change of underclothes that we placed into our shoulder bags. After eight hours on the train, the first step was to get food and wine. Walking toward a commercial area, she picked out one of those cafes replicated in numerous American movies, where we sat outside, watching people rushing by as we toasted with our wine glasses.

"So, where to next, *fraulein* Brenda? The more we walk, the more of the city we'll see."

"*Das is richtig, meine liebe, aber . . . mais, maintenant nous devons parler seulement francais!*"

"Ah . . . okay. Whatever you said."

We walked for a couple of hours before deciding to find the hostel. I scanned the lobby area as she spoke to the clerk. The furniture looked uncomfortable as it did in most *jugenberges*, but sitting my sweaty body in a cushioned chair was a treat. I was just about to close my eyes when Brenda walked over.

"Bad news, *meine liebe*."

"*Scheise* . . . damn."

"Seems the men's section is full, but . . . there would be room for me. But let's look for something else."

"Naw, go ahead and get a space here, and . . . I'll find a park," I offered heroically. I thought back to my long, uncomfortable night in Zurich.

"But you don't have a sleeping bag. Let's find a hotel."

My thoughts jumped to my limited budget, but I put up a confident front. As we walked the streets to find a hotel, I counted my money silently in my head.

"We'll get one room with two beds," she suggested. "That way, we save money. What do you think?"

"Sure thing," I responded.

We entered the first hotel we saw. The lobby was small and dimly lit. I didn't see any chairs, so I stood close to Brenda at the desk. The man behind the desk had a jaded, washed-out appearance, and the cigarette he puffed curled smoke rings into his peppered hair. As Brenda spoke in French, he glanced at me and then back to her. He mumbled something, and Brenda stiffened. Suddenly, he became loud, gesturing with both arms.

"What's wrong?" I asked.

"Come on, let's go," she responded.

"Go? What did he say?"

"Nothing," she said, her eyes brimming with tears.

The man yelled again, tapping his forefinger on the counter.

"Please, let's go, Mel!" Brenda pleaded.

"Something to do with me, right? What did he say?"

"He told me . . . to take my business elsewhere and not to use his hotel."

I looked at the man and sprang forward to grab him across the counter. He leaped backward, shouting in French. I kept reaching for his throat, cussing him out in English. Brenda pulled me toward the door.

"Let's go!" Brenda urged. "Please, Mel, let's go!"

Outside, she cut along one narrow street, and then another. I followed her until we slowly relaxed. Then, we both broke into nervous laughter. It took us two more hotel lobbies before we found a vacant room. The room wasn't impressive in its bareness, and it possessed a distinctive aroma and atmosphere, reminiscent of nothing but itself. There were two narrow beds on either side of a rickety nightstand that held a lamp.

There wasn't a shower, although I needed one. The bathroom wasn't a separate room, but the sink and toilet were hidden behind a partition. Brenda took her turn in the space behind the curtain, peeing and washing up in the sink before slipping beneath the sheets in her bed. I, too, took my bird bath in the sink, turning off the ceiling light before dropping onto my bed. Looking over at her in the darkness, my eyes focused on the silhouette of her body.

Then, it began—that churning, anxious feeling of indecision. For minutes, I struggled against the horny-headed satyrs dancing in my head. I called her name, and she rolled slightly in the bed. I suggested we should get naked in one bed and have wild sex to celebrate our only night together in France. She chuckled, whispering that she would if it wasn't for Mark, her boyfriend at Boston University. Silence. I told her I didn't know. She confessed that they'd been involved for some time, and she listed his personality traits—nothing of particular importance that I wanted to know. However, I offered a few supportive words, not meaning any of them. I rolled on my side and embraced frustration. I couldn't sleep, and I couldn't get her out of my head. So, I began counting backward from one hundred. By the time I got to number ten, I gave up. Once I gave up, I went to sleep.

The next morning after breakfast, Brenda and I took the three-hour train ride to Luxembourg City, taking a local train to the international airport. When we reached the Icelandic Airline's check-in desk, there was only one seat remaining on the standby waiting list. We looked at each other, and Brenda suggested we flip a coin. However, I knew I couldn't leave her alone in the airport.

"So, what will you do?" she asked. "The next Icelandic flight is tomorrow night."

"I'll check my suitcase into a locker . . . hitchhike back into the city," I said. "Spend tomorrow taking in the sites . . . sample a few glasses of wine."

"I didn't know it would be this crowded," she remarked. "Listen, I have your address and phone number, and you have mine. We have to see each other this summer, *mon amour*."

"Sounds good to me."

"Do you have any money?"

I knew exactly how much money I had. After paying for breakfast in Strasbourg, I had one twenty-dollar bill that was folded and placed inside my sock. The plan was to use seventeen dollars to buy my one-way bus fare from New York to Hyannis. That would leave me one dollar to catch the subway from Kennedy Airport to the Port Authority bus terminal, and two dollars for a coke and a bag of chips to eat during the seven-hour bus ride home.

"Sure, I'll be fine," I told her.

She hugged me tightly.

"Thanks for being my friend, Mel."

She smiled, and before joining the passenger line, she slipped some paper into my hand. I looked down and saw a folded twenty-dollar bill. She was already boarding with the passengers before I could call out her name.

I was hungry, and I didn't want to sit around the airport. I saw young White kids who didn't make various flights forming groups to figure out their next moves. It would be easier being alone and certainly easier to hitch a ride alone. I slipped my suitcase into a free locker and key and quickly lucked up to hitch a ride into the city.

I walked several streets, finding a restaurant with an inviting window seat. I used the twenty dollars that Brenda gave me to order a full meal with wine, and I pulled out my journal and jotted down some thoughts. The food was hot and tasty, filling my stomach's growling emptiness. The wine was splendid, as was my buzz. I hit the street again, maneuvering my way back toward the park I'd passed.

The park wasn't lit well, and the benches were in view of the streets. So, after using the park bathroom, I reversed my path back toward the business streets. After an hour of walking, I stood at a closed photography shop that had a large window display of various equipment. To the right of the showcase, I saw two doors with clear glass panes. The door on the left was the locked entrance into the darkened store itself, and the door on the right hid a dimly lit stairway. I assumed that the right door was locked as well, so I claimed the dry cement area in front of both doors. I huddled for warmth and to keep from view.

It grew chilly for a July evening. I adjusted and squirmed, searching for sleep. Time assumed a strange, unnatural quality, and every position was an indefinite state of discomfort.

When I heard the footsteps, I thought they were only in my head. The French voices rose loudly in laughter. Whether the couple saw me was unclear, but I watched them stagger and laugh in their drunkenness. The man turned the handle on the right door—it was unlocked. The woman followed him inside, and they ascended the stairway into the darkness.

I feared that once they reached their love nest, they might call the police to report me. I listened for several minutes for police sirens, but I breathed easier when only the city sounds pierced the darkness. The couple didn't see me. Then, it struck me. They opened the door without a key. I stood and turned the doorknob, heard the click, and stepped inside. Before me, a wooden stairway inclined to a single dim overhead light. I saw a door on either side of the narrow landing. Perhaps doors to apartments . . . business offices?

I moved inside and claimed a wooden step, which wasn't as cold as the concrete. I leaned against the wall and contorted my body as best as I could. It was a long night of broken sleep, and the next morning, my back and legs ached. I hit the bathroom in the park before walking a wider circle around the city, making a point of passing the outdoor cafes. No luck. Breakfast seemed to be a meal that people felt obliged to complete.

By the early afternoon, my shoulder ached from my full bag. I hitched a ride back to the airport, planning to search the terminal's café for food before journaling to pass the time. Entering the terminal, my heart dropped as I saw more White kids sitting in small groups around the terminal floor. I strolled to the Icelandic Airlines lounge area and saw the evening flight's schedule in large letters above the counter. I confirmed with a busy agent that my name was on the waiting list.

I toured the airport's café area, but the kids had swept the tables like locusts, leaving only crumbs on empty trays. I retraced my path back to the lounge, claiming a corner space to sit on the floor. Leaning my head against the wall, I wondered how Jesus fasted for forty days, and Gandhi for twenty-one? All I could think about was food!

Then, I noticed this White guy approaching me. He looked as restless and disheveled as everyone else loitering at the airport. When he stepped to me, I knew he wanted to talk. He had long, scraggly hair and a beard, and he flashed a dingy smile at me. His jeans were beyond faded, as was the wrinkled Pink Floyd T-shirt he wore. He begged for a cigarette, but I admitted I didn't smoke. He swore aloud and slid along the wall to sit next to me. He confessed he saw me writing in my journal, and he claimed to be a writer also, traveling abroad to get some experiences to write about. He continued his oration by asserting his love for Vonnegut, Roth, and Updike, confessing that John Barth's *The End of the Road* was the *truth*. I hoped my silence would signal my preference for solitude, but he rambled on about his Boston parents suffocating his efforts to find himself.

Asking again for a cigarette and receiving the same answer, he stood and looked around the terminal. He mumbled beneath his breath, and I caught a whiff of his stench as he moved toward a cluster of White kids playing cards. I leaned my head back, drifting into a light nap. When I opened my eyes again, the lounge area was filled with waiting passengers. I had drifted into a much deeper sleep than I thought. The clerk at the desk announced the flight's number and destination. Hearing my name, I hurried to the counter, showed my ticket, and informed the clerk I had to get my suitcase from the locker. I ran the long hallway, seized my luggage, and returned quickly. Finally boarding, I was self-conscious again about my clothes and odor when assigned to take the middle seat between two businessmen. My stomach growled. I longed for the flight to be in the air and cruising for the Iceland stop. Thirty minutes later, the flight attendant finally wheeled out the cart with drinks and snacks. I devoured the bags of pretzels and nuts before they touched the tray before me.

I slept all the way from Iceland to New York, waking only once for a bathroom run. The expansive interior of John F. Kennedy International Airport was welcomed, and I searched for signage leading to the shuttle for the Port Authority Bus Terminal. Once there, I bought my ticket for Hyannis, leaving me a couple of dollars for a soft drink and chips. After hours of waiting, I was finally on my way to Cape Cod. After more hours of riding and stopping and riding, I arrived in Hyannis, using my final quarters to check my suitcase and shoulder bag into a locker. My plan was to walk home, shower, and collapse for a few hours before driving back to the station to gather my luggage.

I angled up the hill from the bus station to catch North Street, which would lead to Mama D and Papa D's house on Mitchell's Way. As I walked the familiar streets, they appeared small and narrow, and I noted that the buildings were unadorned and plainly designed with no centuries-old architecture. I had seen so many different things during the past ten weeks. Met people from around the world. Tasted life in ways I never imagined.

At that point of reflection, a car slowed next to me, and I saw three White teenagers. They all flipped me the finger, and the one in the passenger seat yelled out, *"Hey, nigger, nigger!"*

The car bolted away as I searched for a rock to fling at them. Nothing. I continued walking and mumbled under my breath, *"Well, I'm home."*

CHAPTER FIVE

## Like A Winding Sheet

After experiencing months in Europe, Cape Cod was depressing. I ached to be back in Germany with my friends. To be surrounded by the city and rural landscapes that held such deep history and beauty. Those months abroad were immeasurable to my independence and self-reliance. With all of its twists, challenges, and revelations, I didn't want that European experience to end. However, I had to accept that Germany was just one of the brilliant pearls on my necklace of experiences.

During the remaining months of the summer, I worked for Papa D's Cleaning Service while living in my parents' basement. As I shared time with my family and friends, I knew my senior year at Bates College awaited with obligations to fulfill. I recognized I had invested too much time and too much of my parents' money not to complete the degree. I remembered the truth I accepted years before—my college success wasn't just about me, as I represented family members and friends. However, the coming year held the pressuring requirement to complete my undergraduate thesis to graduate and enter the job market.

Returning to campus, I faced two semesters before graduation. I decided that my thesis would focus on the Harlem Renaissance works of Langston Hughes, Countee Cullen, and Wallace Thurman. Although I wanted to work with Dr. Leamon, I chose Dean Carignan as my advisor, knowing his knowledge and experience teaching African American Studies would help me develop a detailed thesis. As the fall semester began, my classes and thesis immediately siphoned my energy, so I leaned into my radio show and stage theater to help me cope and revitalize myself. Along with my radio show as an outlet, theater provided a break from apprehensions about my future. I hadn't taken any acting classes, but I auditioned for two plays that year and received roles in both.

The first production was the one act play *The Private Ear* by playwright Peter Schaeffer. The three-character comedy required a British accent, which was a challenge since I had a difficult time speaking in an American one. In *The Private Ear*, the important goal was for me to develop the interior and exterior dimensions of a fast-talking bloke who tried to seduce his roommate's girlfriend. Eventually, I made my character click, and the local newspaper gave the play and me personally some positive comments, which indeed brought satisfaction after those many hours of rehearsals.

The other play was *The Devils*, a three-act play written by John Whiting, based upon an alleged demon possession of nuns in a seventeenth-century convent. The priest accused of this enchantment was Father Grandier, played by my talented classmate, Rick Porter. The priest was a man caught between his spiritual and human longings. My character, Father Ambrose, was the elderly priest who appeared late in the play to save the Grandier's soul. The challenge with the character was both physical and aural. My makeup, gait, physical gestures, and vocal tones had to resonate the age, wisdom, and temperament of the elderly priest. Again, the reviews from the city and campus newspapers were good, and I was singled out for my brief appearance as one of the outstanding performers in the play. I received the Bates Theater Award for best supporting actor for that year, and I was elated. These creative, theatrical endeavors balanced my academic duties, providing me a needed diversion as educational demands pulled me into the quicksand of suffocating deadlines.

\*\*\*

I took an English class in the spring semester with Professor John Tagliabue, an internationally-known poet who was affectionately called "Tag" by his students. Walt had developed a rapport with the professor through previous classes, and Tag inspired me as well—through his facility with words and images, his alacrity to be himself in front of the class, and his flowing references to numerous authors, dead and alive.

That semester of reading and writing during Tag's class reacquainted me with the power of being a wordsmith. One of the poems I wrote in class connected to my feelings about the significance of music in my life, and Tag encouraged me to re-work and revise the poem to submit it to a national competition. To my surprise, my poem, "I Am . . . Music," was accepted into the 1973 *National Anthology of Student Poetry*, marking my first publication.

\*\*\*

My friend and brother, John Jenkins, lured me into the martial arts through long discussions about blending my spiritual self with my mental and physical attributes. His leadership in the Golden Fist Academy in Lewiston and his impressive demonstrations of Shotokan karate opened the doorway to a regiment that pushed me to physical exhaustion while deepening my self-confidence.

Many Americans were confronted with martial arts at the same time through the television series *Kung Fu*, but young men like me were astounded that year by Bruce Lee in his Chinese-made movies that hit American big screens. Although Lee had appeared as a supporting character in *The Green Hornet* television series (1966-1967), the movies *Fists of Fury* (1971) and *The Chinese Connection* (1972) featured Lee as the protagonist. He became a Chinese hero with a unique screen persona, and the rapture of viewing *Enter the Dragon* (1973) was indescribable.

Part of the impact of those Bruce Lee movies were that they offered an alternative screen hero—a skilled and strong Asian man. By the time I graduated, men of color were the popular, dominating images on the big screen, particularly the emergence of Black male characters. These included Sweet Sweetback, Shaft, Gravedigger Jones, and Coffin Ed Johnson (*Cotton Comes to Harlem*, 1970), and Priest (*SuperFly*, 1972). Despite the questionable moral behavior of those protagonists, they possessed the boldness and swagger necessary to navigate their inner-city challenges and the *Man*, i.e., the White-dominated political and legal systems. My fanatical connection to Sidney Poitier didn't waiver, but in the late 1960s to the early 1970s, a wider pantheon of Black actors surfaced: Melvin Van Peebles, Richard Roundtree, Ron O'Neal, Jim Brown, Bernie Casey, Ivan Dixon, Jim Kelly, Paul Winfield, Richard Pryor, and others.

From some perspectives at the time, those representations of Black men reinforced racial stereotypes. By contrast, for me and younger Black viewers in the 1970s, those Black male screen images underscored a variety of roles that exuded strength, sexuality, aggressiveness, and on occasion, tenderness. During that same decade, the television and cinematic images of Black women with brown or cinnamon skin tones, large or short afros, and shapely bodies emerged. Judy Pace, Pam Grier, Tamara Dobson, Sheila Frazier, Gloria Hendry, Carol Speed, Paula Kelly, Lola Falana, and Jayne Kennedy offered a panoply of Black women characters affirming their beauty, sexiness, and toughness. Those portrayal of Black women assured me that somewhere beyond the state of Maine, there was a host of Black women that I could still possibly meet.

\* \* \*

Early in the fall semester, Dean Carignan encouraged me to consider graduate school and a master's degree. I appreciated his encouragement, but graduate school required two more years of classes, library research, and academic writing, which all seemed overwhelming at the time. So, I met with the campus career counselor, who shared the exciting, people-based world of selling life insurance. As he spoke and suggested the myriad of benefits of a profession in insurance, I gagged. He tried to get me to sign up for interviews with various company representatives coming to campus, and I hurried to the library to explore graduate schools.

I enjoyed American history, Black literature, music, movies, theater, poetry, and short stories, but I didn't find programs that would allow me to get a degree that included all of those. However, I settled on two Midwest campuses that had studies close to my interests: the Film, TV, and Broadcasting program at Indiana University and the American Studies program at the University of Iowa. So, I applied to both programs and waited.

By the spring of 1973, an unexpected twist occurred. Paulette, in her senior year at Barnstable High School, informed me that my alma mater was looking for Black teachers as a response to demands of students and parents. Black Power had reached Cape Cod. Paulette, a leader on the High School Student Council, led the charge for more ethnic representation on the faculty, as there was just one Black male teacher, whose only subject was woodworking. I never considered teaching. I didn't have any teaching training, experience, or credentials. Still, I applied for the job as another option.

When May arrived, I was feverishly completing my thesis. With no response from graduate schools and no interest indicated from Barnstable High, I began reflecting on the virtues of selling life insurance. Abruptly, toward the end of the month, I got the letter from the high school inviting me to come for an interview. I was surprised, but I submitted myself to the *Twilight Zone* feeling of driving four hours to Hyannis to enter my old high school. I observed the familiar buildings as I parked. Glanced around the old corridors. Interviewed extensively with my former principal.

So, with the fading dreams of radio broadcasting, revisiting Germany, or pursuing theater in Boston or New York, I accepted the high school's offer to teach. I took the job in desperation and fear of an unknown future. I signed a one-year contract and obtained an emergency teaching credential. Within the following week, as the ink dried on my signed contract, I received acceptance into both graduate programs at Indiana University and the University of Iowa.

\*\*\*

My Bates College graduation was a blur. It came and passed in a series of hugs and handshakes. My parents were extremely excited, and I dedicated the entire ceremonial day to them. The summer following my graduation, before I began my teaching job, I worked with Papa D for his cleaning service. At that time, he had a small flatbed truck and two vans with his business name stenciled on each. With two later shifts covered by his other workers, Daddy and I worked the day shift together from eight-thirty a.m. to five p.m., which had a routine of cleaning a variety of businesses throughout the many villages of Cape Cod. Interspersed between those regular stops were the various tasks in private homes: window washing, floor mopping, and waxing. It was tedious, monotonous work, but I did my best, never wanting to let my father down.

Even as I wondered how he tolerated such physically taxing work, the answer was right in front of me. Though tedious, the work provided a feeling of satisfaction and accomplishment. In the time applied to doing the work, the payoff was the completion of the job. The knowledge that a problem had been solved in a given amount of time. Unlike my years of study in academia, where I waited at each step for someone else's approval, there was a defined beginning and ending when my father assessed his work and felt satisfied without waiting for someone else's acceptance. He found pride in the tasks he fulfilled at each job along the way. Then, the bonus—it was *his* business.

One of the private homes scheduled for window cleaning was in a new development in Hyannis. Daddy worked the windows at the front of the house as I took the rear, the plan being to complete the outside windows before lunch. As I moved my ladder and blaring transistor radio from one window to the next, a woman with short dark hair and a wide smile appeared inside the room. She insisted that we introduce ourselves when she asked if I wanted anything to drink. Somewhere in that conversation, it turned out that Ginny Neuben-Cassara was a psychology teacher at Barnstable High, and when I told her I was contracted to teach in the English Department, she insisted that we become friends. Ginny possessed an irresistible personality; she was an intelligent, loquacious woman with no filters. She was engaging and overwhelming at the same time. Moving forward, she would remain one of my most supportive and closest friends over the next fifty years.

That summer brought another person into my life: Jason Richards, a Black man four years younger than me who had an athletic, handsome look I never possessed. I met Jason through Paulette, as they were graduating in the same high school class. He was smart, articulate, hungry for knowledge, and had committed to Bates College. Paulette arranged a meeting between us to discuss the particulars about Bates. I was honest about what I assessed as the best and worst aspects of the campus, and Jason paid me with appreciative nods and sincere embraces. He and I easily moved into a friendship that continued through decades of personal losses and professional achievements.

*\*\*\**

At first, my assignment at Barnstable was to teach both Black History and American Literature, with the latter duty based upon the publication of my poem, "I Am . . . Music." The thinking, I guess, was that getting a poem into a national anthology qualified me to teach poetry and fiction to high schoolers. However, over the summer the school's administration decided to add two more young Black teachers—John Reed in history and Bruce Gaines in sociology—and I was assigned to teach only in the English Department. Fortunately, that decision simplified my position, providing me the time to prepare for teaching literature selections in my assignment of five classes.

At eight a.m., I was teaching a poetry class to seniors. I was twenty-one and teaching students who were eighteen and nineteen. In my suit and tie, I entered the class and saw those White kids looking at me, and it took me some moments to find my voice. Using my theater experience and improv deejay techniques, I survived the first and the remaining classes for the day.

Even more surreal during that first week back at my old high school was that some of my former teachers were still working there. Those instructors, that I previously addressed with the formal title of Mr. or Mrs., were now my colleagues. I felt uncomfortable early on, but eventually I adjusted to that peculiar aspect of the job. However, that shift was quite easy when it came to Alice Owens. Having been a mentor in my high school days, Alice became my life-saving colleague in the English Department—a friend who welcomed talks about literature, the byzantine developments at Barnstable High, and on most occasions, my aspirations. Alice was married to Scott, a journalist who suffered from cancer. He was tall, extremely slim, with a thin pencil mustache and a patient disposition.

After weeks of searching, I stumbled onto a vacant studio apartment. On the second floor of an old Cape Cod style house, the space had a tiny bathroom with a shower stall; four coiled burners atop a mini-refrigerator and no oven; a combination living room area with a twin bed in one corner; and a separate storage area. My portable television and turntable were crammed into the corner of the living area, close to the single window that offered a view of the harbor. It was an addictive view, and in the coming months, I treasured the boats meditating on the gentle waters, and I often allowed my thoughts to be moored there as well.

\*\*\*

John Reed, Bruce Gaines, and I were extremely opposites in our personalities, but we were so compatible when it came to our sense of responsibility as Black teachers to the Black students at Barnstable High. Despite our young ages, we committed ourselves to being the best teachers and mentors possible, relying heavily on our shared conversations to navigate our roles as Black educators. In turn, the Black students welcomed us, including the Cape Verdean and Portuguese kids who, due to the Black Power movement, had transitioned to a Black identity.

At the same time, I developed a tribe of friends among White teachers—a comfortable, fun-loving group of eight of us. We weren't hedonistic, but we enjoyed a good time, often shaped by deep conversations over cocktails. They were a rather motley collection of personalities, the exact ingredients I needed to make my cake of a new life in Hyannis. They helped me tolerate my return to my former home. My tribe supported and tolerated me professionally and offered valuable, welcomed friendships.

And then there was Helen Winters, a fellow English teacher with long brown hair and high energy. Helen was articulate and perky, always moving through the hallways as if hurrying to some event being held in her honor. Despite my efforts to keep her at a distance, our paths intersected as English Department colleagues and sociable singles.

Due to my one publication, everyone perceived me as a poet, and no one was surprised or offended if I arrived late to a function because they understood I was writing. This tribe of friends gathered often for an after-school softball game or at one of the favorite watering holes in and around Hyannis. I never knew that high school teachers drank alcohol so much and so often. With my childhood friend, James Tobey, added to the mix on numerous occasions, I was connected to the best friends that Hyannis had to offer.

I rounded off this connection to friends and family with my continued immersion into the martial arts. Even as I maintained my Shotokan style, I signed up at a local Tae Kwon Do studio, where I could merge my Japanese techniques with a Korean-based system. The physical challenges were exhausting, but I was rewarded with a confidence and discipline for challenges yet to come.

\* \* \*

I first met Gwen Fulbright the summer before my senior year in college. When I returned from my trip to Germany, I settled down into a non-eventful passing of months in Hyannis before starting my senior year at Bates. Gwen worked as a maid at Smuggler's Beach Motel—the only White woman amid the Black faces of my mother, aunts, and cousins. Originally from North Carolina, Gwen was a third-grade teacher who took the summer to work and play on Cape Cod. She was four years older than me with an endearing sense of humor. She disliked the South, but with family and friends still there, she was tethered to that environment, which she probed with razor-sharp blades of criticism. She soon became a third wheel to me and James when we enjoyed summer nights with movies, seafood restaurants, and bottles of wine.

With German phrases and French expressions still swirling in my head, Gwen offered a patient friendship as I slowly transitioned back into my American world. Soon, our laughter rolled into embraces, slipped into kisses, blended into touching—both physically and emotionally. And as I resisted the pull of our romantic involvement, she promised she would write to encourage me through my final year at Bates College. And when she decided to take a year away from her classroom teaching in North Carolina to explore a lengthy residence in Hyannis, Gwen made it clear that the possibility of me being in her future inspired her migration North.

When I resisted any kind of commitment due to my upcoming senior year of academic classes, thesis project, and future life questions, she assured me that I was worth the wait. When the academic anxieties and pressures steam-rolled my waking hours, her letters lifted my spirits to face the upcoming week. After graduation, when I settled back into Hyannis to teach, I didn't articulate to my family and friends what they already knew: Gwen Fulbright had become an inextricable part of my life.

\*\*\*

Working and living in Hyannis again, my extended family members and people I frequently met in public saw me as that brilliant, young Black leader who would carry a torch to illuminate the pathways for political and community directions. However, I *wasn't* that person, nor did I want to be. As I envisioned the years before me, I didn't know the exact path I would follow, but I couldn't circle backwards and move forward at the same time.

At twenty-two, I didn't know exactly *what* I wanted, but I knew who I *didn't* want to be. Yes, I understood that many saw my accomplishments as a source of collective pride that would inspire young Black kids in the community. I felt honored, but I selfishly rejected the obligation to sacrifice the possibilities unknown, in my future. I wasn't a Black Jesus nor a Martin Luther King, Jr. My need at that stage in my life—no matter how selfish—was to discover and follow my own path. I still didn't know exactly *where* I was going, but I knew I couldn't stay in my hometown.

In particular, I wasn't expecting the personal meetings with students and parents. Once students felt a trusted connection, they confided experiences that intersected emotional and psychological minefields about family encounters, sexual abuse, religious experiences, alcohol abuse, illegal drug consumption, sexual experimentation, and the fears of not fitting in with their peers. I wasn't prepared for the role of a therapist.

On one occasion, I received a phone call from a parent requesting to meet me in my classroom. She was a White woman in her late forties who looked more like the grandmother than the single parent of a student named Daniel. Meeting in my homeroom after school, she began to cry as she took a seat. With her husband deceased, she raised Daniel by herself. But having just turned nineteen, Daniel informed her he was leaving school to join the army. Distraught with the fear of losing her son to the Vietnam War and facing a life alone, she begged me to help her. Daniel told her that I was his favorite teacher—a surprise to me since he only spoke to me when questioned. I listened until there was a silent space filled only with her sobs. In my best performance as a mature man, I said something that I probably heard in a movie: *"The most difficult thing for a parent to do is to let a child go. But that day has to come when a child determines his own path. But . . . no matter what Daniel finally decides, your love and caring will be the guiding forces in his life."* Silence floated loudly over the room. Her sobbing ebbed, and she seemed to find some solace in what I said. After that meeting, I never heard from her again. Daniel disappeared from class, so I assumed he made the decision to enlist. I never knew what happened to him, but he entered my thoughts often during that semester.

\* \* \*

"You're one of the most self-sufficient people I ever met, Mel."

"I am? I'm afraid to ask you exactly what that means."

Alice Owens, my former teacher and current friend, sipped her wine, smiling.

"You know a lot of people," she continued, "but you don't *need* a lot of people."

"Oh, yeah . . . I do know folks . . . been lucky that way." I sipped my wine and saw her continued smile. "What are you getting at?"

"She has some real feelings for you . . . Helen."

And I understood where Alice was going in the conversation. She was saying out loud what everyone in the English Department was thinking: Helen Winters and I were a couple whether I wanted it or not. Helen made it easy to be attracted to her. Whether at a restaurant sharing hors d'oeuvres with Harvey Wallbangers, or kicking back at her house with amaretto and conversation. We flowed easily into discussions about *Roe v. Wade*, Patty Hearse, Richard Nixon, current movies. Her most memorable movie of 1973 was *The Way We Were*. For me, it was *The Exorcist*. Those film choices were a testament to our differences.

And Helen knew about Gwen Fulbright because I was honest about that relationship. But she didn't press me with commitment, though she explicitly stated that her preference was to spend more time with me. I only disliked one thing about Helen: she was a chain smoker, lighting one cigarette and then another. Her house, her car, her clothes, and her hair smelled like smoke; her kisses tasted like ashes. Our conversations drifted back repeatedly to that territory of concerns—for her health and for my preference of smokeless smooches.

Yet, at the same time, Helen and Gwen had something in common. Their attitudes about race were not anchored in ignorant biases and curiosities found in many White people, male or female. Helen and Gwen were genuine and comfortable with the reality that we were of different cultural and historical backgrounds. Race was not the problem. Rather, it was something much more fundamental to my primary concern at the time: each woman served as a tightening chain to Hyannis.

As I committed myself to entering the master's program at the University of Iowa, I knew those friends and lovers in Hyannis would become anchors that I would eventually disdain if I stayed. Even James couldn't hold me, but as a true brother, he never attempted to do so. Instead, he encouraged me to head off into a future that I desired. Perhaps much of my restlessness could be traced back to those years of traveling with my family between Florida and Cape Cod. Perhaps it was that flame that still flickered from my short exploration of France, Germany, Austria, and Switzerland.

After one year of teaching at my old high school, I packed my Toyota—my cassette tapes tightly organized in a box in the passenger seat; turntable on the passenger floorboard surrounded and stacked by my vinyl albums; and boxes of books, clothes, and a typewriter. In August 1974, I headed for the Midwest, leaving behind all the possibilities. Knowing I had to make it to the next destination. To keep moving forward. To catch and explore my next dream.

## CHAPTER SIX

## Landlocked

Nothing could have prepared me for Iowa. In August 1974, the state assaulted me with its distant horizon lines that framed fields of corn stalks, remote farmhouses, and roads that stretched into nowhere. Iowa City was a city only in name, as the university with about twenty-two thousand students at the time was *the* oasis, the primary landmark that connected to what might be called a cultural landscape.

To me, I had entered another universe of Whiteness, and in this case, a world of conservatism. On campus there were semblances of diverse peoples as students of various backgrounds—domestic and international—interacted with one another. But once I left campus, my cautionary feelings spiked as White people were still in their "Negro" or "Colored" labeling of Black people. So, I kept my butt on campus, which wasn't difficult since university housing had placed me in a dorm that housed single graduate students with senior undergraduates.

Instead of a harbor view from my own small studio apartment in Hyannis, my early morning views were of a naked Martin Mahoney—my White, gangly, long-haired senior roommate who came from somewhere in northern Iowa. He was a nice enough guy with numerous questions about me and my background, but his friends who dropped by our double room nightly were not as . . . polished. It became evident that my room would *not* be a place to read, study, and write. Additionally, Martin and his friends' musical tastes undulated across pop, country, and rock: Gary Puckett and the Union Gap; John Denver; Merle Haggard; Lynyrd Skynyrd; the Electric Light Orchestra; and Paul McCartney and Wings. So, I kept my R&B and jazz albums in the corner unless I was alone in the room, and Martin and I found a neutral ground of appreciation through Joni Mitchell's *Court and Spark* album.

The one friend of Martin's that I liked was Kip, a long-haired Iowan who was more complex in his personality, and he and I found a common connection through the martial arts. He was new to the arts but had some background in Tae Kwon Do. Our discussions were peppered with Bruce Lee, fighting techniques, and the Tae Kwon Do class offered through the campus's Physical Education Department. Eventually, I joined that class, and it gave me a twice-weekly excuse to be out of the dorm room.

I missed going to movies. I craved the big screen movie fix. On rare occasions, I allowed myself a weekend screening on campus, the only time I would permit myself to stray from my studies. I longed to see *Chinatown*, *Cabaret*, *Death Wish*, *The Godfather II*, and other movies I heard my roommate and his friends discussing. However, I didn't have the money to spare for a ticket, gas, and popcorn. Instead, I would take in any movie shown on campus, usually an older Hollywood Studio film from the 1940s or 1950s that would be screened for free. I would sneak in as the movie began, avoiding anyone who might want to go for a beer afterward, which I couldn't afford.

Part of my campus world revolved around my effort to obtain the promised funds from the university. The small scholarship awarded to me hadn't been delivered, and consequently, I was financially broke. My savings were depleted in covering gas, food, and motels to journey to the university from Hyannis. So, I approached the supervisor of the dorm's cafeteria and got a job as a general worker—collecting, scraping, washing, stacking, and placing dishes in their receptables at the food lines. Observing that I was reliable, the supervisor promoted me to the next level—maintaining the drink dispensers, connecting tubing to drink canisters, and cleaning the troughs of spillage.

However, the important reason for being at the university was to earn my master's degree. I selected a variety of classes that underscored the intentions of the American Studies program: an interdisciplinary exploration of American society. Thus, I connected my interests across the humanities by choosing African American Studies, American Literature, and American Film History.

\*\*\*

His name was Wilfred Samuels, but everyone called him Pepie. Pepie was a Black PhD student who was generous, charismatic, and intelligent. He had a Costa Rican background, but he grew up in Pasadena, California. He was a favorite of the ruling Black Scholar at University of Iowa, Dr. Darwin T. Turner. For whatever reason, Pepie and I hit it off when we first met, and while I was there at the University of Iowa, he saved me on many occasions. In the years after leaving the university, he became a significant Scholar, eventually serving as the chairperson of the African American Studies Department at the University of Utah—editing texts, lecturing, community organizing, and writing critical nonfiction about Black Studies, including his book, *Making Crooked Paths Straight: Crossroads and Conversions in The Interesting Narrative of the Life of Olaudah Equiano* (2015). And after meeting at the University of Iowa, Pepie remained a life-long friend.

\* \* \*

Without question, it would be difficult to measure the impact that Dr. Darwin T. Turner had on the University of Iowa *and* the development of African American literature in academia. Dr. Turner was viewed as a prodigy after earning his BA at sixteen, his MA at eighteen, and his PhD at twenty-five. His anthology, *Black American Literature* (1969), was considered a seminal work in assembling the contributions and achievements of the significant Black American writers from the eighteenth through the twentieth centuries. That publication was followed by numerous tomes analyzing and celebrating the various genres of the African American literary tradition. He was the chair of the African American Studies program when I arrived on campus, and he had a particular interest in Black Drama.

Dr. Turner preferred his doctoral students, and out of his impressive list of graduate students, Pepie was his jewel. As a mere MA student, I soon learned to listen to the doctoral students who had experience in the program and navigated the campus *and* the community. Pepie did his part to keep me involved, though it was difficult for me to breach the camaraderie among the Black doctoral students. But I understood the closeness they shared and the acceptance I would have to earn.

Some of the students who were in the doctoral program went on to teach at various universities. However, one student stood out to rival Dr. Turner in his first-hand, personal knowledge of Black literature: Sarah Webster Fabio. While Dr. Turner was the academic scholar and editor, Sarah—with her MA in hand and working on her PhD—was known for her poetry and the distinction of having contributed to the establishment of the first Black Studies Department at UC-Berkeley. She was in her mid-forties when I met her, but she already had three books of poetry and numerous vinyl recordings of poetry—a spoken word artist of her time. But closer to my heart were the experiences she shared of reading poetry with Langston Hughes and Gwendolyn Brooks in the mid-1960s at an arts festival in Dakar, Senegal.

In the Research and Methods seminar taught by Dr. Turner, I sat next to Sarah and Vashti Lewis, a professor in her late thirties who was on leave from the University of Kansas, Wichita, to earn her doctorate. Among Dr. Turner, Sarah, and Vashti, I was in the orbit of brilliant Black people. When Dr. Turner mentioned a noted Black writer, Sarah often knew that author personally, and Vashti had taught that author's work in her university classes. It was a singular, academic immersion into Black culture that I never experienced before. I listened, learned, and valued the complexity, longevity, and significance of Black culture to the United States and to the world. It was a striking contradiction—to be surrounded by such brilliant Black people in one of the Whitest states in the country.

\*\*\*

I met Lynn Klamkin by accident. We struck up a conversation one day after leaving a creative writing class. I signed up for the class as a way of developing my poetry, but after two meetings, the class struck me as a gathering of literary terrorists bent on destroying anyone attempting to use the label of poet. Lynn sat in on the class, but she was actually a fellow in the famous University of Iowa Writers' Workshop, a two-year program that awarded a master of fine arts. She was in her early twenties, blonde and loquacious, wearing a pair of dark-rimmed glasses that made her look like a cute librarian. She appreciated my poem that had been dissected in class without anesthesia, and she explained her involvement in the Writers' Workshop, indicating she had published her first novel, *Hello, Goodbye* (1973).

Lynn and I became friends, and we often connected over discussions about writing. I was impressed with her accomplishment as a novelist, and she revealed some of the eccentricities of the published authors-professors who taught seminars in the Writers' Workshop. Eventually, she shared that she was having an affair with one of the workshop's noted professors, a nationally-known author who she found alluring. She was a Sapiophile, but she knew that his personal life and ego wasn't going to lead to a relationship with any longevity.

\*\*\*

Mail arriving from home became a source of much-needed spiritual uplift. Letters from Mama D and Papa D, often with money enclosed. A note from Paulette to let me know that she was doing well and working toward her BA at Cedarville College in Ohio, a private university about 500 miles east of Iowa City. And a weekly letter from Gwen Fulbright, updating me on her life on Cape Cod and her affection for me. I welcomed every word received from everyone, lifelines to my former world.

As the semester moved closer to Thanksgiving, I hungered to get out of the dorm. I still received no indications about any grad housing, and though my university's semester check finally made its way to me, it merely replenished the savings I had used to survive. I began looking for a small off-campus apartment within close proximity to the university.

Traveling back to Hyannis for a long Thanksgiving weekend wasn't practical. Even the six-hour drive to see Paulette would be a challenge, and I didn't want to impose on Pepie as he already had plans. So, Lynn Klamkin came through and offered me her off-campus residence while she traveled back East. There was no hesitation to accept the offer, or else I would be staying in the dorm for the holiday. I picked up a Cornish hen, rice, canned vegetables, two cans of beer, a quart of milk, and cereal. It was a small but homey place with a large area serving as a living room and a kitchen area in the corner. The bedroom was a separate smaller room with an even smaller bathroom. When I woke up Thanksgiving morning, it was snowing. The thick blanket of quiet snow reminded me of the first snow of the season that covered the Maine landscape.

The remainder of the day provided two unexpected events. First, with no turntable at Lynn's place, my option was to watch the television in the corner. To my surprise, Bryant Gumbel appeared on the screen, giving sports news on an NBC station. I hadn't seen him since my freshman year at Bates. If he could make it, then there was hope for me, wherever I would land after obtaining my master's degree. The second event was more nauseating—I undercooked the Cornish hen. My Thanksgiving became Thanks-suffering as my knotting stomach led to an afternoon of curling up near the toilet. I hung on waiting for the volcano to erupt again. It wouldn't be the last time I was sick in Iowa City.

\*\*\*

Final semester papers were due for all my classes, but my time was monopolized by completing an annotated bibliography for Dr. Turner's Research and Methods seminar. I packed up my belongings and left the dorm for a place I found about three miles east of the campus. It was a closet masquerading as a studio apartment on the ground floor of a two-story building.

Walking inside, on the left were large windows that faced the busy street. Beneath the windows, a silver radiator stretched along the wall. The thin curtains allowed natural light inside, which was good considering the absence of a ceiling light. The major light in the room was a cheap floor lamp I picked up from a Goodwill. Off from the main room was a small bath with a toilet and shower stall. Another smaller space held a mini fridge, stove, and sink. But I was ecstatic to have my own place.

By mid-December, I was driving to the East Coast, stopping to pick up Paulette in Ohio. We agreed to drive straight through for twenty hours to reach Cape Cod as quickly as possible. I drove the first twelve hours, stopping only for gas and bathroom breaks. She drove the last eight hours while the snow assaulted our efforts. When we reached Hyannis, I dropped Paulette off at Mama D and Papa D's house and continued another twenty minutes to Yarmouth where Gwen Fulbright lived. After five months, I needed to kiss and embrace to resurrect that part of me incarcerated by months of reading, studying, and essay writing. I stayed at her place for two days.

During that Christmas visit, I conversed endlessly with friends and my parents. I called Helen Winters, sharing a lengthy phone call, but I didn't want to jeopardize what seemed to be an imminent commitment to Gwen. The truth was I was in love with Gwen. However, I still resisted any discussion that would anchor me to Hyannis.

\*\*\*

By the time my sister and I returned to the Midwest through the snowy, ice-crusted countryside, I was a moody man. I enjoyed *what* I was studying, but I didn't like *where* I was studying. I was depressed. Strapped for money. Entombed inside my studio apartment. Within a couple of weeks, I was physically ill, the flu aggressively attacking me. At some point, I sat up, the bed sheets knotted around me. I stared at the clock, but I didn't know which day it was. I limped to the curtained window and peered outside. A frozen landscape. There were no people. No cars. I switched on the television and returned to the wet sheets, watching the television as a local commercial reminded me I was in Iowa. I hobbled to the shower, but there was no water through the frozen pipes. I returned to the bed. Laid down . . . cried . . . prayed. I remembered that peaceful day of solace at the Staffelsee in Murnau, Germany, and drifted back to sleep.

After my episode of sickness, the reality was that my financial situation hadn't changed. I was now waiting for my spring semester payment from the financial aid office. But I knew I had to do something more than loiter in the university's hallway of disappointment. So, I remembered pieces of conversations among graduate students about teaching part time. I knew I couldn't get a teaching assistantship on campus because those positions went to the doctoral candidates and were awarded at the beginning of the academic year.

I located a phone book in the campus library. Fingered the pages until I found a community college located about twenty miles away. I searched the listings for the college's English Department. I didn't mention my plan to anyone on campus, and my confidence came from my one year of teaching experience at my high school. When the community college operator transferred my call to the English Department, I asked for the chairperson who, of course, was unavailable. I requested an appointment, indicating that I was calling from the University of Iowa's English Department. That lie worked to get me a fifteen-minute appointment with the chairperson at the end of the week. In the days that followed, I shaped my resume to emphasize both my high school teaching experience and my current master's program.

Wearing a dress shirt and tie beneath my winter jacket, I drove to the community college and found the English Department's office. The pale, balding chairperson on the opposite side of the desk appeared attentive to my verbal presentation, his nodding suggesting his approval. I mentioned the seminar with Dr. Turner, which I milked to strengthen my qualifications to teach on his campus. By the beginning of the following week, I was proven right. A phone call delivered the administrative assistant's voice, offering the position to teach a 20th Century American Literature class. I was elated, and I felt the world had promise again. The university's spring semester check finally arrived, and I was resurrected. Calculating my new budget, I could make it until the beginning of June before returning to Hyannis to work for the summer.

And then the phone rang.

"I'm sorry, Mr. Donalson," the community college's chairperson repeated for a third time.

"But you already offered me the position. I'm supposed to drive to campus tomorrow to sign the paperwork."

"I know, I know, but I'm sorry," he said yet again. "You see, when we phoned the African American Studies Department to check your references, I spoke to Dr. Turner."

"Yes, he can testify to my position in the program and my grades."

"Oh, yes he did, but . . ."

"But?"

"Dr. Turner recommended someone else from his doctoral program who he felt could better teach the class."

I raced to campus, furious as I waited for a half hour before Dr. Turner returned to his office from teaching a seminar. I followed him into his office, watching him light a cigarette and organize his files before he gave me his attention.

"Dr. Turner, *I* found that teaching job! *I* interviewed! *I* was given the position!"

"Understood, Mr. Donalson. But I had to do what was best. I recommended Chris Ferguson for that position."

"But why would you do that? I need that job! I need the money!"

"Mr. Ferguson is a doctoral candidate and more prepared than you to teach American Literature."

"But Chris has never taught full time. I've taught American Lit for a year!"

"As a high school teacher, Mr. Donalson. But this is college level. And I need to make certain that one of our best is going to represent us!"

"This isn't right, Dr. Turner!"

"I have to do what I know is best. Sorry."

He gave me a tight smile of dismissal and returned to the files on his desk to indicate the discussion was finished. I fumed. I wanted to grab him and cuss out loud as I beat his ass. I knew the hand techniques I perfected in the martial arts. I wanted to hurt him until he bled. Instead, I drifted from his office, held back my tears, and tried to make peace with the rage that pounded in my chest.

It took time before I gained a perspective on what Dr. Turner did. Something that became clear as I found myself a Black professor in White academic settings. The pressures, disdain, and insults that targeted a Black professor were aimed directly for the jugular. Racially-biased and jealous colleagues who watched and judged. The deans who promised but often undermined efforts to uphold the significance of African diasporic experiences. The campus provosts and presidents who smiled during a closed meeting while harboring a pre-set plan to dismiss everything discussed during that meeting. Darwin Turner was *the* Black scholar on campus who possessed a national reputation and carried—in that Black Power decade—the heavy burden of representing and fighting for the inclusion, respect, and honor for a field of study still being debated around the country. Turner's decision to recommend a Black doctoral student who he'd known for several years—as opposed to an MA candidate he'd known for only one semester—had very little to do with me personally. His decision was about the best way to serve African American Studies, both on campus and out in the community.

I was blind to those truths at that time. I wasn't familiar with the hostile terrain of White institutions of higher education that consistently weighed the value of Black Studies in reference to the traditional hierarchy of White male authors and professors. After all, it was assumed that the great and essential books, essays, and creative genres had allegedly been written and shaped by White men. Despite the arguments made by the Black Aesthetic intellectuals and Black Power advocates, academic institutions were still battlefields where reform and diverse representation were debatable by the existing power structure. For many campuses, the allegiance to academic sanctity and tradition was not debatable, and any residue of race, ethnicity, and culture immediately tarnished and reduced the value of Black literary works and those Black professors who attempted to argue otherwise. More systemic lessons were still to be learned, waiting for me in the decades ahead.

\*\*\*

"I'm pregnant."

Gwen's voice was emotional over the phone, but not hysterical. It took some time to find my voice.

"What? Pregnant! When did you find out?" I asked.

"Several days ago," she said. "Been thinking about it . . . about us . . . so much to think about."

"Yeah . . . there is! So, are you feeling all right? I mean, are you feeling sick?"

"Listen, Mel . . . I know you're not ready to be a daddy. I don't know if it's the right time for me to be a mother. My job situation is not really the career I wanted at twenty-seven."

"Yeah," I agreed. "I know. So, what're you thinking?"

"I'm . . . I'm going to have an abortion. But I wanted to see how you felt about that."

"I guess . . . I can't think clearly right now. I mean, it has to be what you decide."

There was a long pause on her end. A deep breath.

"When's your spring break?" she asked.

"The second week in March, I think."

"Okay . . . I'll get an appointment for then."

"Yeah, all right. I mean . . . I'll come back and be with you when you go in."

"I would like that."

"Yeah. Okay."

The remainder of our conversation evaporated swiftly. I was numb, and her words touched my ear faintly. Long after hanging up the phone, I stared at the curtains that appeared like threatening shrouds. I was empty and uneasy, questioning what I didn't say and what I was strongly feeling. I was afraid.

\*\*\*

Two years after the *Roe v. Wade* decision, Gwen and I sat together in a Boston clinic, waiting for her to be called for the procedure. Despite the decision we *both* made after many phone calls, we sat as solemnly as the other couples and single women waiting in the lounge. My apprehension, though I didn't articulate it aloud, was for Gwen's safety and health. I didn't want her to be physically hurt, given the emotional journey she had endured.

For me, I supported Gwen's choice to have an abortion. Truth was—I was selfish. I wasn't prepared to be a twenty-three-year-old father still determining a career path. In our three years of being physically intimate, we had always been careful in using protection. She was on the pill until I left for Iowa, deciding to stop taking it when I was away for those five months. When she knew I was returning at Christmas, she began taking the pill again before I arrived, but her body followed its own path.

I talked to James Tobey about it, and he was supportive of our decision. He was the only person I told at the time. It was a life decision for Gwen and me to make, including any consequences that might follow. In those twilight moments when I wrestled with our decision, public discussions at the time were clashing loudly. Pro-life voices used the word "killing," as the pro-choice voices argued for the woman's right to decide what should happen to her body. As I did my reading and reflecting, it was clear that American women had been having and inducing abortions for decades, from eighteenth-century rural towns to contemporary cityscapes. Women sought out midwives for potions and doctors for clandestine operations. Other women ended pregnancies by deliberately falling downstairs, tumbling from horses, or inserting foreign objects into their bodies. By the early twentieth century, politicians, Protestant preachers, and the Catholic Church denounced ending pregnancies from their campaign stumps and pulpits, but by the early 1970s, activists for the Women's Liberation Movement of the time supported "a woman's choice."

But I had to contemplate what *I* thought, standing at the junction of "yes" or "no." And at that time, I realized that it *was* about a woman's choice—even before dealing with such abhorrent causes of pregnancy, such as rape and incest. The decision had to fall on the wishes of the individual woman—not some politician, preacher, or pundit. Basically, *Roe v. Wade* was allowing for that choice. The law itself wasn't *requiring* women to have abortions. It was simply allowing for a woman to make that personal, private decision at a particular time in her life.

And I prayed and thought and prayed about the decision that Gwen and I made. I came back to the same mix of emotions and the same decision. Abortion had to be contextualized to the specific situation at hand. Pregnancy could be seen as a blessing, but it had to be understood in the real time of life—not in some intellectual, political, or religious debate. Each pregnancy, and time of that pregnancy, was distinct and required a decision intrinsic to that pregnancy. And as I looked closely at myself, I knew—though difficult to admit—that I was too selfish and not worthy enough to be a caring and responsible father.

When I returned to Iowa City, I decided two important things. First, I was going to take classes during the summer in order to finish my master's degree by December 1975. I had to get away from that campus and out of that state.

Driving alone back to the Midwest, I was resolute in pushing forward as quickly as possible. Second, Gwen and I decided to be together, and we began planning her move to join me in Iowa City.

\* \* \*

Following a suggestion given by several grad students, I searched for an on-campus work-study job that could bring in some additional income. I took several trips to the financial aid offices, looking over work-study job announcements that allowed twenty hours of work a week while I continued to complete the degree early. I came across positions that didn't seem to be too demanding of my energy and time, but one position appeared to be the best—working at the information desk in the University of Iowa's Student Union. The only problem was—I didn't know the geography of the campus or the locations of all the academic departments and function halls.

Doris Gamble was the supervisor responsible for the information center. She was in charge of the desk staff as well as updating handouts about campus's social, educational, and cultural functions and contacts of dozens of campus locations and staff leaders. She was a vivacious and outgoing woman, endowed with a plump appearance possessed by many Iowan women. But I was glad when she offered me the job, which gave me the chance to step out of the shadow of Dr. Turner and his power circle.

The first two weeks on the job were nerve-wracking. I double-talked with lost people who stood before me, prompting answers from my coworker at the desk. I often sent people in directions that led them in circles, and I learned to speak with confidence about things and personnel I didn't know. I figured that if people came back to confront my faulty information, I would blame them for misunderstanding my instructions. I suspected that Doris knew my faults, but she liked me for some reason, even inviting me to her home to have dinner with her husband and kids. But I always made an excuse and continued to juggle classes and papers that I needed to finish.

But Doris wasn't the only person who helped me. I took a 20th Century American Literature class with Dr. Roberts, an accomplished White professor, who I mistakenly assumed was lesbian because of her short hair style and wardrobe of blue jeans, mismatched tops, and hiking boots. I was still a work in progress at the time! But Dr. Robert's teaching methodology, informal lectures, and racially diverse literary selections were impressive. There was a rumor going around about her having difficulty with the English Department regarding tenure, but her classes never reflected any professional difficulties. She wrote positive and encouraging feedback on my required papers, and she agreed to be on my master's committee, pledging to compose the required American Literature question for my comprehensive exam.

The second professor who provided immense encouragement to me was Peter Nazareth. Dr. Nazareth and I met at a social gathering for the African American Studies program, where he taught classes in Black literature while also teaching courses for the university's International Writing Program. He was born and educated in the East African country of Uganda. He was an intelligent and extremely well-read scholar, writer, and editor of Black and Third World authors, and our initial conversations drifted into creative writing. After a number of additional chats, he read my short story I had stumbled through for months, titled "The Thirteenth Hour." Using Genesis 18:16-33 and coalescing Abraham, Lot, and Jason (from the Greek epic poem) to shape my White protagonist, my story followed the main character who confronted Black Power revolutionaries planning to attack and kill all the White people in the wealthy town of Sodoma. Lotman argued that there were good White people living in the town who didn't deserve to die just because they were White. He proposed that if he found ten good White people, the Black revolutionaries should spare the town.

Dr. Nazareth read the story, provided positive feedback, and helped get the story published in an international journal. In the same way that John Tagliabue at Bates College helped me with publishing my first poem, Dr. Nazareth believed in my fiction. Sadly, he and I lost contact when I raced away from Iowa City with my master's degree, but he was priceless to me and my writing.

\*\*\*

Kip Brezsky remained in touch with me after I moved out of the dorm room that I shared with Martin Mahoney. Kip joined the Tae Kwon Do class, and occasionally he and I sparred one another when my time allowed. His enthusiasm and genuine love of martial arts was tangible, and when I asked him to help me with a personal project, he didn't hesitate.

I was taking an American Film History class, and I decided to try my hand at making a film. I read up on filmmaking particulars and gave time to discern the details of an 8mm movie camera. Since I wasn't a filmmaking student enrolled in a class—and therefore couldn't borrow a university camera—I searched out a photography shop that would rent me the equipment and set me up with one reel of film, which was all I could afford.

The story had to be simple, as it would only be a silent movie that would possibly last for five minutes. With Kip's help in recruiting another martial artist, I wrote and shot *Karateka*.

Opening on a close-up of Kip reading a martial arts magazine, I lingered on his smile as I blurred the image. From there, I showed Kip and the other martial artist fighting on a grassy landscape. I was cognizant enough to set the camera in different positions to capture the two at battle, knowing that I had to edit the various angles to reveal their fighting movements. At the end of the fighting, I cut back to a blurred close-up of Kip's face as he cried. I pulled back to a wide shot to show Kip sitting in a wheelchair. Despite all of the aggravations and mistakes with the camera, as well as begging to use campus editing and splicing equipment, I was pleased with my brief immersion into filmmaking. The final, edited film—with no dialogue, music, credits, or captions—took me away from my academic obligations and personal pressures, if only for a short time.

* * *

In early summer, I flew back to Massachusetts to gather Gwen and her belongings. We drove to Iowa City in her yellow Mustang and moved into a furnished, one-bedroom apartment across town and away from campus. Lakeside Manor was a large community with a swimming pool and recreational area, a location where university couples with and without children settled.

I was pleased we were together, but one issue became a dominating one. I was obliged to be on campus for long hours during the work week, taking seminars and still working the Information Desk job. Consequently, Gwen was alone during the days and some evenings. She didn't know anyone but me, and when there was a social gathering among the grad students, she wasn't familiar with the writers, books, and other references that seeped into conversations. As an elementary school teacher, she didn't have a graduate level experience that helped her connect at social gatherings. Eventually, she took a job at a department store to keep busy and bring in additional money.

At the same time, the ongoing issue was the optics of our relationship. There I was—a Black graduate student in a committed relationship with a White, Southern woman. It was *Gone With The Wind* meets *Shaft*. With some of my Black colleagues, I read the thoughts that wrinkled their faces: I personified the least tolerated stereotype of a Black man—one who chose to have a relationship with a White woman. I had navigated that critical zone in my undergraduate days at Bates College when seen with various White girls. However, at the University of Iowa, that marker was more visible, given my emphasis on African American Studies. My choice of a White woman was taken personally by Black women in my program as a rejection of Black women everywhere. How could I be a credible Black scholar with a White woman on my arm? The stares, the sneers, the smirks—all validated a dismissal of our relationship.

I knew I had to reconcile my personal decisions about my relationship with Gwen with the prevalent spoken and unspoken attitudes. However, the truth of my feelings was evident when I made the decision to ask Gwen to join me. I realized that the proximity of someone real cancels the fantasy of someone afar. Yes, it would have been ideal to have a committed relationship with a Black woman, but at that time in my life, that was not my truth. Gwen and I chose to be with one another due to our experiences together and our feelings for one another. I wouldn't select my relationship partner to pacify or confirm what others—Black or White—preferred to accept. It was my life and my choice.

As for Gwen, it was extremely difficult for her to concede the life she once knew in order to be with me. In Iowa City, she was isolated physically and emotionally. The judgmental stares directed toward her denoted silent dismissals. In particular, it was debilitating to her that people felt she wasn't good enough for me. And though I never felt that way, my lack of time and attention to her suggested that she wasn't the most important person in my life. By the end of the summer, storms arose between us through heated discussions, heavy silences, and suffocating resentments. She felt abandoned, but I was burdened with finishing my studies and preparing for my comprehensive exams in December. There was a bit of jealousy as well. She insisted that I spent more time with the grad students on campus, including the women grad students. But I had no interest *in* and no time *for* anyone else. I was overwhelmed by answering too many obligations at once. Gwen was my girlfriend and my close friend, but she needed and wanted more. By the end of October, our relationship was splintered beneath the weight of doubts stacked atop our unsuccessful efforts to maintain even the friendship we had over the years.

When she announced she was leaving, I was unable to give her an argument from my heart as to why she should stay. At that point, our relationship was built upon the past. She stated she was returning to Hyannis, and she wouldn't be waiting for me anymore. She was going to move forward with her life—without me.

And once she left, I immediately missed her. Yet, I argued to myself that it was for the best. I had to finish my degree! I was too close to the finish line to let even our love and broken relationship distract me. I was exhausted emotionally, conflicted with giving up my relationship, and disappointed about what happened between us—but I was committed to fighting the last round of my educational quest.

\*\*\*

My reality shifted again. I had to give up the one-bedroom apartment when Gwen left because of my humble income, but with five weeks before my exams,

I needed a home base. I packed my Toyota again—with most possessions placed snugly in the trunk and a cheap blanket covering my back seat items to avoid tempting passersby. The books and files I needed to complete my seminars and study for the exams were stacked on the passenger seat and the floorboard beneath. There were scattered nights when I returned to my former studio apartment building, parking in the rear lot to keep off the streets. I slept in my car and drove to the campus gym in the early mornings to shower and dress, spreading my wet towel atop the back seat blanket to dry during the day.

I was still working at the Information Desk, and could forage for food in the building, as breads, fruits, and cookies were prevalent during the holiday season. Doris was kind enough to invite me to join her and her family for dinner on the weekends, but I didn't want to impose or attempt to make conversation. I wanted to be alone to prepare academically and to avoid any questions about Gwen or my future plans.

I was quite happy when I caught a break. Moutala, a grad student from Nigeria, had become an acquaintance of mine from social gatherings. He reminded me of Minkah Kuwarte, the African brother I met in Murnau, Germany. Moutala planned to visit a friend out of town for Thanksgiving, and he offered his apartment during the five-day break. When he returned the Monday after Thanksgiving, he allowed me to sleep on his couch during that week leading into my exams.

I entered the exams a bit ragged, but I was confident in my knowledge. Over three consecutive days, I completed essay exams, allowing three hours for each—American Film History; American Literature; and African American Literature. With each one, I connected historical and contemporary themes and symbols, revealed meanings, and assessed political and cultural perspectives. In the following days, I paid a last visit to all three department offices to leave my forwarding address. I delivered dozens of borrowed books into the library deposit bin. I filled my Toyota's gas tank, and I left Iowa City.

\* \* \*

"landlocked"

the sun doesn't set in iowa,
embarrassed, it hides behind the nearest hill,

no ocean air into which to melt,
no salt air to fondle
its edges to a purple mist,

the darkness comes
without ceremony
to a land best suited
for the whims of the wind,

howling, staggering over itself
in an uncompromising attitude of arrogance,
knocking against my window, uninvited

it grins with lewd delight,
promising to return
with snow,
a comrade without wit or mercy,

my spirit is incarcerated within these rolling
plains,
where dying grass grows
from old testament soil,
and woodpiles reek of republican rodents,

where thoughts are chained
to corn fed beef, Sunday school socials,
and tractors broken down,

yet beyond these hills
awaits the magic of the horizon,
and the sun, ancient and humble,
knows this truth, as I do

CHAPTER SEVEN

## Dreams, Ideals, and Stars

Christmastime in 1975 was a disconcerting season. I slept most days, stayed in my parents' basement, hung out with James, and attempted to see Gwen. She was open to getting together on occasion, but she made it clear that she was "dating" other guys. She had read Erica Jong's *Fear of Flying* and decided to free herself from the imprisonment of a relationship with me. For me, I was burned out and not too sympathetic to her new-found feminism.

My basic solace was to write and inhale the creative high that emerged when I immersed myself into poetry and fiction. I spoke to my parents and told them of my plan to leave again, which confused them. Since I had a second academic degree, they figured I would settle back in Hyannis and resume teaching at the high school. Not knowing my next move clearly, I still rejected the option to plant myself in Hyannis. When I spoke with James, he noted my uncertain future and rationalized that I would be fine as long as I wasn't in Iowa City.

I reached out to John Jenkins, who was living in Lewiston, Maine, and I asked if I could stay with him for a while. My plan was to write a novel during the winter months since living in Lewiston wouldn't offer any distractions. He agreed, and his enthusiasm to see me was encouraging. That Christmas, I also connected with Jason Richards while he was visiting his sister and brother-in-law in Hyannis for the holidays. We had a lengthy discussion about his Bates College experiences and living as a Black man in Maine. He welcomed my planned move to Lewiston, promising his help when needed.

As the new year began, I returned to Lewiston, and not much had changed since I was there since 1973. Yet, I knew the uneventful environment and the escape from the pressure-filled graduate student life was the space I needed. Lewiston was a cold, grey world, and my plan was to write and let the sunshine in.

It was good to see John again, and he offered his couch and fridge to me without hesitation or rules. I left most of my belongings covered in my Corolla and brought in one suitcase to be as non-intrusive as possible. John had completed his Bates College degree, worked in the college's housing office, and was the Sensei and owner of the Golden Fist Academy. He was as unique as he had been during our undergrad years, with his ebullient personality that soaked in experiences and knowledge.

Welcoming the opportunity to study my initial Shotokan style again, I was at the brown belt level, and along with other students, I followed John through his demanding dojo workouts, public martial arts exhibitions, and several martial arts tournaments where we competed and won trophies at all belt levels. The Golden Fist Academy grew in numbers, and I, along with fellow Brown Belt Pam Wansker, began instructing lower-level classes to pay for our membership in the academy. Before the year passed, Pam and I earned our Black Belts at the same time.

As John kept me busy in one area, Jason Richards kept pulling me back to Bates College, proudly introducing me to the recent Black student arrivals. The number of Black students had tripled since my freshman year, and I dropped in on campus events and occasional parties. I also met Marcus's girlfriend, Rose Holiday, who was a smart, pretty woman who had grown up in Switzerland, though her parents eventually moved to Delaware. Her father was a chemist for DuPont, but her experiences of living abroad gave her a sophistication and confidence missing in other White women her age.

I dove into reading, researching, and writing my novel—not to complete academic materials to prepare for an exam or a seminar essay. It was a liberating time, and I felt my decision was a good one as pages of narration developed and characters spoke loudly in my head. The working title for the novel was *Walking Among the Gods*, and as I outlined the story of a Southern Black father moving his preteen son to the North following his mother's death, I tapped into my memories of Florida and Georgia.

Through John's contacts, I eventually found my own one-bedroom apartment, and I signed up as substitute teacher for the school district in Lewiston. I had a phone line installed, and I purchased a couple of dress shirts and ties. I didn't necessarily want to teach, but it would be the easiest job for me to do, particularly since substituting would be babysitting without the responsibility of class preparations. The annoying aspect of the position was that I would receive a phone call early in the morning requesting that I be at a selected school within the hour. These last-minute requests often spoiled my writing plans and forced me to quickly shovel out my snow-filled driveway to reach my car.

That first day of substituting placed me in a junior high school where a flood of White faces stared at me in the main office and along the hallway on my way to the assigned classroom.

As I walked into the classroom, the thirty or so White students suddenly went quiet. They all stared in disbelief and curiosity. Then, from the back row, one kid shouted, "Look, it's Fred Sanford!" Without missing a beat, I joked back, "You could at least call me Lamont. Fred is old, and he walks funny." The class laughed again, I wrote my name on the board, and we were off and running. They took the first twenty minutes of class to ask all manner of questions about me personally and Black people in general. I then followed the lesson plan left by the teacher. The same process occurred in the remaining classes for the day.

I pitied those kids, staring and questioning, trying to fill their cultural void and racial curiosity. The Black population in the state of Maine was still less than 1 percent, and for those students, their primary points of racial reference were television shows, movies, and music. There were no daily interracial encounters for them, so their knowledge was piecemeal and fed by popular culture.

The substitute teaching was infrequent, and it was clear that I needed something more to keep me until the summer when I could return to Hyannis—with the first draft of a novel—and jump into a steady summer job. The opportunity came when Jason told me that the local bookstore, Bookland, was hiring for a full-time position. Stewart, the manager, and Jessie, the assistant manager, were welcoming and courteous. They were well-read and embraced a more diverse vision of the world. The job was not overwhelming, but it required a level of alertness. As a clerk, I had to stock and restock; maintain and organize the books on the shelves; greet and assist the customers; and work the cash register. The latter duty bore the most pressure when customers crowded the lines, and any returning change in coins required calculations in my head. I was a writer, not a mathematician.

By the spring of 1976, I fell into a manageable lifestyle: working as many hours offered at the bookstore, writing as much as I could, holding lengthy discussions with John and Jason, and accepting that my relationship with Gwen was over. The realization chained me to an emotional wall, and I hoped the physical distance from her would allow me to slip from the limiting manacles of *love*. Concerned about my personal life, Jason introduced me to the new assistant dean at Bates, Debbie Thomas, a confident, articulate Black woman who had attended Middlebury College. Some people immediately thought the two of us would make an ideal couple—being Black and single in Lewiston. She was very attractive and perhaps a year younger than me, but her administrative duties placed strenuous burdens on her on campus. Being the only Black administrator, she worked in a fish bowl, and her off-campus life kept her in the spotlight as an anomaly. As for me, I was attempting to get over my years of involvement with Gwen. However, Debbie and I became good friends and shared conversations about the limitations that Lewiston held for us both.

As that winter dragged along, an inspirational moment occurred at the bookstore. Since Bookland was the major chain and the Lewiston-Auburn area was the most populated after the city of Portland, our store was scheduled to host a book reading by author Stephen King. Mr. King was touring with his newest bestseller, *Salem's Lot* (1975). The anticipation among the store's workers was infectious, and the customer turnout for his reading was impressive for a weeknight. Along with the other clerks, I met Mr. King as he entered, but I was assigned to the cash register while Stewart and Jessie took the lead in hosting and talking to the author. Since the book reading was set up at the rear of the store, I only caught occasional words that filtered to the front. Bursts of applause complemented ripples of laughter, until a long, sustained ovation led into a Q&A session. Finally, after the customers and fans drifted away, I was able to edge up to Mr. King before Stewart ushered him out to the parking lot.

"Mr. King, hello," I began, shaking his hand. "I'm writing my first novel now. I just wanted to see if you have any suggestions as I'm working on it."

King looked at me, tilted his head, and said, "Write. Write as much as you can."

He shook my hand, but I wanted more, watching him follow Stewart out of the store. I was disappointed and upset. He had just published a 600-plus page novel, and his only advice was seven words. I shook my head and folded the row of chairs filling the rear space. As I drove to my apartment afterward, I thought about other questions I wanted to ask Mr. King. I had met other authors before who were successful in poetry and academic texts, but Mr. King was the first popular fiction writer that I met. I hoped for some insight from him to sustain me through the cold mornings with my typewriter and bowl of oatmeal. I wanted him to stoke my dreams about writing with the promise that there was a personal rainbow of success waiting for me. I wanted some validation that what I was doing would lead to fulfilment through public recognition.

Years later, his words still resonated, and they became the cornerstone of the lessons I would tell students as I taught creative writing classes. Mr. King was correct and precise—*write!* As I matured as an author, that simple word served as the tool for shaping my imagination and passion into paragraphs that washed across endless blank pages. A writer must *write* and minimize the distractions that often enter that space where ideas germinate and require a nurturing sweat before blossoming. To write is to offer light to the darkness of experiences and emotions that haunt a writer's sleeping and waking hours.

Talking is *not* writing. Wishing is *not* writing. Dreaming is *not* writing. The only vessel that brings writers closer to that golden fleece that they search to embrace is the process of wrestling with and determining the words that give flesh to a haunting skeleton of ideas. Demanding and draining, suffocating and strangling—it is a solitary journey toward a speck of a destination on the horizon. A writer must *write*!

* * *

Jason and I often dove into some deep waters of conversations. We discussed religion, race relations, personal relationships, family, and sex. He was majoring in religion studies and was considering the ministry as his future. However, he was anxious about committing to such a burdensome calling as being a pastor—the leadership responsibilities, the neediness of a congregation, and the complications of possibly being a Black pastor with a White wife. He and Rose were quite serious in their relationship and aware of what they would face after graduating from Bates. Their concerns were amplified when Jason shared his older sister's reticence in accepting his future marriage plans. His sister and her husband had raised Jason, and as a strict, religious woman, she had her list of reasons against her brother's interracial union. The resistance was more visceral alongside the opinions of Rose's father, who opposed their plans for marriage. Jason was a deep-thinking man with a great deal on his mind during his senior year at Bates College, and his desires for his future were matched by the uncertainties of that future.

However, in late winter, Jason came to me with an idea that he had brought to the campus's Black Student Society.

"So, Mel, here's what we've been doing," Jason said, smiling. "We've talked to Dean Carignan about some changes we need here with the faculty. We have no Black professors, and we need . . . actually we're demanding that the school brings in Black faculty. So, on behalf of the Black Student Society, would you consider teaching a Black lit course here at Bates?"

"Me?" I questioned. "I . . . well, I hadn't thought of it."

"Hey, man. You're an alum . . . you have a graduate degree . . . you know Black lit."

"Yeah, but . . . this is Bates College. What did the dean say?"

"He said you would probably have a snowball's chance in hell of teaching here. That's why we're not giving up."

I knew Dean Carignan since my undergrad days, having taking a class with him and then working with him as my thesis advisor. Hearing his response didn't give me much hope. But the Black students—some of them I had met socially since returning to Lewiston—continued to pressure the administration. After a few weeks had passed, I received a call from Dr. Carl Straub, the dean of faculty. We met and discussed my interest in instructing *one* class during the eight-week, "short term" in the spring. He made me an offer, and I was too excited to refuse.

The weeks before that session gave me time to over-prepare to teach an African American Literature class. As I expected, the class was full, and it went extremely well. The class was comprised of both Black and White students. I led the class through the late nineteenth to late twentieth-century body of Black American literary expressions. I used Dr. Darwin Turner's anthology, *Black Literature in America*, supplemented by selected essays and Dudley Randall's *The Black Poets*. Randall's book was published in 1971, containing selections from slave songs to contemporary authors, including the four popular Black poets at the time: Don L. Lee (Haki Madhubuti), Nikki Giovanni, Sonia Sanchez, and Etheridge Knight. The huge anthology—*Black Writers of America* by Richard Barksdale and Kenneth Kinnamon—was a comprehensive and expensive book at the time, so I placed a copy on library reserve reading. The White students enjoyed the class—an examination of Black culture and creative expressions that most knew little about. But the Black students *loved* the class—reading and talking about literature that represented them.

Following the success of the course, I was invited to a meeting again with Dean Straub. Our discussion was comfortable and genial, as he praised the student evaluations and my success in teaching the class. He seamlessly eased into an invitation to teach in the English Department beginning in the fall for the 1976-77 academic year—with an asterisk. Since I didn't have a PhD in hand, the college would only offer me a one-year contract as a three-fourth position, instructing only three classes instead of the required four for a full-time position. The job offer was welcomed, but I immediately thought the three-fourth position was similar to the practice of Black people being assessed as three-fifths of a human during American slavery. Yet, the steady pay, which would be more than the bookstore, and the ability to attain teaching experience would be rewarding financially and academically.

With the Bates position beginning in early September, I remained in Lewiston for the summer—writing, working at the bookstore, and planning my classes. It was an enjoyable season, spending time with John and Pam, as well as Jason and Rose who were both working summer jobs as servers at a local restaurant. My novel was moving forward, but always in the back of my mind was the impending fall semester where I'd be teaching college-level classes on my former undergraduate campus.

\* \* \*

At the first scheduled faculty meeting, I walked into a room dominated by White faces that greeted me with amused gazes and slight smirks. Many of the faces didn't know me at all, as colleagues reconnected over handshakes and shared jokes. From the waves of conversations that washed over me, I was saturated with boastful phrases about traveling, completing a book, and diving deeper into research. Out of the 110 professors, I was the youngest one. Out of the 110 professors, I was the *only* Black one. It was a rippling ocean of discomfort.

"So, Professor Mel Donalson . . . how are you?"

It was Dr. James Leamon extending his hand. Except for some visible grey hairs spiraling his mustache, he looked the same—lean, physically fit—the professor we used to call Jungle Jim. Although he served as an unofficial advisor while I wrote my senior thesis at Bates College, I hadn't kept in touch with him during the years following graduation.

"Dr. Leamon! It's really great to see you again!"

"Well, there's a rumor going around with your name attached to it."

"Yes, of all people," I said, nodding. "I'm back on campus as a faculty member."

"So, tell me what's been going on in your life since we last saw one another."

I briefly explained my sojourn since leaving Bates, noting my death row depression in Iowa City. It was an elliptical account, emphasizing the teaching and academic experiences. He listened, nodded, and delivered some encouraging remarks about the need of the students to have someone like me—a young professor who embodied the values of a scholarly profession.

"Y'know," he continued after a pause. "I still remember that day in my Colonial History class when you shouted out your comments about Thomas Jefferson. Such anger . . . arrogance! And I still disapprove about *how* you said what you did. But . . . because of *what* you said, I began to review the ways in which I taught Jefferson. And you were right. My admiration for the intellectual man . . . avoided who he was *as* a man. So, I've been teaching Jefferson in a more . . . complete manner since that day."

At that moment, I didn't recall how I responded, but I knew that I was floored by his honesty. At the same time, I felt that I *did* belong in that gathering of august White men. I didn't have their degrees or publications, but I had influenced the manner in which one of the smartest professors I ever knew reassessed what he shared from his professorial platform. I felt that if nothing more were to come of the academic world, I had truly accomplished something significant.

\* \* \*

When I taught high school, I was only three years older than many of my students. At Bates, I was beginning to show my age—I was six years older than some of my students. As I was scheduled for several lower division literature classes, I taught freshmen and sophomores, many of whom had been educated in prep schools in various parts of New England. In small classes of fifteen to twenty students, their private school educations paid off. In general, they were well-read, efficient writers, and critical thinkers. Importantly, they made me work harder to anticipate questions and to shape responses that were informative, thoughtful, and provocative. These were "book smart" White kids, with only a few who flaunted a pedantic demeanor to prove they were smarter than the young Black professor standing before them. But I was prepared, and being more arrogant than the small number of challengers, I won the verbal battles and wielded the power of the pen when grading their essays.

\* \* \*

During the fall semester, several faculty members made the same suggestion: get my PhD so I could teach and earn tenure at the college level. I didn't resist the idea, nor did I race after it. With my novel completed and undergoing revisions, I saw my future as pursuing a writer's pathway, even though I wasn't exactly sure how that would be achieved—journalist, playwright, novelist, poet? The only thing I enjoyed more than writing was watching movies, and the only thing I loved more than watching movies was listening to music. Unfortunately, I had no pathway for succeeding in movies or music, and writing came easily.

It was Dr. Leamon who told me that he had attended Brown University and thought the education there was excellent. The only thing I knew about Brown was that it was an Ivy League school, which seemed way beyond my grasp, particularly financially. However, as a way of creating options for myself, I applied to Brown and Yale, believing that those two campuses would be the best fit for me, specifically with the interdisciplinary approaches offered in their American Studies Departments.

I received another level of encouragement during the spring semester when I met with Dean Straub. Attempting to create options for my future, I inquired about the possibility of teaching another year at Bates. He assured me that the administration at Bates was quite pleased with my teaching and my commitment to the students, emphasizing that my presence on campus had made a measurable and positive difference for undergrads—Black *and* White. But . . . it would be a challenge for the administration to award me another one-year position. In short, he was confident that Bates would welcome me back to the faculty—if I earned my PhD.

\* \* \*

Winter came boastfully to Maine in 1977, a climate clashing in confusion between cold and comfort. My classes went well, both challenging and rewarding as I fulfilled my position as a professor. I made certain that I was always prepared, organized, and available to my students, whether Black or White.

At the same time, I understood the responsibility I had to the Black students, and I encouraged and advised their efforts to bring Black culture to the campus. In February for "Black Arts Week," I organized a stage production in the campus theater for members of the Black Student Society to participate in and develop. Assembling poetry, speeches, and excerpts from essays, I directed the students in performing a historical progression of Black creativity and leadership. The program, despite the frustrations and headaches that arose during rehearsals, was successful with a full audience attending the performance.

Additionally, I helped bring two outstanding Black alumni to campus. First, the poet, playwright, and novelist Owen Dodson gave a reading of his verse and dialogued with audiences about his literary career and his years as a Bates student. Dodson was a memorable speaker, inspiring attendees with recounts of how he overcame numerous systemic challenges on his journey to a career as a writer and educator.

During that same week, Black alumnus Benjamin E. Mays came to campus and shared a panoply of experiences. He was known for two outstanding reasons: he served as the president of Morehouse College for twenty-seven years *and*, he had a mentoring friendship with Martin Luther King, Jr. Dr. Mays's Bates visit demonstrated that he was a masterful speaker, and his discussion with the students was inspiring. The following morning, I had the privilege of taking him to the Portland International Airport, and during our drive, Dr. Mays congratulated me for working with the Black students on campus as a professor and mentor. We discussed the current state of Bates's Black student community, and he was extremely encouraging—urging me to continue being a mentor *and* professor while continuing to pursue my dreams as a writer. The one-hour ride ended much too soon, but I was moved by the magnanimous person that he was. I reflected on the thoughts written by Dr. Mays in his 1971 book, *Born to Rebel: An Autobiography*: "The central questions confronting every black man are what he can do to enlarge his freedom, to create in himself a sense of his inherent worth and dignity, and to develop economic and political security . . . There is no easy way: there are no certain answers."[3]

---

3. Benjamin E. Mays, *Born to Rebel: An Autobiography*, Athens, GA: The University of Georgia Press, 1971, pp. 308–309.

\* \* \*

Yale sent me a rejection letter, leaving me mute with disappointment. I couldn't tell all those supportive people who kept encouraging me to prepare for New Haven. So, I clutched the hope that Brown University would save me from falling into an abyss of misery. But like a heavyweight boxer fighting an amateur lightweight, Brown delivered the knockout punch—rejection! I laid there on the canvas, a melancholy buzz filling my head. I entered a fog of distance from everyone, trying to maintain positivity on the outside while wrestling with my inner sadness. I eventually got around to sharing the news, and everyone was stunned. Yet, I didn't have a rubber soul to bounce back from my despondency.

I shared the news with several friends, including Gini Cassara. We had kept in touch since teaching together at Barnstable High School. With her divorce, Gini reclaimed her family name and moved from Hyannis to Madison, Wisconsin.

"That's impossible!" she said over the phone.

"Yeah, yeah. I really thought I would get in. Particularly with Dr. Leamon being a Brown graduate and writing me a recommendation."

"Doesn't make sense," she stated. "You should write someone at the campus and complain."

"Well, the letter came from the dean of the grad school."

"Go over his head if you have to!" Gini urged. "Tell someone they made a mistake. You should've been accepted!"

When I hung up, I reflected on Gini's words, hearing them in my head throughout the night, and by the following morning, I constructed a plan. I phoned the office of the dean of the graduate school at Brown University and asked if he would be available the following day. Getting a confirmation, I rose early the next morning, and I put on a shirt, tie, and dress jacket. I then drove four hours to Providence, Rhode Island. I arrived at the campus by early afternoon, and following the map from the college catalogue, I parked as close as possible to the graduate offices. I found the specific center needed, took several deep breaths, and entered with my best Clint Eastwood scowl.

"Good afternoon," the secretary smiled. Her silver hair was swirled in a bun. Her complexion was pale. "How can I help you?"

"I need to see Dean Wilkinson, please," I responded through clenched teeth.

"Do you have an appointment?"

"No!"

"Well, can I tell Dean Wilkinson what this is about?"

"There's been a terrible mistake made!" I asserted.

"I see . . . well, just a moment."

She angled to the closed door behind her and knocked before slipping most of her plump body inside the office. I held my ground and stayed in character until she returned.

"Well, he really has a tight schedule," she offered, "but he can give you just a few moments."

Inside the dean's office, I took the offered seat, shifting from my fierce Clint Eastwood demeanor to my cool and confident John Shaft attitude. Reaching for his notepad and pen, the dean angled his chair toward me. I began firmly. Attitude in place. I invoked the significance of my undergraduate studies, including writing a thesis. My year of teaching high school. The graduate program at the University of Iowa. The year of teaching at the distinguished Bates College. My published poem and short story. My completed but unpublished novel. I made certain that I hit every possible high note in the symphony of my academic and creative experiences.

Silence. A moment that lingered for several heartbeats. Dean Wilkinson looked over his notes and then questioned me about the particulars of my application to Brown's American Civilization Department. He inquired about the *why's*, *when's*, and my future plans. I emphasized the facts and possibilities of my academic background, adding the verbal encouragement from Dean Straub to return full time to the faculty at Bates College. He wrote continuous notes on the pad and asked me for the best contact information, indicating he would review my application file and speak with the chairperson of the American Civilization Department. He shook my hand, and I hoped he couldn't feel the sweat running down my arm and into my palm.

I hurried from the building and broke out in a slight run to my car, my heart pumping. I drove away from campus before uniformed security guards chased me for impersonating movie icons. I didn't breathe until my Toyota merged onto the expressway heading toward Boston and Maine.

Two weeks later, I received a phone call from Dean Wilkinson's office, followed by official letters of acceptance from the graduate school admissions office and the American Civilization Department. I finally exhaled and muttered overdue prayers to God. And as I shared the good news with my family and tribe of friends, I realized that my life was moving in an academic direction. It was scary. I had won another battle in a war I was hesitant to fight, but I allowed the geyser of joy to erupt from inside and wash over me.

Mama D, Papa D, and Mel, 1954

Mel, Mama D, and Paulette, 1957

Mel, Quonset Hut, Hyannis, 1963

Mel, High School Senior, 1969

Cousin Betty, Mel, and Mama D, High School Graduation

*Dreams, Ideals, and Stars* 131

Bates College, Study Abroad Group, Spring 1972

Lois Philips Tolis, Train Fun, Study Abroad Group, 1972

Humberto Torres, Train Jokester, Study Abroad Group, 1972

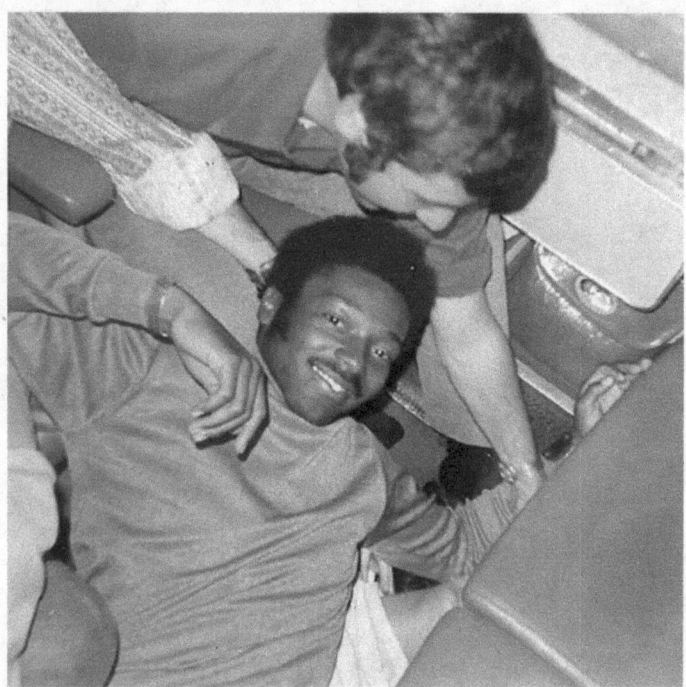

Mel, Train Prankster, Study Abroad Group, 1972

Dreams, Ideals, and Stars 133

Berlin Wall Section, Spring 1972

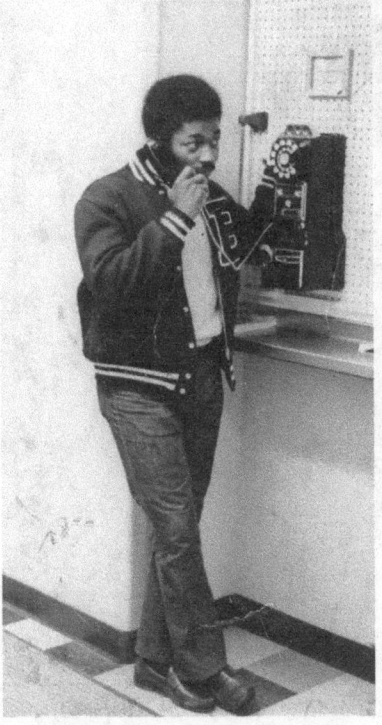

Mel, Bates College Dorm, 1973

Bates College Buddies, John Jenkins and Ira Waldman

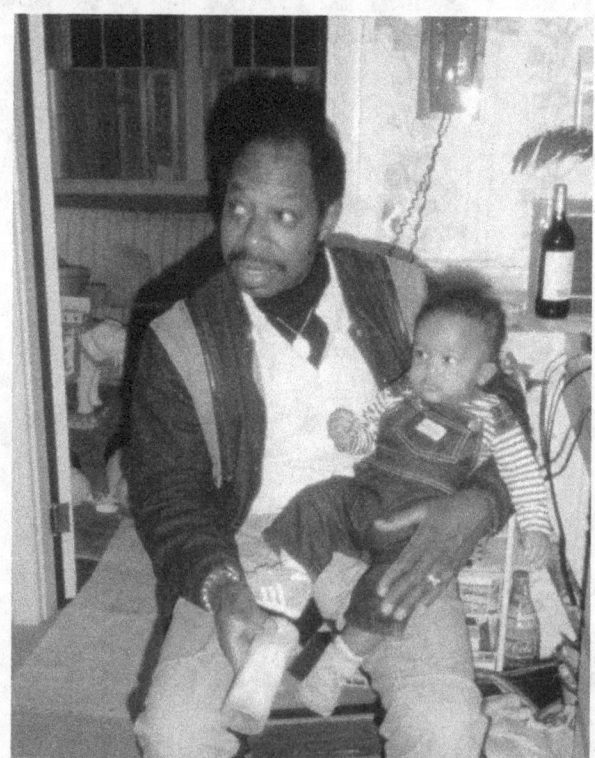

Baby Derek and Granddad Wilbert (aka Papa D)

Dreams, Ideals, and Stars 135

Toddler Derek and Dad

Beverly and Mel,
Maui Marriage, 1995

Jackie George, Friend and Producer,
*A Room Without Doors*, 1998

Actor Michael Beach,
*A Room Without Doors*

Actor Dick Anthony Williams,
*A Room Without Doors*

Mel, Paulette, and John Jenkins, Late 1990s

Reggie McDowell, Friends for Decades

Virginia Cassara and husband Tim Hunter, Friends for Decades

Fred Lamster and wife Fran, Friends for Decades

Harry Smallenburg, Professor, Photographer, Musician—
Friends for Decades

My Loving Parents, 60th Anniversary

Mel and Beverly at Pasadena Event, 2000

The Donalson Men—Brian, Derek, Wilbert, Mel, 2002

Producer David Massey, On *Performance* Set, 2008

Raymond Forchion, Casting Director, *Performance*

Actor Art Evans, *Performance*

Actress Nisa Ward, *Performance*

Mel Giving Lecture about Black Directors in Hollywood

Beverly Shares *Being Grace*, Her Children's Book

*Passage* Short Film Poster, 2021

Mel and David at Screening for Cast and Crew

Derek and Marisol, Engaged

Mel, Panel Member, 50th Bates College Reunion, 2023

Ben Guillory

Reyna Grande

Jim Henderson

David Massey

Luis Rodriguez

CHAPTER EIGHT

## The Cultivation of Talent

The summer before I started my studies at Brown in 1977, I was in Hyannis, living in a cottage behind the house of my parents' friend. During the day, I worked alongside Reggie McDowell for Papa D's cleaning company. Reggie, my childhood friend, was shaping his future plans for working in the hospitality business, and he and I appreciated the trust that Papa D had in sending the two of us to complete jobs together.

My free time was spent begging banks for an educational loan and searching for a small apartment in Providence. The summer in Hyannis also gave me time to spend with James and his band, as they covered pop songs at various clubs. He was one of the most talented men I knew, but he was *still* in Hyannis—always encouraging me to follow my dreams, but not taking those significant steps in his music and personal life.

After numerous trips to Providence, I finally found a ground floor, one-bedroom apartment at the edge of College Hill, which was a convenient area, but not within comfortable walking distance to campus with a full book bag. My new place had a separate, closet-size bedroom, but the entire space was as small as my Iowa City studio apartment.

The American Civilization Department—which it was labeled at the time—was on Waterman Street. It was housed in a detached building that held a reception area, small offices, and student mailboxes. I was in a cohort of sixteen graduate students who hailed from a variety of backgrounds—including Debbie Thomas who had been an administrator and friend at Bates College. Debbie and I were pleased to see each other for another reason: we were the only Black people in our cohort.

The program was strenuous, submerging grad students into the theoretical, research-related expectations of a PhD candidate. I balanced the required Research and Methods seminar with my choices of graduate-level classes, ranging from literature, history, and cinema. The interdisciplinary approach to exploring the United States appealed to me, examining those intersections of academic disciplines often separated into divisions of study, such as the humanities, social sciences, physical sciences, computer sciences, and engineering. Outside of my cohort, there were those students in the department who had completed their required courses and were preparing proposals for and/or writing their dissertations. Being new to the department, I spent my time with those in my cohort, but I was fortunate to connect with two other students who influenced my journey at Brown.

One was fellow poet, Peter Balakian. Peter and I shared conversations when crossing paths in the department offices. We exchange ideas about verse, our favorite poets, and writing projects. He was encouraging and patient with my questions. Significantly, Peter was Armenian, which opened up an entirely new world of ethnicity for me, and to Peter's credit, he explored his own ethnic-cultural background through his grandmother's experiences as a survivor of the Armenian Genocide of 1915. Peter's researching and discovery of his family's history led to his memoir, *Black Dog of Fate* (1997). His book inspired Armenian American communities across the country and led to his future activism. He went on to publish numerous books of poetry, including his collection *Ozone Journal* (2016), which won a Pulitzer Prize.

The second person who made a difference in countless ways was Fred Lamster. I first met Fred when I signed up for a film course he was teaching. I assumed he was a junior professor at Brown, but discovered he was completing his PhD program and serving as a teaching assistant at the same time. When we first met, we discovered our mutual love for films, and we have been talking ever since. Fred guided me through the particulars: details about the strengths and weaknesses of the department and insights about who was who on the faculty and among the graduate students. We met weekdays in the Special Collections section of the university library. I was there to read, research, and develop seminar papers, and he was there to write his dissertation—a study of the 1940s filmmaker Frank Borzage. Borzage was an actor turned Academy Award-winning director who helmed movies from the late 1920s to the 1940s. Fred's disciplined, focused, and productive work ethic inspired me, as he finished his PhD at twenty-eight years old and eventually published his book on Borzage, *Souls Made Great Through Love and Adversity* (1981).

Fred grew up in a Jewish neighborhood in Queens, New York, and possessed an infectious energy and expansive reading background. He inhaled books and exhaled boundless ideas. He was my close friend, a confidante who propped me up and told me the truth when necessary. He became and still is my brother.

\* \* \*

My bank loan helped out immensely during that first year at Brown, but it wasn't enough. The department offered me a research assistantship that I eagerly accepted. Consequently, I worked with an English professor who was working on the poetry of Lafcadio Hearn, a truly forgettable nineteenth-century poet whose writing neglected to connect with me. Yet, I met with the professor, heard his adoration for Hearn, and received his instructions to find critical essays about the poet hidden in dust-covered anthologies. The work was not exciting, but it strengthened my skills with the research process. I learned to patiently peruse library catalogue index cards and stacks of books; read quickly but critically; and make notes that captured significant points and perspectives from the text. Between reading and writing for my classes, seminars, and my research assistantship, my life as a graduate student was a seven-days-a-week pursuit.

The evenings that I took off were to catch an on-campus movie with Fred, usually a vintage Hollywood film. Those relaxed evenings were balanced with early morning weight-lifting workouts in the gym or chasing balls on the tennis courts. Unfortunately, there was no nearby martial arts studio where I could worship. On occasion, the one-hour drive to and from Hyannis was reprieve from the monotony of graduate life, but it required gas money. Ultimately, the best thing for my humble budget was to spend the weekend reading and studying, with an hour break on Saturday afternoons to watch *Soul Train* on my twelve-inch television screen.

\* \* \*

One of the required seminars during that fall semester was American Civilization, basically a theory and methodology class to explore cultural analysis through the lenses of literature, history, anthropology, and sociology. The intent was to introduce the research, theory, and practices of notable scholars for examining the comparative structures and systems of various cultural groups. The professor teaching the seminar was a disciple of Claude Levi-Strauss, a twentieth-century sociocultural anthropologist. With the two-hour seminar meeting in the late afternoon, the biggest challenge was remaining awake, so I contributed verbally as a strategy for keeping my eyes open.

To survive the tortuous weekly experience, I approached the professor with the idea of shooting a short film to complement my required seminar paper. My film's focus would use interviews to demonstrate a comparative analysis of racial and generational traditions among people from the same Southern state: Georgia. I titled the film *Generations from Georgia*, which included interviews with three sets of people: my grandmother, Ella Mae Donalson; my parents, Wilbert and Dorothy Donalson; and a White doctoral student in Brown's American

Civilization Department named Susan Donaldson—*with* a second "d"—whose family background was also in Georgia. Although Susan and I discussed the probability that we were somehow related, our interests in confirming a possible familial connection were never pursued.

With Fred's help, we filmed interviews in Hyannis and in Providence using a Super-8 camera for the footage and borrowed equipment to edit the piece. The fifteen-minute film had inconsistent lighting and sound, but when showing it in the seminar, my fellow students were thankful for the break from the sleep-inducing, monotoned lecture from the professor. With my seminar paper and film submitted together, I squeaked out an excellent grade, but more importantly, I never had to retake the course.

\* \* \*

Another professor entered my life that first year at Brown, and the impact was irreversible. I first encountered Dr. Mari Jo Buhle during my search for a class that would complete a full course load. Having taken classes in American literature and American history throughout my master's program, I knew those areas in detail. When I saw a course called The History of American Women, I figured it was the easy choice to make. After all, how much information and content could comprise a historical examination of women?

When Dr. Buhle entered the classroom, she shared a brief smile and wrote the outline of the day's lecture on the blackboard. She was a thin woman physically, appearing to be a long-distance runner with short, auburn hair. As she lectured, her voice was smooth and even, delivering her content in a conversational manner. Dr. Buhle delivered the most organized, detailed, and comprehensive lectures, which she matched and often surpassed from class to class.

It was a jolting, alarming class that forced me to confront a history that I didn't know. Having filtered all women through my limited, awkward, pain-filled, and emotionally draining experiences with girls, the class forced me to confront truths about America's history and about myself. I didn't know as much as I thought, and the little that I *did* know only skimmed the surface of decades of materials, achievements, and facts that had been omitted from previous literature and history texts. It was the revelation of the many reprehensible actions taken against women and the remarkable resilience and creativity that sustained women in the face of adversity. And yes, Dr. Buhle's lectures also noted the flaws within a fragile sisterhood when unity often buckled beneath the weight of sexism, racism, and classism. In her class, I actually became *educated*, but I was upset that I had reached a doctoral level of studies before experiencing such books, essays, and knowledge.

I seized the opportunity to push my research further for the course's required term paper, enthralled by and focusing on the expressions and fortitude of nineteenth-century Black poet, Frances Ellen Watkins Harper (1825-1911). Harper was born a "free Negro" in Maryland, and she worked as an abolitionist, lecturer, teacher, and author—writing poetry, short fiction, and a novel. I came across her poems "Bury Me in a Free Land" and "A Double Standard" when taking African American Literature at the University of Iowa, but in the Special Collections section of Brown's library, I was able to access Harper's original manuscripts, letters, and handwritten drafts. It was a remarkable experience to reach across centuries to encounter a Black woman who navigated America's racially oppressive nineteenth century.

Dr. Buhle continued to be an inspiration for my future decisions about academic studies. She was the scholar who demonstrated the integrative pathways to understanding American society. During that year, I knew that she was the professor with whom I wanted to study. I was the typical "work in progress" as a man, and many authors, activists, and politicians still needed to be explored and assessed. Dr. Buhle lit that candle of awareness and investigation, allowing me to glimpse into the darkness of America's systems that I knew firsthand regarding race but would now have to comprehend regarding gender and sexuality.

\* \* \*

By the time the winter of 1978 assaulted Providence, I was neck-deep into my studies. At a low point in my spirits, the city was pummeled with over fifty inches of snow. On one distinct afternoon, urged by hunger and empty cabinets, I braved the elements to walk several blocks to the corner market. Hills of snow were packed onto the sidewalks. I crunched and slipped my way along the street, following the boot prints of others before me. I angled up one snowbank and saw the white landscape blanketing the streets. As I stepped gingerly, I looked down at the roofs of cars abandoned at parking meters, snow-plowed into four-wheeled popsicles. When I reached the market, a line of people snaked around the corner. Joining the back of the line, the whispered update was that the market was selling each customer only one loaf of bread and one carton of milk or juice.

In another forty-five minutes, I paid for my rations and retraced my path across the packed snow. I entered my apartment, feeling depressed but appreciating the radiator's warmth. With bread slices in hand and a carton of orange juice, I turned on the small television and found a hazy broadcast of *Soul Train*. I looked at the beautiful women gyrating on the screen, at the snow-laced windows, and back to the dancing women.

"Damn, this is crazy!" I said aloud. "Why am I here?"

And though I had considered the thought numerous times before, on that day I said aloud, "I'm going to California!"

* * *

Two developments lifted my spirits during the winter semester of that first year. I was informed that my short story, "The Thirteenth Hour," would appear in the February 1978 journal, *Commentary*, published by the University of Singapore. Dr. Peter Nazareth, from the University of Iowa, was true to his promise to get the story to a reading audience. I was grateful and excited with a mixture of emotions. I was a published fiction writer.

The second development was unexpected. I took a cinema class that utilized Semiology as the critical methodology for analyzing *The Godfather* and *The Godfather II*. We viewed each film numerous times, breaking down sequences to explore the "signs"—any component and elements communicating meanings and messages to viewers. It was dense and theoretical, but engaging. The course was taught by Dr. Greg Colombo, a professor who resembled a young Francis Coppola, and he shaped the syllabus to require an extensive investigation that explored some intersection of Semiology and film. Although a seminar paper was required, as the submission deadline edged closer, I went to Dr. Colombo and begged him to allow me to do something *different*.

"I can bring in several graded papers that I've written that demonstrate my ability to complete an analytical, academic paper," I told Dr. Colombo. "But . . . I'm just so tired of dealing with this abstract thinking and talking. But, of course, I don't mean to be disrespectful of your seminar."

"Okay, I think I understand," he smiled, hearing my weariness. "What do you have in mind?"

"Well, maybe I could try writing a script . . . you know, based on some aspect of *The Godfather*. Something creative. A story that would reveal significant underlying meanings in the film."

"I see," he said. "Well, tell you what. Think it through some more and bring me back an outline by next week. Your script, of course, would have to be the same required length as the seminar paper."

"No problem. I understand. I'll get something to you by next week."

I was elated by his openness to my academic exhaustion, but then fear overtook me—I'd never written a screenplay before. So, I transitioned into another kind of research, excavating the library and campus bookstore to find titles that would guide me through this unknown writing terrain. I couldn't find a book about screenwriting, so I followed the familiar format and dialogue of a stage play to complete my assignment. I drove myself through this fog of a new territory and came out on the other side with a twenty-page script. Using the film's opening wedding sequence as my blueprint, Michael, the favored son in uniform, arrives at his sister's wedding with Kay—whom I wrote as a Black woman. By changing that one character, I forced the other characters to deal with the outsider on more than one level. It was no longer just about the Corleone's tolerating a woman outside of their Italian background; rather, they were forced to also engage race and gender in a different manner.

Dr. Colombo liked what I submitted and where I took the sequence, awarding me an A-. In addition, he did something quite helpful.

"Have you ever heard of the AFI, Mel?"

"No, I haven't."

"The American Film Institute . . . in LA," he explained. "It's only about ten years old. A graduate-level program that specializes in several film-related areas. One is in screenwriting."

I perked up, thanked Dr. Colombo, and hurried away to research the AFI. I read the institution's mission to train future filmmakers to enter the film industry, and I phoned the AFI offices for more info and application papers—which, upon receiving, I completed immediately and mailed back, including my 8mm film, *Karateka*, that I made at the University of Iowa.

By April, I received a phone call from AFI, scheduling me for an interview in Boston with its representative who indicated that he was the chairman of the faculty. At that meeting, he revealed nothing about the status of my application, but he used the time to explain the screenwriting program in detail and the Institute's workshops. I still had no definitive answer, but I felt I did well in passing the personal audition.

\* \* \*

By the end of the academic year at Brown, I faced a challenging decision. I received acceptance into the American Film Institute. It was a golden opportunity to study, learn, and enter the movie-making world that I dreamed about since I was an eight-year-old kid in Fort Pierce, Florida. However, there was no tuition money offered, leaving me with the familiar challenge of finding funds before classes would begin in the fall. At the same time, having earned my master's degree and completed my coursework at Brown, I only needed to pass my oral exams and write my dissertation to receive my PhD.

Fred Lamster gave me useful advice that shaped my direction. He suggested I move forward with planning the next year at Brown—deciding my dissertation topic and choosing the four faculty members for my oral exams committee.

Then, take the summer to go out to Los Angeles and visit the American Film Institute in person to negotiate tuition. Fred's plan made sense.

I approached four professors, inquiring if they would work with me in preparing for my oral exams at the end of the 1979 spring semester. At the same time, I moved out of the tiny College Hill apartment in Providence, storing my meager possessions in Mama D and Papa D's basement. My folks suggested getting in touch with the Whitted family that they had visited earlier in the year. Julian Whitted, our landlord when we rented his Quonset hut, had a brother and family living in Los Angeles. I had never met them, but reached out as encouraged, finding that their son, Michael, was open to me staying with him until I found my bearings.

\* \* \*

In June 1978, I drove to California, and I had three months to figure out my future direction. Rolling through the smoggy Los Angeles air, I noted the downtown buildings and the long, extended freeways congested with cars. Following the directions I received, I exited onto Western Avenue, traveled north to Pico Boulevard, turned west to reach St. Andrews Place. For two blocks north, I gazed at the buildings bordered with wild hedges that needed manicures. Old, sunbaked cars and trucks peppered the curbsides as the heat and smog sat indifferently like a hazy dome. The belching brakes of city buses assaulted the air, as Black people moved off and on, flowing in and out of a corner market. Older two-story apartment buildings lined a long block of sidewalks with discarded papers and crushed soft drink cans.

Although meeting Michael Whitted, his parents, and son for the first time, they were all very generous and polite, treating me like a long-lost family member returning home. Michael, who was about my age, allowed me to crash in his apartment on St. Andrews Place, where he served as the building manager, but he worked full-time for the Alcoholic Beverage Commission. Michael was an energetic guy, a dedicated father of the son he had with his estranged Japanese-American wife. He lived a busy life, one where working hours were a diversion from his full social life. He belonged to the Black Porsche Club and the Black Ski Club, which gave him weekends filled with attending meetings, partying, and often traveling.

By the second day in the city, I mapped my way into Hollywood, following Sunset Boulevard west to Doheny Drive, then heading north to the Greystone Mansion, where the American Film Institute was located at the time. After explaining to the receptionist that I was an incoming screenwriting fellow, I soon sat in an office with a well-dressed woman wearing a casual smile. It was the same smile she maintained while explaining that a deferment of admissions for a year was *not* possible. In anticipating that response, I countered with my plan to get a job to pay tuition while attending AFI. Through the continual welcoming expression, the administrator discouraged me, indicating that industry professionals would be lecturing in classes during the day and at other events in the evening. Due to my required attendance day and night, I wouldn't be able to be a full-time fellow *and* work a job. There was only one option: I needed to have enough money by the fall to study at the Institute for the coming year.

There was no pressure for me to leave Michael's apartment, but certainly I had to get my own place for the summer. The first step was finding a job, and in my naivete, I thought my university experience would be to my advantage as I applied at nearby dry cleaners, department stores, and grocery stores. Unsuccessful with my first days of looking, I studied the classifieds of the *LA Times* and followed up on an opening at a warehouse—the Imperial Billiards Company—in Glassell Park, located northwest of downtown LA. During the interview, I lied, suggesting a previous job at a hardware store and claiming only a high school education.

The masquerade was successful, and I was hired to be a shipping clerk. Working in a small room with three other guys, I filled purchase orders—selecting items from the warehouse shelves; packing the items in the appropriate boxes; weighing and addressing the boxes; and placing them in the bin to be sorted into the delivery trucks. Two of the shipping clerks—older, White, and married with children—had been with the company the longest, while the third guy—Javier, a young Latino, single guy—was, like me, new to the position. Javier was Chicano and introduced me to a whole new perspective of the Los Angeles area. I was able to learn some of his Spanish words, and he helped me identify specific food items in Spanish during our morning breaks at the food truck—what we called the "Roach Coach." The fifth guy who manned the forklift was Chuck. He was a lean, front-tooth-missing, cowboy-hat-wearing Black man from Arizona, who enjoyed talking and laughing loudly. By the second day on the job, I had it figured out. Eight hours of the same repetitive motions, pierced with loud-talking; sex-laced stories; and corny jokes from the two older White workers. A forty-hour, Monday through Friday work week—it was a new kind of hell.

I luckily found an apartment on the 900 block on South Gramercy Place, in the mid-city area between South Wilton Place and Western Avenue, just a ten-minute drive from Michael's apartment building. It was a tiny, one-room space with a Murphy bed that had to be pulled down from its vertical position behind a closet door. Most times, I slept on the couch to maintain the illusion of a larger living space. The couch also offered a better vantage point of the muscle-bound roaches that insisted on sharing the apartment with me. The roaches were not bashful nor afraid of my name-calling and occasional victory at swatting several with a newspaper. There were some nights when I was certain I heard the insects whispering and organizing inside the closet. So, each morning before dressing, I followed the ritual of shaking my clothes and checking my shoes for members of the steroid roach community that had lived there before I arrived.

However, I wasted no time in addressing the challenge before me—rushing away from my eight-hour warehouse job and dropping into banks to apply for a loan to attend the AFI. On those efforts, I shifted back to my academic persona—changing into a shirt and tie, hoping the bankers would be swayed by my background and aspirations. But no success. I was recent to my present job, I didn't have any local history, and I had no collateral. All I had were dreams and roaches, and neither had much value in LA.

As I walked the indifferent streets, I was heavy with self-pity. I reflected on my treasure of skills and talents, wondering why it was so difficult to move forward. The world appeared to be selecting me as the recipient of frustration and closed doors. Why was it so difficult to use and develop the God-given talents that flowed inside me? How long would I have to demonstrate to the universe that I was anointed with certain skills—gifts. Drifting into a depressed mood while sitting in my car's hot interior, the smoggy air suffocated my hope of studying at the American Film Institute.

It was difficult to let go of the AFI opportunity, but I knew I had to put it in perspective. Perhaps reapply? I wasn't certain. However, I knew that the only way to cultivate my talent was to work and develop my skills—consistently and faithfully. Regardless of the obstacles. Despite the setbacks. Without the American Film Institute for training as a screenwriter, I did what I suspected dozens of other aspiring screenwriters did at that time: I read about and went to the Larry Edmunds Bookshop, an independent business in Hollywood. I strolled aisles and fingered instructional books. Additionally, the store clerk informed me I could buy a copy of a screenplay from a recent movie. He showed me the list of titles, but he didn't share the details of how the store obtained the copies. So, I purchased a book and a script, knowing I had to teach myself.

I worked my eight hours during the weekdays and wrote at night. I allowed myself to relax on the weekends by learning the freeways, surrounding cities, and locales highlighted on sightseeing guides. I attended Sunday services at the First African Methodist Episcopal Church, located at nearby Harvard and Adams Boulevards. The church kept me connected to my faith, and the service reminded me of Bethel Baptist Church from my Florida days.

Unexpectedly, I also connected with Bruce Gaines, who taught at Barnstable High School with me and had migrated west to live in the coastal town of Hermosa Beach. Bruce and I hadn't seen much of each other since I left Hyannis for Iowa City, but through my parents, he reached out to me. His studio apartment was located on the Strand, which was the wide, concrete thoroughfare separating the buildings and the beach. Filled on the weekends with walkers, cyclists, roller skaters, bikini-clad women, and tourists speaking various languages, the Strand was home for Bruce and his coterie of beach pals. Bruce and I fell back into the friendly banter we shared while teaching at Barnstable. He loved his relocation to California, and whenever time and money allowed, we dropped into The Lighthouse, the jazz club that showcased both local musicians and marquee jazz makers.

The Los Angeles area was a magnet for an array of personalities—a place where anyone could reconfigure or improvise a sense of freedom and irresponsibility confirmed by leisure time, fancy cars, designer clothing, facelifts, and tanned, muscular bodies. Yet, there were those real markers of turmoil and desperation via the graffiti-riddled, inner-city neighborhoods; nightly television news headlines; *Los Angeles Times* mastheads proclaiming city crimes and political animosities; police sirens whining in the late-night darkness; and the downtown streets peppered with rootless people.

But as September drew near, I had to follow the only path that made sense—returning to the East Coast and preparing for and passing my oral exams in the spring, the last step before writing my dissertation. I would miss the Whitted family, especially Michael's energy and friendship. I would miss the guys I worked with at the warehouse. I would miss the spontaneous, laughter-filled hours with Bruce in Hermosa Beach. I would miss the LA freeways and landscapes that changed so drastically as I drove from downtown to the west side of Culver City, Westwood, Santa Monica, Playa del Rey, and Marina del Rey. But, for certain, I would *not* miss the roaches.

CHAPTER NINE

## Seekers and Saints

As that week-long drive East neared its end, I was pleased to see the Sagamore Bridge leading onto Cape Cod. I had solidified an arrangement with my parents before leaving LA. They agreed to let me live in their furnished basement, and I would contribute to food and help pay the utilities. That agreement allowed me to avoid maintaining an apartment in Providence, yet provided personal space to concentrate on my studies. I would make the drive to Providence when necessary, and the Cape Cod Community College library was close by to provide basic reference books.

Dr. Buhle agreed to be my dissertation director, working with me on one of my four areas of concentration, The History of American Women. Dr. Colombo would work with me on American Cinema. English professor, Dr. Walter Blake, worked with me on American Literature, and Dr. Charles Nichols, my sole Black professor, would helm my focus on African American Studies. My proposed dissertation topic blended these four areas together as required by the department. It was titled, "The Representation of African American Women in the Hollywood Feature Film, 1915-1949." At the end of the academic year, I would have to take a two-hour oral exam, and upon passing, submit a fifteen-page proposal describing the critical approaches to my dissertation topic and the significant films I would view and analyze.

My plan was simple: study intently, defend my areas of concentration, apply again to the American Film Institute, and save money. That way, I could return to LA and write the dissertation as I matriculated at the AFI. Despite the Institute's warning, I would find a part-time job to support myself. So, I dove head-first into the plan, hoping not to drown in the details while buoyed by my California dream.

\*\*\*

Once I organized the required bibliographies for each of my four areas of concentration, I scheduled a monthly meeting with each professor, driving into

Providence once a week to meet with one professor each week to discuss the designated area of focus. As I drove in each week, I relied heavily on Fred Lamster for an overnight stay when necessary, as he was sharing a two-story, four-bedroom house with three other grad students. If the couch wasn't available in the downstairs living room, Fred allowed me to crowd him out by sleeping on the floor in his bedroom. He was a life saver, particularly as the winter months came with snowstorms to challenge a drive back from Providence to Hyannis.

As the academic year progressed, I applied for a part-time teaching assignment in composition at Cape Cod Community College, and the campus was desperate enough to hire me. The one class brought in some needed funds, but it also delivered piles of student papers to read. With that teaching gig, I made just enough money to remind me that I was still poor. I rationed my money to cover gas for traveling to and from Brown, purchase necessary books, and go to an occasional movie. When I allowed myself free time, I'd sit in on one of James Tobey's band rehearsals or hang with some of my tribe of friends.

However, on one occasion, when James and his band were out of town, I glanced through the local paper to see if there were any music performances scheduled in Hyannis. There was one club on Yarmouth Road near the railroad tracks that advertised live music and no cover charge. The featured performer was a duo called Jade and Sarsaparilla, but I wasn't familiar with their music. However, it was a weekend, and I needed a break from my routine. I decided to splurge, taking fifteen dollars from my nest to spend on a couple of hours at the restaurant/club.

When I entered the club's dark ambience, the venue was crowded. I angled to the bar, took a seat, and ordered a draft beer from the woman bartender. The two performers were already into their set, covering some R&B and Soul classics, such as "Ooo, Baby, Bay," "Since I Fell for You," and "It's Gonna Take a Miracle." Before they ended the set, they added some original pieces. The tall woman played the piano skillfully, her long hair teasing her shoulders, while the other, shorter woman caressed the microphone, her dark hair just as long. Their voices blended well, and the shorter vocalist—attractive and sexy—stole my attention. When they took a break, the shorter woman came to the end of the bar. As the bar lights fell across her face, I saw that she was indeed pretty. She chatted briefly with the bartender, but I caught the bartender's attention with a wave of my hand.

"I'd like to buy the singer her favorite drink," I told her.

The bartender nodded as she reached back to lift the large bottle of Disaronno's Amaretto, pouring it over light ice. I did some quick math in my head, guessing that the liqueur would cost about six dollars, but the register rang up eight dollars, and along with my three-dollar beer and tips, I had only a few dollars remaining. The bartender delivered the drink, spoke briefly to the singer who nodded at me. I returned the nod and was surprised when she lifted her drink and eased along the bar to sit beside me.

"Hello, loved your set," I praised. "I'm Mel."

"Linda," she said, lifting her glass in a toast.

"Here's to you," I returned, clinking her glass. "My first time here . . . you did Smokey's song justice."

"Thanks, you can't go wrong with R&B."

"Are you from the Boston area?"

"Mmm, no. Janet and I are from the Cape," she responded, nodding back to the pianist near the stage.

"And you brought out the crowd tonight," I complimented her.

"We're lucky. We have a loyal following."

"So," I continued, attempting to angle into her personal life. "What do you do when you're not on stage?"

"Well," she smiled, reading where I was going. "Tell me what you do when you're not listening to music."

I launched into name-dropping—Brown University, PhD, Women's Studies. She nodded thoughtfully.

"I don't think I've met any man who's into Women's Studies."

"Well, I'm not any man," I returned with as much male bravado as possible. Linda smiled again.

"Do you know where you are?" she asked.

"What do you mean?" I said, not fully comprehending.

I looked around, and with the lights raised, I saw the audience. Tables full of women—talking, drinking, leaning forward in conversations, and some sitting close with their arms wrapped around one another. The plurality of them were White, with a few Black women sprinkled around several tables. At a couple of tables, some women were kissing.

"Thanks for the drink, Mel," Linda said as she smiled again, moving back toward the stage.

I called for the tab and paid as the next set began. As I moved toward the door, I felt everyone was looking at me, perhaps laughing at my obvious stupidity. All I saw were pretty women with long hair, which Linda certainly was. But I didn't see *her*, or the dozens of women populating the room. Their levity resonated with freedom and unregulated expression of being with other women.

As I drove home with a few dollars in my pocket, I realized that I paid for a brief but important lesson that I needed to add to the bibliography of my life.

From my perspective, a pretty, feminine, long-haired woman had to be what I thought she *should* be. Even with open eyes, I was blind to my own ignorance. I still had much to learn and accept. If I didn't widen my vision, my PhD would merely stand for "Privileged Heterosexual Dimwit."

\*\*\*

In November, I received a letter postmarked from North Carolina. It was from Gwen Fulbright—she was getting married. I was very pleased that she had found what she sought. Certainly, there was a hint of sadness, as I meditated on the years we had known each other. I had expectations too, but not in the same manner as she. In one of our many deep discussions, she called me a "dreamer," hypnotized by something always beyond my reach. There was truth in that observation, though I couldn't put a specific name to it at the time.

Then, in December 1978, Jason and Rose were married in Maine, and I was privileged to serve as their best man. They had to fight to be together in a manner that Gwen and I never did. Rose battled with her father, an educated man who rejected his daughter's commitment to a Black man. Then, Jason argued with his sister, whose strict Protestant background fed her reservations about his union with Rose. As I witnessed Jason and Rose exchanging vows and giving up family ties for one another, I realized how much sacrifice their love demanded.

Gwen and I never ran the hurdles that Jason and Rose were forced to jump. On my part, I fully accepted the selfishness that shaped my choices about being with Gwen. Looking honestly into the mirror of my life, I had no vision about the commitment and compromise demanded by a marriage. I was wedded to elusive dreams that demanded my time, energy, and creativity, leaving very little of *me* to share with anyone.

Life is but birth and death balancing on the scale of years. The significance and the purpose between those polarities are rooted in the experiences of fulfilling one's sense of being. I knew that if I didn't attempt to reach beyond the ordinary, I would be lost. I would merely be imitating what everyone else was doing. There *had* to be something more than the pre-ordained, expected elements of what a fulfilling life should look like. If I couldn't step out of line and follow my own path, what would be the importance of *my* life? Yes, I was feeling both regrets and elation for Gwen, Jason, and Rose. They were able to find fulfilment in their commitments to others. But to give a lifetime commitment to someone else is to give that person priority in your life. And in my honest moments, I knew I just wasn't ready to relinquish my selfishness.

\*\*\*

By the end of January 1979, I was chin-deep into my studies. Like an academic monk, my days were cloistered to the routines of reading bibliographical texts, critical essays, and books; conferencing with my professors; and making more notes. I had removed myself from anything resembling an existence outside of the walls of academic preparation.

However, an unexpected respite was imposed on me when I had a visit from three of John Jenkins' friends—Tory, Julie, and Susan. Actually, Tory was the only one I knew, having met her previously when she and John Jenkins were dating and making a summer visit from Lewiston to Hyannis. I gave the women my basement fortress, while I took the sofa upstairs in my parents' domain. Their visit forced me to take two days off from my academic studies and lose myself in spontaneity. The three were nurses who decided to leave Maine and journey to California via points of interests along the way to reach San Diego. The second night of their visit, we went out to a local dance club, moving to the music spun by a deejay shadowed in a corner. We danced together as a group, sometimes alone, and cheek to cheek for slower tunes. It was a refreshing breakaway. Before they left, Tory shared the news that she broke up with John because he wanted a commitment she wasn't ready to make. I understood those words too well, and she told me to drop into San Diego when I returned to the West Coast. I promised I would, and I longed to have that freedom that pulled the girls into a future they would carve out as they went along.

\*\*\*

I was twenty-seven in mid-May 1979 when I rallied my skills to face the four professors for my oral exam. My nerves revved at a high gear, as the cups of morning coffee oiled my intellectual engine. Meeting in a campus building's conference room at a large round table, the niceties and introductions were brief as the questioning began. Each professor had thirty minutes to interrogate me on any of the 200-plus selections on *each* specific bibliography for that given area of study. I was the most concerned about the Women's Studies area because it was my longest list, and I wanted to do my best for Dr. Buhle. Surprisingly, as I responded to her questions, I relaxed and allowed myself to articulate in a calm, informed manner. The remaining areas of discussion carried me into the fields of American Literature, American Cinema, and African American Literature.

Finally, after two hours, it was over—the years of reading academic texts, the seminars, the numerous academic papers, and the sacrifices in my personal life. I thanked all the professors and made my way to my car—exhausted. I whispered a prayer. I looked around the campus. I wanted everyone to know that I had completed the foundation for the imposing structure of my PhD: years of classes and seminars; endless hours of reading, note-taking, and writing critical papers; immeasurable time in libraries; and the sacrifices of personal relationships. Was it all worth it? Had I made the best choices? And looking into the year to come, I would research and write my dissertation. More sacrifices, more poverty, and more financial concerns. Why had I given so much power over me to others? How long would I continue to put off living my life by living the role of a graduate student?

\* \* \*

A week after passing my oral exams, I received a rejection letter for my reapplication to the American Film Institute. I reread the letter several times, sinking into a deep disappointment. My dream of writing, filmmaking, and living in LA was torched by one letter. What happened? Why was I outside a world I longed to participate in? I was confident that I could contribute and excel in both the creative and academic domains.

I placed my emotions on the back burner and approached my desires logically. To complete my orbit in the academic universe, I needed to write my dissertation—my study of the images of Black women in film. I was too close to completing my degree to walk away from it. So, I decided to push forward and complete the task. At the same time, I decided I would return to LA in the fall. I contacted Michael Whitted and asked him to keep an eye out for an apartment, particularly if anything opened in his building. Even without the American Film Institute, I had a better chance to create opportunities in writing scripts and making films if I resided in LA.

However, I decided to remain in Hyannis for the summer to work and make money for my return trip to the West Coast. I applied for and received a job working for the city of Hyannis, becoming the supervisor at Veteran's Park and Beach, the same recreational area where Paulette and I spent our summers as youngsters. As the park supervisor, I was responsible for a staff of four lifeguards; the adjacent John Kennedy Memorial; and a young student worker.

Although the job gave me more responsibility than I wanted at the time, it was ideal in allowing me to be at the beach six days a week. In the moments I stole for lunch, I hid inside the office to write and to organize my trip back to LA, researching and planning stops at museum archives and film libraries in New York; Washington, D.C.; and the University of Wisconsin to view films for my dissertation. Through letters and phone calls, I located films from the early decades of Hollywood that were archived and available to screen for research purposes.

My immediate and extended families had become accustomed to me returning to Hyannis for short visits before driving away again. Even as they shook their heads at my rootless life, they encouraged me to follow whatever dream drew me away from a settled life in Hyannis.

My first stop was in New Haven to visit Jason and Rose. He was studying at the Yale Divinity School, and she had a position as manager in a popular restaurant near campus.

Jason was driven by his plans to become a minister, and Rose sacrificed her personal goals to support his dreams. I stayed with them for a couple of nights, which allowed me to take the train into New York City to the Museum of Modern Art to view two films in its collection. My next stop was Washington, D.C., where I stayed with Reggie McDowell while he was a manager at a major hotel. During the two days there, I accessed the film archives in the Library of Congress, viewing seven films from the 1930s to the 1940s that I wouldn't find elsewhere.

From there, I took a serpentine route through states I hadn't seen before: Missouri, Wisconsin, Colorado, and Arizona. Angling into San Diego, I connected with Tory, Julie, and Susan. The three of them were busy with their duties as nurses, enjoying their Southern California home. Tory had kept in touch with me after their short visit to Hyannis, and it took little convincing to get me to stay for the weekend before heading north to LA.

During that visit, Tory explained that she felt restricted in her past relationships, and she decided to follow a different life once she reached San Diego. She didn't want to be the "main event" in anyone's life. Then, she confessed that she wanted to see me whenever we could get together. As she put it, she could be my "muse" as I wrote my fiction and dissertation. It was an unexpected offer, and I wondered why she found interest in me. She simply explained that she wanted me because I didn't *need* her. With my focus on my doctorate, I wouldn't place any restricting demands on her. She wanted to be a free spirit. So, she promised she would occasionally drive up to LA whenever we both wanted. Since my primary focus was my dissertation and writing, her offer was too good to refuse.

When I finally took the two-hour drive north to LA, the heavy brown air and busy freeways welcomed me. I camped out with Michael Whitted, who informed me that he had saved a vacant apartment for me in the St. Andrews building. I released a big breath of relief and settled into the familiar surroundings as I planned my next steps.

\*\*\*

Once again in LA, my immediate goal was to get a job and create an income to add to my meager savings. At the same time, I needed to maintain a steady commitment to the dissertation, researching and writing daily to keep the project on track to arrive at the final destination of the PhD.

Even as I knew what I had to do, I felt myself questioning the reasons *why* on several occasions. I definitely wanted to complete my academic journey, but I wondered how much was for me and how much was wrapped within my "Black man's burden" to represent my immediate family, extended family, and all Black people in America. Since high school, I carried that sense of responsibility to affirm my personal achievements as a community accomplishment. However, it was a quest to prove *what* to *whom*? Why was it incumbent upon me to be another Black beacon of success? At that juncture in my life, I needed something for me—for my creativity to be fulfilled. Perhaps, at its core, my creativity was driven by my basic belief in meliorism, that somehow my writing would help to make a better world. Naïve—perhaps. Sincere—absolutely.

As I meditated on such lofty thoughts, I completed several job applications with the appropriate lies and half-truths to look like the person the companies sought. While waiting to hear about the jobs, I continued to work on two parallel worlds: my dissertation and my creative writing, specifically a screenplay. One particular story remained in my head since reading it years earlier in a seminar—"The Monster" by Stephen Crane. Set in the late nineteenth century, the story focused on the relationship between a White doctor and the young Black man who worked for him. During a devastating fire, the young Black man was disfigured by the flames when saving the doctor's son. His physical appearance became repulsive to the White townspeople who demanded that the doctor send the Black man away.

To take a break from the daily work of the dissertation and the script that summer of 1979, I splurged and bought a ticket to the Playboy Jazz Festival at the Hollywood Bowl, an outdoor venue that seats over seventeen thousand people. So, I purchased a nosebleed seat for one night in the rear section, and I enjoyed Herbie Hancock and Joni Mitchell performing together, as well as an impressive set by Flora Purim and Airto Moreira. I had my poem about Purim published a few years earlier in a *Bates College Journal*, so the event took on added satisfaction.

At that point, I had viewed my selected films relevant to my 1915–1949 time frame. However, I was still reading and noting critical assessments of the films, as well as the analyses of relevant gender tropes and racial markers inextricably integrated into the settings, characters, and themes. On the weekends, I included my creative side, carrying my script pages along the Pacific Coast Highway to Coral Beach, just beyond Pepperdine University-Malibu. It was a narrow strip of beach with no parking lot, but there was ample room between the highway and cliff to park my car before I descended a short slope onto the sand. With my beach chair in one hand, my writing pad and pen in the other, I worked consistently on my screenplay.

\*\*\*

Frequently, as she promised, Tory traveled from San Diego to LA for a weekend visit. We often hung out in Westwood, in the shadows of UCLA—catching a movie, trying a new eatery, or drinking cocktails as we watched passersby. Tory always covered our costs without complaining or hesitating. On those weekends when Tory didn't visit, I sometimes took a day from writing and caught up with East Coast friends who had also moved to the Los Angeles area: Bruce Gaines in Redondo Beach and Fred Lamster in Long Beach. Bruce was still teaching high school, while Fred had gained a teaching position in the English Department at California State University-Fullerton.

When December arrived, my academic research and creative writing were both going well, but I was still unemployed despite filling out numerous applications. As my savings raced toward depletion, I was down to my last $200, with monthly bills still not paid. I reached out to my mentor and friend, Harold Perkins, in Hyannis. Harold continued to encourage me to be faithful to my goals, insisting that a job would soon appear. Surprisingly, his $500 check arrived within the week, which brought me humbly to tears.

During the week following my twenty-eighth birthday, Papa D, Mama D, and my teenage brother, Brian, flew out from Hyannis to spend a week with me. They were concerned that I was perhaps sliding into an abyss of depression. Their expressions of love were an additional lifeline intertwined with the support already provided by my tribe of friends.

I continually meditated on why so many gave me such loving care. I was not extraordinary in any way, nor was I attempting to reach goals that others had not already achieved. I was certainly blessed by family and friends who tossed me lifelines of love to keep me from sinking beneath the surface of challenging waters. And I knew that the best way to thank them was to fulfill the goals I sought.

As I reached the first week in February, I completed the first draft of my script, which I titled *The Veil*, and I had two job interviews scheduled.

\*\*\*

Century City is a business and entertainment area west of Los Angeles, located between Beverly Hills and Fox Studios. Answering an ad for a job, I journeyed to one of the towering high-rise buildings where the law firm was spread out over two floors, containing about seventy lawyers.

After a successful interview with the human resources office, I was offered a job working in the firm's duplicating room, sharing the space and the copying duties with two California natives who had no interest in movies, politics, sports, or anything else other than lunch. The big, state-of-the-art duplicating machines were in constant use during my eight-hour shift. The position wasn't difficult once I became familiar with the process of completing duplication orders, arranging multiple copies for delivery to lawyers, and attending to an occasional malfunction with the machines. The department was in a basement space, far below the carpeted hallways with cubicles, secretarial staffs, and lawyers offices.

I was pleased to be receiving a salary and keeping food in the fridge, but two weeks into the job, I was surprised by a summons from the firm's librarian. The library was on the seventh floor that housed an assortment of lawyers, and it was located in a small space that allowed for an administrative office and an adjoining room with several long tables and full bookshelves.

Monica Buckley was a vivacious White woman with short, auburn hair. She was quite smart with a graduate degree and a comprehensive knowledge of the firm's library holdings and demanding lawyers. Her assistant, Linda Fontaine, was a taller, bubbly woman with sandy-blonde hair, equally smart and a few years younger than me. The two maintained the busy library space, but Monica needed an assistant to replace someone who recently fled the firm. She wanted to hire from within, and after glancing over recent applications, she saw something in my paperwork that prompted her to interview me. As she asked me questions about my background, she smiled at my responses, perceiving that I was far more accomplished than my application suggested. When she offered me the position, I accepted because it paid more than the duplicating room position. Simple enough, my job would be sorting and delivering the incoming mail, while picking up outgoing envelopes and packages. Additionally, I was responsible for restacking law books abandoned on the library's tables and occasionally driving my car downtown to the Los Angeles Law Library on 1st Street, to borrow and return books requested by the firm's lawyers.

As I moved from the basement to the higher floors with partners and associates, one thing was clear—there was only one other Black person among the firm's sixty-plus lawyers. She was an older support staffer that I seldom saw, but we always smiled and nodded when our paths crossed. Somewhere behind her nod, I sensed there were some revealing stories to share about the firm, but we never had that private conversation.

So, my new schedule was set. I was at the firm by eight thirty a.m. Monday through Friday; taking notes for my dissertation from an essay or book during the half-hour lunch; and leaving by five p.m. for the gym to grab a brief workout. Then, I'd buy and eat a fast-food meal by six thirty while driving to the USC campus. I'd settle into the undergraduate library from seven thirty to ten to skim documents and take notes for writing an early draft of the dissertation. With little variation, the schedule kept me on task and forced me to maximize the Monday through Friday time frame I allotted to the dissertation.

About two months into my library position at the law firm, something unexpected happened—I had a date with Faith Stern. When I began my new job, which included delivering mail from one cubicle to the next, I first noticed Faith because she resembled a young Liza Minnelli. She was professional, but more personable than other lawyers, and as a junior associate, her desk was always piled with folders and binders. Our conversations began with general references to the firm, politics, music, and, of course, movies. The short quips developed into longer discussions, particularly when she confessed her frustrated, creative side. She played piano and wondered whether her legal direction was what *she* really wanted or if she was following a path preferred by her East Coast parents.

From lunches to happy hour cocktails, to an invite to dinner at her house—I moved slowly with no expectations. I was too committed to my dissertation and screenwriting, and I wasn't certain whether dating someone from the job was a smart move—especially for *her*. I was just a library assistant, and she was targeting an eventual partnership in the firm. However, accepting her initial invitation, I followed her directions to Venice Beach to reach her second-floor apartment on Rose Avenue. Inside her place, a baby grand piano was snuggled tightly at a corner window, allowing a gorgeous view of the beach and the distant ocean. After a dinner filled with laughter and serious statements about what she called her "rigid Jewish family expectations," I confessed my blessings of having a supportive family. We carried a blanket, a bottle of wine, and glasses onto the beach, hearing the surf whispering through the refreshing ocean air. In those days, one could safely walk the Strand and hang out on Venice Beach after dark. By the time we finished the bottle of Sauvignon Blanc, we migrated back to her apartment.

I felt obligated to tell Tory about Faith, but Tory stated it wasn't an issue for her. She was glad that I met someone who pulled me away from my demanding dissertation. And as I told Faith about Tory, Faith stated that it was too early to set up boundaries and rules. She was dating other guys but with little enthusiasm. The truth was that Tory welcomed the freedom to see whomever she wanted, while Faith enjoyed the companionship of another creative spirit. And, for me, I was obsessed with completing my academic work and fostering my creative writing. The three of us were all getting what we wanted.

\*\*\*

It was during that year that I had one of my "inspiring moments." On one of my many trips to PIP Printing near my apartment building, I met Carl Weathers. Mr. Weathers had been a college football star and eventually played for the Oakland Raiders. Pursuing his aspirations to be a professional actor, he had done a number of television appearances, but he gained popularity through his role as Apollo Creed in *Rocky* (1976). His presence grew even bigger as he reprised his role in the sequel, *Rocky II* (1979).

When I entered the store, Mr. Weathers was chatting with a White man, an obvious fan, and he shared the "brother nod" with me when he caught my eye. I eased over as he talked about working on the *Rocky* films, but I was first impressed by his athletic build—his muscles were thick, stretching the athletic shorts and shirt he wore. I had never seen anyone in person who possessed that kind of physique. And as he pulled me into the conversation, I threw a couple of questions at him about Sylvester Stallone and the filmmaking process. He was gracious by sharing twenty minutes to talk with me, and when I told him of my screenwriting aspirations, he was encouraging, urging me to keep writing. He cushioned my access to him, however, by declaring he already had a writing team, but he insisted that "we" needed more Black writers to "tell our stories." Those were words I heard before and would hear for decades to come, but even from his position of success, he spoke with sincerity. At the same time, I knew I would be in the gym the next day. I still had a long way to *grow* through my bench presses and squats, and I had a hell of a long way to go to reach his kind of success.

\*\*\*

By April 1980, during one of my scheduled trips to the USC undergraduate library for research, I glanced through journals to see what jobs were being advertised in the Los Angeles area. When I came across a job description for the University of California-Santa Barbara, I noticed that there was a Black Studies Department. So, I decided to deliver a similar performance as I did when applying to Brown University. I took a sick day from the law firm and drove the two hours north to the coastal city and was impressed by what I saw. Located on the Pacific Coast Highway, Santa Barbara boasted a mountain range to the north and the ocean south of its downtown area, with Stearns Wharf serving as a business area and tourist destination. The university campus was another fifteen-minute drive beyond the city, situated on a mesa overlooking the Pacific.

I located the Black Studies Department, and in my dress shirt and tie, I entered and asked to meet the chair, Dr. Gerard Pigeon. He had a Caribbean background, and he was quite gracious as I explained my visit to his office. I argued that though I was only ABD—All But Dissertation—I was scheduled to have my first draft of the dissertation completed by the end of the summer. There was hesitation in his voice, even as he was impressed with my Brown University background and the courses I could teach in his department, including Black Literature, Black Americans in Cinema, and Creative Writing. He knew that the university would only want to hire a candidate with a PhD *in hand*, but he agreed to keep me in his files. I glanced around the grounds on my way out, and I savored the possibility of having a university teaching experience at such a beautiful campus. I placed the visit on a hopeful shelf in my head and drove back to LA.

\*\*\*

It took Faith three glasses of wine and a tide of tears to wade me into the deep waters of her recent past. Before we met, she was raped by a guy she was dating. Her words entered my ears, but they stuck in my throat, stealing my breath and voice at the same time. She shared the tragedy with me in an emotional narration. I listened quietly and embraced her as she cried. I wanted to do more, and I hoped my presence gave her some comfort. I asked her about reporting to the police. Seeing a therapist. "No" and "no" were the answers. I was angry and ready to destroy the guy—to leave him crippled on the sidewalk with body parts missing. But I held my emotions in check and encouraged her to express as much or as little as she wanted.

Later, as Faith slept, I stared through the living room windows. The ocean glistened in the distance. I reflected on the movies that I had consumed, such as *Two Women* (1960), *Midnight Cowboy* (1969), *Last Summer* (1969), *High Plains Drifter* (1973), and *Death Wish* (1974), that used rape as a plot point without exploring the magnitude of the violation for the victimized women characters. Fortunately, in the following decades, some films would prioritize the effects of the crime on women. Reflecting on the devastating effects of rape on girls and women at the time, two literary voices crept into my thoughts: Maya Angelou's *I Know Why the Caged Bird Sings* (1969) and Susan Brownmiller's *Against Our Will* (1975).

However, Faith was a survivor who was reconstructing her life. I acknowledged her trust in me, but I wasn't certain how to respond. I listened as she exhaled elliptical phrases and cried again. I wanted to do *something*! My rage was beating inside my chest at some male I never met. Some *male* who undermined what it meant to be a *man*. Instead, he was the lowest of the slime, whose privilege and exploitation crushed another human being in ways that he never cared about. A male who shape-shifted into a beast bestowing physical, emotional, and psychological destruction. I was ashamed to be a man.

\* \* \*

By the end of July, I was deep into the last chapter of my dissertation, and the finish line of my rough draft was edging closer. The tedious, persistent reading and writing schedule had paid off, and I was confident that I would hit my target date for completion by the fall.

Importantly, I was also contacted by the Department of Black Studies at UC-Santa Barbara (UCSB) with the positive news that they were offering me a one-year position, with the details of salary and schedule to arrive in the following weeks. I was overjoyed, and as I spread the word about the job, my friends showered me with well wishes. Although Faith realized that the university position and move to Santa Barbara would affect our relationship, she urged me to accept the offer. However, she added that she had feelings for me and wanted to be in a committed relationship. This confession came, of course, as I was organizing to leave. She said the two-hour distance wouldn't be a problem for her. Her confession led to numerous discussions that never seemed to end. The weight of those conversations ached across my shoulders as I packed boxes, and I knew Faith really wanted our futures to be synced before I left.

At the same time that changes were coming into my life, Paulette wasn't pleased with her Pennsylvania radio job. Within our lengthy talks, she revealed she wanted to come out to LA to find work in a bigger market. Consequently, our talks led to the plan for me to fly East and for us to drive cross-country together in her car to LA. I negotiated with Michael Whitted to allow Paulette to take over my apartment when I moved to Santa Barbara.

When I flew back to the East Coast, I was exhausted mentally and physically. I looked forward to the brief Hyannis visit, staying in my parents' basement again, and recharging my travel batteries for two weeks. I made a point of contacting Dr. Buhle to update her, planning to do my revisions of the dissertation to target a final draft by Christmas 1980. As always, she was encouraging about my steady work and felt that the December deadline was possible even with teaching classes at UC-Santa Barbara. Of course, I caught up with my brother, James Tobey, during that time in Hyannis. His music was still vibrant and professional, but despite his previous touring, he seemed resigned to stay with his mother and help her financially.

Visiting some of my former Hyannis hangouts and getting together with friends, I thought about the many people who flowed in and out of my life.

Some stayed longer than others, and some gave me more of themselves than I gave in return. Some of my friends were Seekers like me, searching and adjusting from decision to decision. But most were Saints—patient and kind in their giving, even though they didn't fathom the journey I was taking. They tolerated my continual drifting, and I remained in their thoughts and hearts, even as I moved away just a little bit further . . . wanting just a little bit more.

\*\*\*

### Seekers and Saints

all my friends intersect at love,
looking for what has been lost,
such an endless quest of dreams
that have been smothered, delayed, and tossed
into the pits of dashed hopes . . .
among the moments when they share,
their testimonies reveal the despair
that I can only touch with silence,
knowing that I, too, have walked that path . . .
one that forever binds
one that forever blinds
one that forever winds . . .
all my friends intersect at love

CHAPTER TEN

## The Symmetry of a Creative-Scholar

A writer must jump into the abyss of uncertainty, sweating words across blank pages to reveal the extremities of human experiences. Whether developing creative or academic writing, *sweating words* remains an element of the writing process. Accepting this realization in my writing, I recognized my dual identity as a Creative and a Scholar, acknowledging both the friction between those two polarities and their intersecting elements.

As I arrived in Santa Barbara, carrying in both hands my dissertation draft and the rough drafts of my creative writing—my screenplay, *The Veil*, and my novel in progress, *A Place of Truth*. At that point in my life, I carried no shame in writing screenplays, prose, poetry, and critical essays at the same time.

The ten-week quarter system at UCSB was an academic sprint. My lectures, twice weekly for each of my four classes, had to be delivered, discussed, and digested in a brief period of time. I felt the same time pressures as my students, as the months fluttered away rapidly like a wall calendar in old Hollywood movies.

The campus had about eighteen thousand students, with a majority of White students, followed by Latinos, Asians, and a sprinkling of Black people. The amount of Black faculty members was as meager as the Black student population, but those who were there were impressive academics. In the Cinema Studies Department, Anna Everett was a standout scholar, as was Cedric Robinson, a political science professor who was the director of the Center for Black Studies Research. In the Black Studies Department, Lester Monts was a musicologist with a wealth of academic and performance experiences, and Beverly Tatum was a popular psychology professor who later wrote the revealing book, *Why Are All the Black Kids Sitting Together in the Cafeteria?* (1997). After leaving the campus, she began a tenure as president of Spelman College in 2002. Historian Douglas Daniels wrote pieces on Black history and music, including *Pioneer Urbanites: A Social and Cultural History of Black San Francisco* (1991).

But the professor who became my brother—Bill Edwards—was a singular personality who saved my butt on many occasions. Before coming to UCSB, Bill had used his sociology background to work in an urban planning office in the San Francisco area, but at the university, his scholarship emphasized Black activist Marcus Garvey. Bill was in his forties, and his home was in San Rafael, a northern California city in Marin County, just above San Francisco. He drove once a month, sometimes twice, to his home to see his family—his wife, Virginia, and sons Ronald and Reuben.

Bill kept an apartment in Isla Vista, the small community contiguous to the university campus, where fraternities, sororities, eateries, and apartments sat in congestion with its student population. Bill was my guru concerning the campus personalities, administration, and student body that he'd known over the years. He was a popular professor who had gone through his baptism of contradictions in the university's academic world. Namely, he had managed to get student body support to retain him during an exasperating fight for tenure that I would soon join myself.

In general, Black academics on predominantly White campuses deal with complex relationships as Scholars. They represent the numbers needed by the campus to shore up its boasting about hiring Scholars of color. At the same time, the faces of those Black professors are often prominently displayed in catalogue pages and on websites to entice students of color to attend the university.

During my four years at UCSB, from 1980-1984, a rather peculiar practice existed that attempted to walk a tightrope of blatant racism. The policy was carried out in the following manner. The Black Studies and the Chicano Studies Departments were two of the smaller ones on campus, but their structural status gave each the same autonomy as other departments. The catch, however, emerged when a professor in those two departments sought a tenure-track appointment—the pathway to gaining a permanent position within the department and the university. In order for professors in Black Studies and Chicano Studies to gain tenure, those professors also needed a joint appointment between their primary department *and* a "traditional" department to approve their significance and value in that second department. Bill had been fighting for years to gain support from the Sociology Department, which didn't recognize the merit of his research and analysis of Marcus Garvey.

My first year at UC-Santa Barbara threw that "joint appointment" shadow over my faculty position. Without having a joint appointment, the only offer granted was a one-year position that required renewal each year. This was a different challenge. I wasn't prepared to fight the windmills of the university's policies while simultaneously battling the demands of my imposing dissertation.

For certain, a tenure-track position was not a gift to *any* professor who agreed to a seven-year commitment of excelling in publishing, teaching, attending conferences, and serving the campus community. However, UCSB's institutional provisions were manacles that shackled the advancement of a specific population of professors.

As I focused on my classes for my first year, I was pleased with my schedule—teaching Creative Writing, African American Literature, and African Americans in American Films. As expected, the student populations in my classes were from a variety of White, Latino, Asian, and African American backgrounds. It was enjoyable meeting the students, even the spoiled White ones who felt inclined to challenge my intelligence and composure with their punctilious queries. They lost the battles, of course, as I was accustomed to those challenges from White students over the years.

The immediate joy came from the Black students who filled my classes. Similar to the Black students I taught at Bates College, UCSB's Black students were hungry for professors who looked like them and could relate to the particulars in their lives. One of the Black Studies Department's greatest strengths were the faculty members who, though small in number, made themselves available for *all* of the students coming through the department's class offerings.

Off campus, I found an apartment in Santa Barbara's La Cumbre area, which was only a fifteen-minute drive from the campus. As I settled into my new home, it was another journey through "Caucasian Land." Every location—grocery stores, auto garages, clothing stores, pharmacies, and restaurants—brought me into a setting with White people. Doctors, waitresses, lawyers, surfers, movie theater audiences—everyone was White. It wasn't the environment I had in the multi-ethnic, mid-city neighborhoods of LA.

So, as I settled into my routine of writing the dissertation, teaching my classes, and revising my screenplay, I studied martial arts at Chris Wiedmann's Wu Shu Studio. The studio had some skillful practitioners, and though it was a Chinese-based martial arts academy, my hybrid Japanese-Korean style was welcomed. The physical exertion from the martial arts balanced the mental demands of being a professor and writing my dissertation. Somewhere between those demanding planets, I filled my small galaxy of available time with movie nights, escaping through popular dramas like *Raging Bull* (1980) and *Eyewitness* (1981).

*\*\*\**

With the physical and emotional distance between me and Faith in Los Angeles and Tory in San Diego, my plan was to avoid dating *anyone*. I needed to keep my personal life simple and devoid of drama. My commitment was to fix my eyes on the horizon of completing the dissertation and keep my heart in hibernation.

However, as indicated in one of my favorite novels—*The Man Who Cried I Am* by Black author John A. Williams—relationships are the product of proximity, both physical and emotional. So, how many times could I intersect paths with someone without speaking? That was my situation with Janet Goodwin. Our apartment buildings faced one another, the walkway between them separated by a strip of green plants. Each time we saw one another, we nodded and smiled. Then, the smiles became waves, until the waves led us to stop and talk in the parking lot our buildings shared.

Janet was a waitress at a nearby steakhouse. She loved animals, gardening, horseback riding, hiking, and camping—all things I had avoided in my adult life. She was originally from Montana, a state that never struck me as a must-see territory, but there was a gentle, fragile quality about her. Her blonde hair allowed her to fit right in with the majority of the Santa Barbara community, and her easy laughter was infectious.

As I remembered my time in Iowa City and my relationship with Gwen Fulbright, I reflected on the similar scrutiny I would face by dating Janet. The concerns about my position as a professor of Black Studies would surface once more—the critical stares from Black faculty and students when seeing Janet and me together. And the anticipated scrutiny from those White folks as well—both on and off campus—was inevitable. There would be more than a few whispers. There might be hateful comments and gestures—from all sides!

However, I remembered an old saying my father shared: "An empty wagon makes a lot of noise." Those people who took the time to judge or comment on *my* life were folks who had little that filled up their own lives. In a similar manner, there was a more significant German expression: "ich muss mein Leben besitzen!"—I must own my life!

\*\*\*

Completing my dissertation, my body felt lighter when I mailed off the bulky package containing 175 pages that confirmed years of academic work. Of course, there was drama—the copy I sent through the mail to the university was lost. When I phoned the university office that should have received the manuscript, they had no record of its existence. My heart palpitated with fear, knowing the required submission had to meet the pending deadline. I phoned Debbie Thomas in Providence, and she agreed to personally deliver my back-up copy to the proper Brown University office. I mailed an insured, special delivery copy to Debbie, and days later, I breathed again when she phoned to confirm receiving and delivering the materials to their destination.

In June 1981, when I flew back East for graduation, my short walk across the stage couldn't measure the years of anguish, weariness, and joy I spent to receive my diploma. Mama D and Papa D were at the ceremony, and I couldn't fully communicate the depths of gratitude I felt for them. No one stood in my corner better than those two, lifting me from the canvas before a full knockout count. Healing my emotional cuts and swollen anxieties to get me back on my feet to face the next round. I handed my diploma to both of them and hugged them for being the lifeline that they were.

In Hyannis, my parents organized a dinner, renting a hall and inviting extended family members and my tribe of friends with whom I taught at Barnstable High. As I was showered with their congratulations and good wishes, it struck me again how much my accomplishment meant to them. It wasn't just about *me*, but it was also about how I represented *them*—those older family members who suffered the Deep South, those younger cousins who received the advantages of growing up on Cape Cod and in Boston, and those friends who acknowledged that *my* success was *their* success as well.

\* \* \*

Dr. Kenneth Kragen was the dean of the college where the Black Studies Department was housed. He was White, in his late forties, forgettable in terms of appearance, and he spoke with an Eastern-European accent that weighed heavy upon the ear. During the fall semester, I made a point of meeting with him, and we had a short but pleasant discussion about my travels through Europe while in undergraduate school. From those fond memories, I shifted the discussion to UC-Santa Barbara and the challenges of the joint appointment. He affirmed the university's hardline policy supporting the joint appointment, encouraging me to endear myself to the English Department in preparation for seeking one. His smile was more of a leer, and his vacant gaze suggested he was sitting in front of me but not actually there. He was the worst kind of administrator—a creepy sycophant, angling to be seated one day in the highest level of that same flawed power structure.

Following numerous meetings with Dean Kragen, there was no breakthrough in the university's joint appointment policy. As our future meetings descended into shouting matches, I was incensed with the vacant-eyed dean who, like a parrot, sang the same tune of nonsense. Then, at one meeting, with all of my years of martial arts training, I was losing control. I felt myself sliding closer to the edge of my chair, my voice escalating to a high roar of anger. I knew I was about to explode physically into his body, lunging and striking. It would be so easy to surge forward with a side kick, the edge of my right foot cracking into his neck, sending him backward against the wall, dumping his plaques and framed certificates to the floor.

I found myself standing and edging forward with rage, and perhaps it was the collective voices of family and friends that filled my head. I believe, ultimately, that it was God whispering "*No.*" I grabbed my briefcase, left his office, and never went back.

And for the first time in my life, I went to see a therapist.

\* \* \*

I'm not sure why Janet decided to share her past as she did. We were just chatting and listening to music in her apartment when she grew quiet and began crying.

Janet was in elementary school when her younger brother died. His four-year-old urge to play led him to the driveway with a toy. When his playfulness led him to the rear of the car, he didn't notice his mother sliding behind the steering wheel, starting the ignition, and slipping the gear shift into reverse. It wasn't until his final yell erupted and the rear tire bumped over his body that the mother knew too late what had occurred. In the aftermath of his death, Janet's parents went in different directions, her mother finding medication in an abundance of alcohol. Without the father's income, the drunken binges led to a host of men rotating in and out of the house. Still a youngster, Janet's presence irritated her mother, who then forced her into the closet when spending time with her visitors. After her mother passed out from drinking, one particular man began to visit Janet as she hid in the closet. And those subsequent visits began to diminish any childhood that Janet possessed, leaving an aftermath of fears, emotional insecurities, and self-esteem issues.

Janet's shared memories seemed more the elements of fiction, but her past supplied the reasons as to why she preferred animals to people, solitude to crowds, and an insistence on a commitment from me.

\* \* \*

By my third year of teaching at UC-Santa Barbara, I was teaching Creative Writing and African Americans in American Films classes. At the same time, I organized and taught a Black Women's Literature course, which a roster of thirty-plus women. If the assigned classroom had been larger, the class attendance would have increased as well. But there I was, teaching a class of Black, Latina, and White women—with about four men at the beginning. I was pleased, but at the same time, I was nervous in the position I had formed for myself. At thirty-years-old, perhaps I wasn't the best person to teach that class, but I was also the only professor in the Black Studies Department who could. I over-prepared, making certain I had all possible questions about the texts solidly covered. The fundamental authors and activists were emphasized in assigned readings and through lectures—Frances E.W. Harper, Mary Church Terrell, Sojourner Truth, Ida B. Wells-Barnett, Pauline Hopkins, Jessie Fauset, Nella Larsen, Zora Neale Hurston, Ann Petry, Toni Cade Bambara, J. California Cooper, Maya Angelou, Audre Lorde, Nikki Giovanni, Sonia Sanchez, Angela Davis, Alice Walker, and Toni Morrison. Additionally, there were White women I felt compelled to mention, including Sarah and Angelina Grimke, Emma Goldman, Betty Friedan, Gloria Steinem, and the work that Dr. Mari Jo Buhle had done regarding women and labor in America.

But it wasn't only for that course, as the issues of gender and sexuality permeated all of my classes—whether it was composition, literature, or creative writing. And it didn't stop with the classroom. My fiction and script writing included perspectives, characters, and/or issues that would encourage readers or viewers to meditate on the influential socialization and politicization that shaped both the manner in which women were perceived and treated *and* the manner in which stereotypical, violent notions of masculinity often distorted and exploited our humanity.

\* \* \*

Since my academic life was not set at the university, I kept looking through announcements of college teaching positions, but most were located in the Midwest and the South. Clearly, I knew that returning to either area would render me emotionally and physically ill despite any possibility of a tenured position. So, as I accepted my limited options elsewhere in academia, I continued to campaign at other possible departments for a joint appointment to remain in Santa Barbara.

To keep my creative energy simmering, I began a new script, *The Inner Circle*, a contemporary, political thriller that used the Armenian and Turkish political clash as a backdrop.

As I researched that script, I was encouraged by Bill Edwards and others to explore expanding my dissertation into a book. So, I took a serious re-examination of what I had written, updating myself on Black women's roles on the big screen. In the early 1980s, with the growing spotlight on Black women's participation in history, literature, and popular culture, updating my dissertation made sense. As I researched and queried various publishers, Greenwood Press indicated an interest. So, I submitted a fresh copy to the press and waited.

Before the beginning of the 1982-1983 academic year, I was offered another one-year contract from UC-Santa Barbara, even as I received rejection on several levels. Houghton Mifflin rejected the first half of my novel, *The Shadows of Truth*, and Greenwood Press rejected my proposal for a book based on my dissertation focus of 1915–1949, suggesting it *would* be interested in publishing a book that would cover 1915–1980. However, after years of completing the dissertation, I wasn't prepared for another year of analyzing an additional thirty years of film images, before spending an additional six months on rewriting, copy editing, and obtaining movie stills.

Then, I received an emotional rejection from Janet. It wasn't unexpected as our discussions increasingly included her need for me to be more "mushy," "soft," and "romantic." She was missing certain kinds of intimate expressions in the manner that she desired. I was guilty as charged, and I admitted my intense focus was on writing a variety of works and navigating the university's maze of a joint appointment.

By October, I was surprised by some unexpected developments. First, I received a response from several query letters I sent out, an agent was interested in my work. After reading my completed script *The Inner Circle*, Marcie Wright, an agent in Burbank, wanted to meet with me. Quickly setting up an appointment with her, I drove south to Burbank for a productive meeting that led to me signing a contract with her. It was gratifying to have professional praise of my writing, and Marcie was confident she could interest a studio in the script, particularly since I wrote the protagonist with Sidney Poitier in mind. Although Mr. Poitier stepped behind the camera in the early 1980s to direct—*Stir Crazy* (1980) and *Hanky Panky* (1982)—he still remained a popular screen presence.

I was emboldened by signing with an agent, and I made a major decision—to move out of Santa Barbara and return to my old St. Andrews Place apartment in LA. I would share the place with Paulette and make the drive to Santa Barbara on Mondays, Wednesdays, and Fridays to teach my classes. I would save money by not renting the Santa Barbara apartment, and I would have two days during the week to be in LA to write and hopefully go to meetings. So, I relocated to Los Angeles, moving in with my sister.

Three days a week, I got up at five a.m., grabbed a chilled coke with a donut from the local shop; drove onto the freeways by six to navigate the morning work traffic; and arrived in Santa Barbara by eight in order to teach my first class at nine. I told Bill Edwards about my new plan, asking if I could sometimes stay at his apartment if the weather was bad or if a late department meeting was scheduled. Bill agreed, and I was surprised how smoothly the schedule worked.

\*\*\*

As I adjusted to being a commuting professor, I still hadn't resolved my personal issues with Janet. After teaching classes one day, we scheduled dinner for yet another "talk." So, I cashed my university salary check and fingered enough funds to cover dinner at a restaurant. Driving to Bill's apartment, I left my travel bag and dress clothes for an overnight stay at his place. Janet and I met at a favorite restaurant, but our discussion deteriorated into another heated exchange. Our dialogue returned to the same wall that existed between our opposing expectations and me residing in Los Angeles. We couldn't find a way to avoid parting the Red Sea of our diverging desires.

In my moody discontent after dinner, I jumped in my car, grabbed a can of beer at the convenience store, and drove to Butterfly Beach—the short strip of sand that rested across from the Biltmore Hotel, one of the ritzy locales in Santa Barbara. It was a beautiful spot, made even more engaging by the full moon shining over the shore. Sitting in my car and drinking down my frustrations, I really didn't know what the next step would be in my relationship with Janet. At the same time, I couldn't *make* her into someone that she wasn't.

Suddenly, blinking lights flashed in my rearview mirror. Bright headlights flooded my car's interior. I saw two White officers approaching, one on either side of the car. They appeared to be wearing green Sheriff's Department uniforms. I rolled my driver's side window down, and a flashlight blinded my vision.

"And what are you doing here, sir?" the officer asked.

"Just enjoying the view of the beach," I returned.

"Do you have any drugs in your car, sir?"

"Drugs? No," I snickered. "I don't have any drugs."

"Are you drinking alcohol, sir?"

"Actually, no. I finished this beer about thirty minutes ago. I was—"

"—Would you please step out of the car and throw away the empty can?"

"Sure."

When I opened the door, the officer stepped back—one hand holding the flashlight and the other resting on his gun. On the other side of the car, the second officer took the same pose. A rubbish container was about ten yards in front of my car, so I stepped out, carried the empty can over, and tossed it inside. When I returned to the car, the officer was shining his flashlight inside the interior. Then, he ordered me to open the trunk, which I did. I stepped back to allow him to see my empty trunk. He nodded and stepped back to the opened driver's side door.

"So, what's this?" the officer asked me, pointing the flash back.

"What?"

"In the back . . . on the floor."

I was inquisitive and moved to peer inside my car. All I saw was a stick I had picked up earlier in the week as I enjoyed a relaxing stroll along Cabrillo Beach.

"It's . . . just a stick," I said.

"No, it's over sixteen inches long. It's a felony."

"What are you talking about?" I asked.

"Turn around and place your hands behind you *now*!"

He forced me onto my car's hood, and his partner hurried to help handcuff me. I was pushed toward the rear door of the police car and shoved inside. As I sat up, I was trying to understand what the hell was happening. Was it a joke of some sort? When the two got into the front of the vehicle, we drove away, and I caught a parting glimpse of a beautiful full moon.

On the way to the station, I worried about my car. It was unlocked. Would it be burglarized? Would it be towed away? And then, as I heard the two officers laugh during their whispered conversation, I began to worry about my situation. I had no control and no idea where I was being taken. And as I heard the two laugh again, it was obvious that my feelings and confusion were of no particular importance to them. What was happening to me was a joke they both enjoyed. Did they wonder who I was, and why I was there at the beach? Did they know about my years of sacrificing, studying, and living in meager circumstances so I could sit in *my* car at *that* beach? Did they understand how many books and essays I had read before writing pages of notes and dozens of papers? Did they know that I had a PhD from an Ivy League university? For certain, one thing was evident to them: I was Black and would fit into the scenario they would construct at the booking.

The station's interior was bright and dreary at the same time. The process of surrendering personal items, fingerprinting, and mug shooting was a familiar dance to the balding White officer processing me. My question about a phone call was met with a mumbled response, and the officer moved slowly to get me through a door and along a short cement hallway that led to the holding cell. Inside I saw about ten other men—some sleeping in fetal positions, but most were sitting on the cold cement floor. Numerous Latinos and four White faces comprised the motley assemblage. I was the only Black face, which brought a few glances my way. There were several guys murmuring, but most, like me, sat on the floor trying to disengage from the dingy cell and the slow passing of time.

I guessed it was about ten thirty p.m., and I knew that the person I needed to call was Bill Edwards. So, I waited, hoping I would soon be allowed to reach out to Bill and connect to some sense of normalcy. I wanted to sleep and wake up on the other side of this cold nightmare. Hours went by before the door cracked, and two officers stepped inside. One stood just outside the door, his hand on his weapon. The other entered with a tray stacked with bulging paper bags. He tossed a bag to each man in the holding cell. Inside the bag, there was a bologna sandwich on white bread with a thin layer of something that resembled mayonnaise. I took a bite out of interest more than hunger, but I couldn't swallow more than one tasteless lump. I dropped the alleged sandwich back into the paper bag and leaned my head against the wall. I waited. My legs ached, and there was no way to find a comfortable position.

Eventually, my eyes grew heavy, and I wasn't certain if I should sleep or not. As I debated the issue silently in my head, voices rumbled from my right. Two White men—one skinny and wild-eyed, the other bearded with long, shaggy hair—argued over something that was only important to them. Their escalating voices erupted into grabbing and pushing, and those sitting near them began to move away. The two men wrestled and rolled toward the center of the cell. The skinny, wild-eyed man angled on top of his enemy, grabbing the bearded man by his long hair. Gaining control, the attacker banged the bearded man's head against the concrete floor. The man's skull struck the cement in loud thuds. His screams pierced the air as his blood spotted the floor. The spots widened into thick puddles as the officers rushed inside, shouting orders at the two fighters. A night stick appeared, and the whacking began on both men. It was a bizarre scene as the skinny, wild-eyed man was pulled backward, the night stick across his throat. A third officer appeared and helped carry out the bearded man, his blood pool marking his defeat.

After the fight, everyone went back to their quiet waiting. Staring into space. Locking on some stain on the ceiling. As for me, I looked at the blood, wondering how severely the bearded man was hurt. And for another two hours, I found myself glancing frequently at the blood pool. There was something senseless and empty about the whole night, and I searched for a philosophical way of assessing the past few hours. Then, I heard my last name called, and stomping my feet to get the blood flowing into my legs, I followed the officer to a wall phone.

I phoned Bill and explained what happened. He was upset and in disbelief. And though it was five a.m., he promised to get to me as soon as possible. They returned me to the holding cell, and another ninety minutes passed before my name was called again. Outside the cell, after gathering my personal items and signing paperwork, I was led to the lobby where Bill embraced me and led me to his car. Driving away, he spoke angrily about the officers, but he didn't know how soothing it was to just hear his voice. As instructed during my call to him, he removed $500 cash from my overnight bag, bringing the money to cover the bail. I thanked him a dozen times more. When we reached his apartment, I remembered my morning class. I quickly shaved and showered, rinsing away the residue of anger that crusted my skin. I hurried into my professor's wardrobe before rushing to campus. It was eight thirty a.m., and I had a nine a.m. class to teach.

\*\*\*

Marcie Wright had submitted my script to several studios, including Columbia Pictures and Orion Pictures. Waiting for responses drained my energy, but I was resuscitated when my article about Chris Wiedmann's Wu Shu Studio was chosen for publication by *Karate Illustrated*, one of the top two martial arts magazines in the country. But any celebratory feeling of success was diminished by the court appearance that hung over my head. I spoke with one of the Wu Shu Studio martial artists who was an estate lawyer. He believed I wouldn't have to hire a lawyer, but he told me I could utilize a public defender since I had done jail time. I trusted him, and he was correct.

When I appeared in court, I met the public defender and explained what had happened that entire evening from dinner to jail. The youngish, White lawyer took notes and reviewed the paperwork I gave him. He placed my casework along with several other files he balanced and met for several minutes with the prosecutor in the corner of the court room. It was a sweat-filled, elongated passage of time. When the public defender returned, he nodded at me.

"So, Professor Donalson, here's the situation. You were booked on a felony which you'll have to have expunged from your record. That process will take a few months. Since you're a professor at the university, have no priors, and you spent a night in jail, the prosecution won't take the case any further. You can apply to get your $500 bail back, but there'll be a fee to have the charge removed. Okay?"

"Yes, yes," I responded, breathing again. "Thank you."

"And between the two of us," he added sotto voce, "this was a bunch of nonsense. The two White officers hassled you because you were a Black man in an upscale area."

I nodded and thanked him again for his help. I left the courthouse understanding how that night could have gone so wrong for me. Later at dinner, Bill Edwards and I joked about the incident over glasses of wine. Underneath our efforts to debrief from the racist nonsense, we knew I was fortunate to escape the negative circumstances. I hugged and thanked Bill many times over, and taking a slow, thoughtful drive along the freeway, I welcomed the lights of LA.

# CHAPTER ELEVEN

# Perfect Accidents

With my left brain in Santa Barbara and my right brain in Los Angeles, I led a peripatetic life during my fourth year at UCSB. I no longer believed nor hoped that a tenure-track position would develop, despite having my PhD in hand, positive student evaluations, and positive peer evaluations from my colleagues in the department. I enjoyed teaching and still found it rewarding to work with students. As in previous years, Black and White students encouraged me to keep fighting the appointment battle at the university—several volunteering to write, speak to, and argue my case with the administration.

However, I wanted to transition into a new direction where I hoped to find rewards that the academic life hadn't offered me. After Paulette moved out to find her own space in LA's Echo Park area, I reclaimed the St. Andrews Place apartment. With my old nest recaptured, I was committed to put my energy into writing. Unexpectedly, I was confronted with a setback: my agent, Marcie Wright, dropped me. My screenplay, *The Inner Circle*, wasn't picked up by the studios and producers to which she submitted. And to keep her new agency from sinking, she decided to shift her focus from representing screenplays to selling teleplays. She saw her future success in television sitcoms, drama series, and movies of the week.

Being dropped from her roster underscored a valuable lesson. There was writing as an "artistic pursuit" and writing as a "business." The writing business didn't necessarily revolve around talent, quality of the material, or loyalty. It was an aggressive, competitive pursuit where screen credits equaled future jobs and increases on a salary scale. I was certainly disappointed at my agent's decision because I hoped she could convince the Hollywood powerbrokers to perceive both the talent and commercial value in my writing.

At the same time, Paulette made changes in her professional life as she took a job in Century City at Tri-Star Pictures. There, she met Jennifer "JJ" Levine who also aspired to work in film and television, and who became an immediate family member. The two worked as administrative assistants, searching for opportunities to get firmer steps in the creative world. From Tri-Star, Paulette went to Columbia Pictures as an assistant to the Sackmar-Lindmar production team—writers who had gained attention for their script contributions to various television shows, including *Cagney and Lacey* (1982–1988) and *MacGyver* (1985–1992). Paulette remained with the team when they transitioned to offices at Columbia Pictures, eventually producing the television film, *Out of Time* (1988), starring a young Bill Maher. Paulette invited me to the set to meet the producers and Mr. Maher, which served as one of those inspirational moments.

Paulette's journey as an office assistant at Tri-Star kindled my pursuit as a part-time script analyst. I knew a freelance position would bring in extra money, and importantly, reading scripts would help me to note the characterizations, structure, dialogue, and pacing contained in submitted scripts by agents. I simply reached out through letters and phone calls to script departments and script supervisors at independent production companies, which led me to an interview at New World Pictures with offices in Century City. Established by filmmaker Roger Corman in the early 1970s, the company became known as the home of inexpensive genre movies in the 1950s-1960s and the learning school for future commercial actors, writers, and directors. During my months of being a freelance script analyst, New World provided me a check for each script that I read and assessed. Significantly, working for the company educated me on the qualities of well-written scripts and those that got made into a movie—often not one in the same.

Caroline Winters was the company's script supervisor, a woman whose appearance conjured up the images of the Hitchcock blondes, such as Tippi Hedren, Kim Novak, and Grace Kelly. However, Caroline was intelligent and articulate with an extensive knowledge of American literature—which was our point of connection. She shared the company's "Bible" with me, which contained and described the various elements to be evaluated in the scripts I received. Those elements became the points I prioritized in the screenplays I analyzed *and* the scripts I wrote.

Significantly, I gained a fuller understanding of the chain of decision making at New World Pictures. The entity that possessed the most power was down the hall from Caroline's office—the marketing division. On occasion as I walked the hallway, I saw the man whose name I could never remember. He was a plump White man with thinning hair, who was sadly adorned in disheveled shirts and ties and chomping on a cigar with his stare fixed beyond me when crossing paths. From what Caroline shared with me, he was the gatekeeper in the chain of script advancement. And what she inferred through a wry smile was that his office determined that a "good" script was the one that could be made to bring in the highest box office receipts.

Those facts confirmed why so much junk reached the big and small screens. It also clarified why Black, Brown, Asian, and Native American characters and stories didn't find their way consistently to the screens at the time—no matter how well-written the script was. It confirmed comments I had heard over the years about stories that couldn't sell. The dollars-and-cents formula was so narrow that numerous characters and plots had little chance of getting to an audience. Production, distribution, marketing, and exhibition were inextricably linked to a "product" that could be marketed to a specific audience—preferably a White one.

I benefitted immensely from the experience at New World, but driving to busy Century City while having to read, write, and type a one to two-page assessment took away from *my* writing, which was already being squeezed through a narrow crack of available time. I was spreading myself too thin across the limited number of hours in a day.

So, I prioritized my time, devoting my energy to finishing the revision of my screenplay, *The Veil*, while developing my novel, *The Shadows of Truth*. That's when I decided to try something different. Perhaps the idea came from watching some local television news report about movie stars who lived in the LA area. Perhaps, the idea sprang from the indigestion of eating the cheap, greasy chicken meals from the nearby fast food joint. But one day, I drove to the Beverly Hills Library and found the shelf containing local telephone books. In the days of hard copy phone books, the white pages contained residential names and numbers, while the yellow pages included commercial businesses. I fingered pages and columns in the white pages before finding the name I sought: Lloyd Bridges. During the months of revision on *The Veil*, my writing breaks were filled with the preferred casting I conducted in my head, and Mr. Bridges was the primary person I desired to play the supporting role of the sheriff. Among *Home of the Brave* (1949), *High Noon* (1952), television's *Sea Hunt*, and the personal meeting during a Cape Cod summer—he was one of my favorite actors, and his popularity spiked when he appeared in the comedy film, *Airplane* (1980).

When I returned to my apartment, I dialed the number I found in the white pages. I wasn't sure who would answer or what I would say.

"Hello," he said. I recognized his voice. "Hello."

"Hello, Mr. Bridges . . . well, my name is Mel Donalson! I have a script I've written . . . it's called *The Veil*, and it's based on a short story written by Stephen Crane."

There was an eternal pause. I figured he was questioning whether I was a prank caller.

"Okay . . . ," he returned slowly. "Tell me about the story."

"Um, well, it's set in the late nineteenth century. A young Black man works for the town's doctor, and during a fire, the Black man saves the doctor's son, only to be disfigured himself and physically crippled by the fire. So, well, the doctor takes care of the Black man, despite the townspeople who want to force him away due to his physical appearance."

"Hm, interesting."

"I was hoping you might be interested in playing the sheriff of the town."

Silence. I was certain he heard the fear in my cracking voice.

"Tell you what," he said after a few moments. "Mail the script to me, and we'll talk after I read it."

My hand trembled as I scribbled his post office box address. Hanging up the phone, I couldn't believe what had happened. I was sweating. I looked around, but there was no one to tell. Who would believe me? I rushed to PIP Printing and had several copies made and drilled with three holes in the left margin. Rushing back to the apartment, I secured the pages with brass fasteners, hand-printed the mailing and return addresses, and typed a cover letter to remind Mr. Bridges of our phone conversation. I planned to be the first person in line at the post office the following morning.

Later, when I told Paulette, she was stunned and happy for me. Part of her positive mood extended from the agent she finally found: Marshall Ferguson. She, in turn, introduced me to Marshall, and after reading *The Inner Circle* and *The Veil*, he said he would represent me.

Marshall Ferguson was one of two well-known Black agents in LA at the time. His office was located on South La Brea Avenue, a few blocks below Olympic Boulevard. The second-floor space had an outer area with a couch and chairs before a reception desk, while Marshall's inner office was smaller and crammed with piles of media journals, newspapers, and scripts. Marshall was a short, fast-talking Black man who could be mistaken for a game show host or perhaps a Baptist preacher on a Sunday pulpit. However, Marshall was always generous to me, even when he was convincing me to do him a favor. He was resourceful enough to compete with larger, more formidable agencies that represented celebrity names.

\*\*\*

As I continued to drive back and forth to teach a fourth year at UC-Santa Barbara, my relationship with Janet was at low tide, leaving only the bare, drying sands of our friendship. I knew things would shift in that direction after my night in jail. Months later, when my sister had to be admitted to the hospital to undergo surgery, I paid several visits to see her. On one occasion, I met Cheryl Dawson, who was my sister's hair stylist.

Cheryl was a pretty, petite Black woman with a very pleasant personality. She was only twenty-one, and I was thirty-one. After that initial meeting in the hospital, I pursued her with phone calls and unannounced appearances at the Black hair salon where she worked. The timing was good in that she had recently ended a relationship with a youngish, awkward brother who failed to meet her expectations. Certainly, I wasn't young or awkward, but I was still trying to fit professional pieces of life into place before moving toward a new personal commitment. I was still showing the battle wounds of my previous romantic involvement. However, despite my post-traumatic stress disorder from personal relationships, I pursued Cheryl. As I re-enlisted in the dating battle, I wore the uniform of patience and marched forward carefully.

\*\*\*

A month or so into our contract, Marshall contacted me. He had forwarded *The Veil* to LeVar Burton, who indicated he loved the script. Marshall promised he would set up a meeting between me and Mr. Burton to have us talk. I was elated, walking on clouds of positivity. Mr. Burton was well-known by the early 1980s, as his role as Kunta Kinte in television's *Roots* brought him into the spotlight. By 1983, his audience grew when he hosted PBS's *Reading Rainbow* and widened in 1987 with his role in the series *Star Trek: The Next Generation*. In the decades since then, he has produced, directed, and hosted television shows.

On the night of our first meeting, Marshall arranged for us to connect in Malibu at the Trancas Bar and Restaurant. Of course, Marshall asked me to use my car for the ninety-minute drive from his office to the Malibu venue because his vehicle was out of service. I had never been to Trancas before, but it was obviously a social spot, based upon the packed parking lot on a weeknight. Entering the dimly lit, busy interior, we found a spot at the bar. Marshall went to find Mr. Burton, and I looked down the crowded bar stools to see cast members from my favorite television drama, *Hill Street Blues*. In my star-struck moment, I couldn't remember the actors' names, but I knew their characters' names.

Marshall returned with Mr. Burton, and in my excitement and the noisy background, I heard most of what Mr. Burton told me.

"I really liked your script . . . you can really write. So, I was telling Marshall, I want to be involved with making this movie happen. And . . . I have another project I want to talk to you about. So, tell me a little bit about yourself . . ."

I blurted out a short bio, and we discussed *The Veil* in more detail before Mr. Burton was pulled into another conversation. He shook my hand quickly, promising to be in touch. Marshall and I stayed for another hour—with Marshall hopscotching around the room and me sipping at the bar. On our way out, the parking lot was just as raucous, and I recognized the tipsy man laughing with two others beneath building lights. It was Gary Busey. I remembered his name because I enjoyed *The Buddy Holly Story* (1978), but I didn't approach him since he was deep into some rowdy joking with several men.

During the drive back to LA, Marshall talked incessantly about future plans with Mr. Burton. I was in a happy zone, intoxicated by future possibilities. I made it home and fell across my bed. I remained sleepless for hours, dreaming with my eyes wide open.

\* \* \*

In the weeks following the night at Trancas, I had another film-related experience. I was using my usual PIP Printing store to make copies of a manuscript. I casually struck up a conversation with a White man in his fifties named Hans Nilsson, who, glancing my pages, asked if I was a screenwriter. I made a joke about my efforts to make my way into the business, and he nodded his understanding. He had silver hair, a tanned complexion, and an accent which was later identified as Swedish. As we drifted out the door and continued the conversation on the sidewalk, he informed me that he was a member of the Hollywood Foreign Press Association. He talked about the association's premiere award—the Golden Globes, and he loved his job as a journalist and critic. As we finished the conversation, he asked if I wanted to join him at an upcoming screening at one of the studios. He told me it might be a way to meet some people and to view a film in an ideal big-screen setting. We exchanged phone numbers, and I rushed back to continue working on my manuscript.

Two weeks later, Hans phoned and gave me directions to his home in the hills of Toluca Lake, a neighborhood north of the Hollywood area. His three-bedroom house was snuggled within an attractive area that offered an impressive view of the neighborhood and the Hollywood lights in the distance. He promised me a tour of the house when we returned from the screening, so we took his Mercedes into Hollywood and headed to the event.

The film was *Educating Rita* (1983), which starred Michael Caine and Julie Walters as the titular character. Before the film began, several people were introduced in the audience who worked on the film, but I didn't recognize their names. As the film developed, I was surprised at the engaging comedy with well-placed poignant moments. Afterwards, Hans greeted a couple of people he knew, introducing me as he did.

Opting to have some wine back at his house, we returned to Toluca Lake, discussing the attributes of the film. Once we had our wine glasses in hand, Hans retrieved a large photo album from a small bookshelf and handed it to me.

"So, over the years as I've interviewed actors and actresses, I've taken their photos—sometimes used their head shots—to create my album."

I fingered the pages and was astonished by the popular actors included in the collection. Hans placed his finger on one page and fingered the actor's image.

"He's gay," Hans declared. As I continued turning the album's pages, he added, "So is he . . . .him . . . and him . . . ."

"What?" I said in disbelief. "No way . . . ."

"Yes, they keep their secrets for their careers," Hans explained.

Photo after photo of well-known actors appeared—most of them White and considered handsome heartthrobs. One, in particular, had been the lead on a primetime drama series and had recently starred in two television mini-series.

"So, Hans, how do you know about these actors?"

At that point, Hans eased his hand between my thighs.

"Do you have a girlfriend?" he asked.

The question didn't quite resonate as my mind was still processing his hand on my crotch.

"Yes, I do!" I pronounced, moving away along the couch.

"Have you ever had a man kiss your penis?"

"Hell, no!" I proclaimed. "Not even in my worst nightmares!"

I jumped up, and Hans did the same, following me to the door.

"I promise you, you'll enjoy it!"

"Hans, man, I got to go!"

Whatever Hans said as I rushed from the house wasn't clear. I was in my car, racing down from Toluca Lake. The beauty of the nearby lights dissipated as I wondered why Hans came onto me. I attempted to figure out what I had done or said that triggered his interest in *me*.

In 1983, Julie Walters was nominated for Best Actress for *Educating Rita* for the British Academy Award, an Oscar, and a Golden Globe Award, the latter for which she won. As that night surfaced again in my head, I was certain I should have been nominated for "the quickest house guest to disappear" from an episode of "Educating Mel."

\*\*\*

When I received a note mailed to me from Lloyd Bridges, I phoned him as requested. He was as friendly as in our previous conversation.

"I read your script, and it's a very good story . . . an important story about tolerance."

"Thank you, Mr. Bridges . . . thank you."

"But you want me to play the sheriff. What about the lead role of the doctor?"

I was speechless for a quick moment.

"Well, sure . . . sure!" I blurted out.

He instructed me to contact him when the funding was in place. He would get his reps to make certain his participation was inked in. I thanked him repeatedly. Then, I lifted exuberant prayers as I sped to Marshall Ferguson's office. Marshall, of course, was excited, but reminded me that getting to the finish line was a process. But he told me he had someone else he wanted me to meet, someone he felt I could partner with moving forward in the business.

\* \* \*

Daryl Paxton and I met at Marshall's office. Daryl possessed a gregarious personality—direct but personable, talkative but attentive, imaginative but detail-oriented. He was a bald, six-foot-two Black man who lived in Burbank with his Japanese American girlfriend. Daryl worked as a computer programmer at Channel 13, a Metromedia television broadcasting company at that time. He was an idea man with resources—both financial and personal—that he could utilize for various projects.

We got along immediately, as he appreciated my writing skills and my comfort level when talking to anyone, regardless of their ethnicity and status. As I told him details of my many writing projects, he urged me to let him read my work.

Daryl knew someone who worked at Prentice-Hall publishers, and he offered to send my novel, *The Shadows of Truth*, to that editor. And while we were still waiting on something to develop with *The Veil*, he suggested we form a management company. We would represent about eight actors, including my sister and people he knew. Daryl figured that I could write scenes for the actors we represented to participate in "showcases" at various stage theaters. A showcase was basically an audition step—as talent agents would be invited to attend to observe actors performing soliloquies and two-character scenes.

Daryl purchased a subscription to the *Breakdown Services*, the daily publication that listed calls for submissions of head-shots and resumes for roles on episodic television shows and film productions. As DP Associates (for Donalson and Paxton), there was a wide gulf between the shores of being an "agent" and being a "manager." As managers, we didn't have to establish an office, and our commission could go higher than that of an agent's 10 percent. So, as I traveled back and forth to teach my classes at UCSB that fourth year, the commute was more tolerable, knowing I worked with a partner to move deeper into a creative business.

Just before Christmas 1983, Paulette lost her day job. I was saddened by that development, and I did my best to lift her up from that emotional shipwreck. Giving that support was made difficult by the lack of progress on *The Veil* and the rejection of *The Shadows of Truth*—from Prentice Hall, the New American Library, and Grove Press. The scripts seemed to be running in place—*The Veil* had stalled without any news from LeVar Burton, and *The Inner Circle* was being sent around by Marshall Ferguson without any interest.

Then, abruptly, when Mr. Burton phoned and asked to come by my St. Andrews Place apartment, I was revitalized. When he arrived, our discussion went deep into the possibilities that PBS Playhouse series might be interested, and he entrusted me with a synopsis of a possible television series he wanted to develop and submit to the networks. The central character was a young, Black priest working and living in the inner-city neighborhood of violence, financial challenges, and disillusioned young people. There was nothing on television like it at the time, and he was excited by both the possibilities of his project *and* my writing. But . . . for months after, I heard nothing from him, and I told myself that I had to be patient and hopeful.

\* \* \*

As I leaned into my budding relationship with Cheryl Dawson, I continually surfed Daryl's ideas that came in waves. By the spring of 1984, Daryl wanted to form a three-man company, bringing in the actor Napoleon Hendrix. Napoleon had earned visibility by being in two major films—*An Officer and a Gentleman* (1982) and *Uncommon Valor* (1983). Napoleon had written an original script which we included with *The Veil* and *The Inner Circle*, as we searched for a three-picture deal. With my writing skills, Daryl's selling abilities, and Napoleon's connections and recent success, we targeted production companies with our three ready-for-the-screen stories. Using the first syllable of our last names, we formed HenDonPax Productions, and Daryl began to scout for financial backers. With meetings at Napoleon's house in Baldwin Hills—LA's noted, affluent Black neighborhood—he proved to be a gentle and kind brother who worked hard to translate his recent performances into a lasting career. Despite our efforts, we couldn't get any traction and backing for a three-picture deal.

On the academic side, my relationship with UC-Santa Barbara ended in June 1984, as there was only the offer of another one-year position. I knew that

I didn't want to continue commuting back and forth, and I needed to be rooted in Los Angeles to quickly respond to any opportunity that might surface. By then, I had written two additional scripts—*The Thirteenth Hour*, based upon an earlier short story, and *Twilight Sings with Laughter*, a story of a White woman who runs away from the emptiness of her successful acting career to find connection and meaning with her adopted Black sister.

The additional reason I wanted to be in LA was my growing relationship with Cheryl. We were at a point of acknowledging a commitment, as we shared similar values and priorities about life. My hesitations lay in two areas: first, I didn't have the regular day job to offer financial stability, and, second, she was Catholic to my liberal Protestantism. But we talked about these two areas extensively, both of us trying to reduce any objections and anxieties that would prevent us from forming a lasting commitment.

However, as I planned my disconnection from Santa Barbara, another situation pulled me back in. I received a phone message from an attorney who was working with a team on a communications project. In that initial call, the lawyer asserted that my professional background in education and film made me an ideal person to join their group. I agreed to meet him in Westwood, near UCLA, on the date set. His name was Jeremy Klein, and as a thirty-something, he was much younger than what I expected. He was a confident, garrulous man who began our discussion by telling me of his current business venture.

"Compact discs . . . it's the music form of the future. Their size is much smaller than laser discs, and the sound is cleaner and more precise."

"Really? I still have my cassette tapes when I drive back and forth to Santa Barbara," I confessed.

"I tell you, Dr. Donalson, look into CDs and CD players to invest. The time is now!"

"I'll keep that in mind. So, Mr. Klein, what is this important venture you think I would be just right for?"

"How would you like to be part owner and board member of a new television station?"

He continued speaking in what seemed to be one long breath, confessing that I had been recommended to him without revealing the source. He knew my academic background, my interest in writing, and aspirations in the film business. He spent the next hour explaining that the Federal Communications Commission had approved the licensing of a new television station in the Santa Barbara area, with the stipulation of including minority stockholders at the helm. His job was to identify minority *and* local Santa Barbara ownership—a total of about twenty initial members to form a subchapter S corporation. If I were interested, I would be asked to buy in a minimum of one hundred shares at ten dollars each. In addition, he wanted me to serve as one of the board members for the duration of the licensing application process. When I told Daryl about the deal, he was more excited than me, reasoning that gaining ownership in a television station would open numerous possibilities in the entertainment industry. So, since I didn't have the money, Daryl funded the one hundred shares in my name.

In that initial Santa Barbara meeting of possible participants, there were Latinos, Whites, and a few Black people, including retired NFL player Floyd Little. I recognized Floyd at once, excited to connect with him and discuss his years as a pro running back with the Denver Broncos. He was a three-time All American at Syracuse University before entering the pros, and he had been voted into the College Football Hall of Fame when I met him. Years later, he would also be selected into the Pro Football Hall of Fame. At the time, Floyd was living in Santa Barbara with his wife, Joyce, in a modest home near upper State Street, and he owned a car dealership. Many of our initial board meetings took place at Floyd's house or in the law offices of Ben Renard.

Ben Renard and his brother, Steve, belonged to one of the oldest White families in Santa Barbara. Their family history and city connections would be invaluable in pursuing the license to favor our group. Steve Renard was also a working television director on the comedy series *Family Ties* and *Full House*. We had a formidable team in place to compete for the television station, and we all understood that it would be a long-term process.

\* \* \*

As the months progressed, I weighed and measured my apprehension about a commitment to Cheryl. In endless discussions with myself, I attempted to reconcile my previous personal experiences, emotions, and fears into some kind of clear roadmap for my current life. As I worked, week after week, waiting for *something* concrete to fall into place with my writing and managing efforts, I kept retreating from considering the one relationship I had avoided for years: marriage.

Eventually, still sweating doubts and anxieties, I placed a down payment on a ring. In the summer of 1984, Cheryl and I drove down to San Diego for an overnight trip, and I proposed to her. It surprised her, and it certainly shocked me to hear my voice delivering the question. It was that kind of out of body experience.

As a boy, I didn't trust girls, but as a young man, I learned to listen to women. I stepped out into a frontier that I understood intellectually but feared on an emotional level. I was thirty-two and questioning that leap, looking out through eyes of uncertainty. Cheryl was twenty-two and eagerly taking the step that would define her as a woman through the eyes of her family.

The engagement forced me to look directly into a pressure-filled reality: without returning to UC-Santa Barbara to teach, I didn't have a full-time job. So, Cheryl and I decided we would confirm a wedding date once I secured steady employment—while waiting for one of my numerous projects to fall into place. Cheryl never pressured me, but I placed pressure on myself. And I knew her parents and her older brothers were watching me.

I applied for a job at a Bullock's Department Store in its data processing division. Weeks of indecision from the company submerged me into the misery of waiting. I kept looking, lying on applications about my educational background, seeking anything that would provide me steady income.

In the interim, I reflected on two issues that could become significant to our marriage. First, Cheryl was ten years younger and living at home. Those years of life experience between us were significant. As my wife and partner, was she prepared to face the financial, professional, and daily challenges of living in LA that would confront us? Second, Cheryl was Catholic, and I was Protestant. That particular difference could be reconciled, but it would require extensive listening and compromising from both of us.

Following our engagement, I agreed—as a non-Catholic spouse to be—to attend a series of "lessons" required by the Catholic Church. One issue for me was that the eight or so couples taking the lessons were all White. Additionally, the lessons were led by a White couple in their forties who seemed right out of a *Saturday Night Live* sketch. With their frozen smiles and religious intentions, they spent week after week describing a man's duties, a woman's duties, and the need to fulfill those gender roles given by God. And after a few weeks, they went into the necessity to replenish the earth and be bountiful with children, God's greatest gifts to humanity. I had to fold my arms across my chest and resist my feminist impulse to scream out like an angry heretic.

In our after-lesson conversations, I urged Cheryl not to ingest all the nonsense preached by the ideal couple. We didn't have to follow anyone's catechism about our roles in *our* marriage. I didn't know the Pope; didn't plan on meeting him; and if I ever did, I would request that he be forced to sit through the brainwashing marriage lessons. I wasn't marrying Cheryl for her to be the cook, maid, housekeeper, and nanny. I loved her, and I wanted her to be my partner—not my domestic employee.

About a month before our November wedding, I interviewed for a job with the Federated Group, the major electronics store chain in the city. There was a training session, a lie detector test, and an assignment to the store that was in the west Los Angeles area. I lasted one week.

Then, fingering the newspaper ads, I applied for a teaching position at the Adelphi Business School. The school was located on Spring Street in downtown LA, and my schedule would be five days a week for seven hours a day to make $1,100 gross per month. The last thing I wanted was to go back into a classroom, and certainly not at a private, for-profit business school. But I was thankful to God for the blessing of a job and grateful to Cheryl for being patient with her unemployed fiancé.

\* \* \*

We were married in the Church of the Transfiguration on West Martin Luther King Jr Boulevard. Our wedding ceremony and the reception were held there on the church property, and we honeymooned in Carmel, the charming coastal village southwest of San Francisco. Afterward, we lived in the St. Andrews Place apartment, and Cheryl was hired at a hair salon in Beverly Hills. The establishment specialized in cuts and stylings for children—particularly those in commercials, television shows, and movies. Since Cheryl was driving through Beverly Hills, I had her drive my Toyota. It wasn't luxury, but it was dependable and not the eyesore Gremlin that Cheryl drove. I took the city bus to and from the Adelphi Business School.

It was called a business school, but Adelphi was merely a scam school. The owners hired recruiters to walk along downtown Spring Street and sign up the homeless and others looking for a chance at finding a future in the business world. The school received a portion of the federal money that would be allocated for each student. Some students were reading at an elementary school level—those that could read. Their verbal skills were even worse, though they sought to become secretaries, administrative assistants, high school teachers, and independent business owners. Teaching English, and sometimes basic math classes, I did my best to inspire. Several of us "teachers" talked secretly about exposing the school, but whenever inspectors came to assess the administration, it received passing approval. Increasingly, I knew I couldn't remain. In addition to the terrible infrastructure of the dilapidated building, the faulty curriculum, and the aggressive roaches the size of our Gremlin, I knew I was working in the bowels of education.

I remained at Adelphi Business School for eight months. During that time, I wrote new fiction, while still receiving rejections on *The Shadows of Truth*. There had to be a way that my creative efforts could provide an income for Cheryl and me. I amped up my efforts with Daryl, DP Associates Management, and HenDonPax Productions. I was still traveling back and forth to Santa Barbara for required quarterly board of directors meetings for the television licensing process.

Unfortunately, I lost touch with LeVar Burton, as newspaper articles and television news announced legal issues he was confronting. The issues remained in the public gossip mill for a month or so. Regardless, he never reached out to me again, and with no funding in place through my agent, Marshall Ferguson, or Daryl, I couldn't keep Lloyd Bridges attached to *The Veil* project. I felt the weight of an opportunity loss. I was a man with talent but no resources.

So, during my daily scanning of the *LA Times* classified section, I saw that the Los Angeles Unified School District (LAUSD) was hiring high school teachers. I didn't have a teaching credential, but I mentioned my PhD in my application. With the district's pressing need for teachers, I obtained a waiver for a year, receiving an emergency credential—with the added requirement to attend weekly sessions on "teaching methodologies" with other non-credential instructors. I was ill at the thought of going through those sessions, but I was paid $900 more per month than the Adelphi Business School salary and received health benefits for Cheryl and me.

I leaned into prayers and attempted to understand why my efforts at success continually evaded me. I wasn't seeking riches and fame. I only wanted to be productive in areas where I could use my God-given talents. I wanted to be a husband who secured the best life possible for my wife. My efforts kept colliding against walls of negativity, but I knew I had the Joshua talent and skills to tear down those walls. But . . . I took the teaching position with the LAUSD, and in September 1985, I was in a high school classroom again. In twelve years, I had gone full circle, a dizzying merry-go-round in an educational carnival. I did not ask for whom the bells tolled, but I heard the ringing sadness in my head.

CHAPTER TWELVE

# The Crookeds and the Straights

Cheryl was pregnant! As I began teaching high school again in September 1985, she was a month along with the anticipation of our baby arriving in the spring of 1986. I was excited, happy, and overwhelmed with fear. Despite the conversations with male friends and family members who were fathers, I felt I wasn't ready. I reflected on Papa D and all he sacrificed and achieved in order to secure a good home for me and my siblings. I wasn't sure if I could possibly be the kind of husband, father, and man that he was. I had responsibilities I never had before, and even though I was back in a high school classroom, I searched for college-level possibilities. I was assigned to one of the top three high schools in the huge school district of 600,000 students: University High School in west Los Angeles. Teaching at University High offered a few rewards, as I met some dedicated teachers who, unlike me, were doing the job they really wanted and enjoyed doing.

In general, University High had smart and well-prepared students, many who saw their destined college futures at nearby UCLA. Some students were children of professionally successful parents, including some who were in the entertainment business. I had one such student in my literature class, Samantha Mathis. Articulate and confident, she casually mentioned her mother was an actress, and after pressing her, she shared her mother was Bibi Besch. Ms. Besch was familiar to me from the many television appearances she had accrued, as well as big screen productions, including *Star Trek II: The Wrath of Khan* (1982). Samantha was surprised that I recognized her mother's name, but I stressed that her mother had one of the more familiar faces due to her lengthy career. And Samantha also went on to have an enviable career in both television and film, including *Little Women* (1994), *An American President* (1995), *Broken Arrow* (1996), *American Psycho* (2000), and *The Punisher* (2004).

However, there was one student—Jake Ramsey—who sought *me* out. When first meeting him, Jake explained that the school counselor suggested me and my composition class due to my background in creative writing. Jake had arrived from Riverside, a city about two-and-a-half hours east of LA. He was a slim White boy with curly hair, and he was articulate with an engaging sense of humor. It was evident that he could navigate the class effectively, and it was also clear to me that he was gay. After a few weeks, Jake met with me for a "private conversation," sharing his plan to write his story and asking me to help him.

Jake lived with his single mother in Riverside, until she married a man with a conservative religious background. Discovering that his stepson was gay with an interest in dressing as a girl, the stepfather turned into an abusive, pious man. As a punishment, the stepdad forced Jake to wear girl's clothing and makeup before driving Jake to his high school and dragging him inside for everyone to laugh at and ridicule. At sixteen, Jake moved out and lived on the streets, hustling strangers to survive. Assured he was indeed a girl inside, Jake saved money to get a sex change operation. Busted by an undercover policeman, the arrest led to Jake being placed into a detention home as a minor. He lived in various detention homes until he turned eighteen, when he was emancipated.

After months of sharing his story and his writing with me, Jake disappeared from University High. One day, he phoned my home number, explaining that he was in a phone booth near the corner of La Cienega and Sunset Boulevards in West Hollywood. He was weary of school and attempting to be a boy. His mother agreed to support his efforts to get a sex change operation. He thanked me for being his friend, promising to keep in touch. However, I never heard from him again.

Jake survived a childhood and adolescence I never experienced. Although poor, I was showered with love from both parents and extended family members. I never felt lost and alone as he did. Meeting Jake, I strengthened my commitment to give my child all the affection and affirmations I could. To shower him or her with love. To provide a home. To give my child the security of knowing I would accept him or her with my deepest love.

\*\*\*

As the year at University High progressed, I needed to leave the St. Andrews Place apartment and find a house for my wife and child. I followed up on a tip from Cheryl's brother that a house was on the market in Inglewood, a predominantly Black neighborhood just south of Los Angeles. It was a tiny, two-bedroom, wooden house in need of attention both inside and out. With very little in my savings and borrowing money from Daryl for a down payment, we applied for an FHA loan that pushed us into months of an application process for our $77,000, two-bedroom house. Getting a mortgage launched my search again for a college-level job. With a lack of academic publications, my best chance was finding a community college position.

I researched several colleges in the LA area, receiving an interview to teach composition and American literature with an emphasis in women's literature. I prepared extensively, updating myself on recent scholarship and reviewing syllabi I constructed at UC-Santa Barbara. When I arrived on the community college campus and entered the interview room, there were *nine* people sitting around the table, including a rather sour-looking woman who was the chair of the department. As the committee members introduced themselves, it became apparent that the chair was saving her sour expressions specifically for me. As she dominated the questions and follow-up comments, she searched for ways to expose me as some type of fraud and unprepared academic. The chair's final effort to nail me inside the interview coffin occurred when she asked for my favorite women authors.

"Well, to be honest," I responded, "I would have difficulty singling out just one theme or author. The truth is—women's literature is an extensive and broad discipline."

"*Broad*," she snickered. "Isn't that a *sexist* term!"

"No," I returned without missing a beat. "*Broad* is an adjective."

The committee members erupted into laughter, and as I looked at the reddening face of the chair, I knew I wouldn't get the job. Later that night, I received a phone call from the sole Black male professor who sat at the interview table.

"Dr. Donalson, you know . . . you're not going to be offered the position," he said, chuckling. "But I noticed on your vita that you have a background in American history *and* Black history in particular. Well, my wife is on the faculty at Pasadena City College, and there's a part-time position in the History Department. I think you should apply."

I wanted to kiss the brother, repeating my thanks and gratitude. The next day, I drove to Pasadena City College with my application letter and curriculum vita in hand. While dropping off the material at the appropriate office, the chair of the Social Sciences Department came out and looked over my paperwork. He invited me in for a discussion about my experiences, promising he would get back to me by the end of the week. He followed through with his promise, and I was hired to teach American History beginning in August for the fall semester.

\* \* \*

My son, Derek Albert, was born on May 7, 1986. I was a father!

Cheryl and I had prepared ourselves beforehand—reading information for new parents, taking birthing classes together, buying new clothing, and selecting a crib. We planned to stay at her parents' house for the first month after the baby's arrival. That way, Cheryl could have her family's help as I returned to work. We chose the name Derek because, in German, it meant "the leader of people," and his middle name—Albert—was a merging of the first syllable of Cheryl's father's name—*Al*len—and the second syllable from Papa D's name—Wil*bert*.

Inside the delivery room, I thought I was ready. However, ten minutes into the theater of childbirth, the doctor indicated that Derek was in the "occiput posterior" position—head first but facing Cheryl's back. That position could cause Derek to have breathing difficulty, brain damage, and a peculiar shaping of his head—*and* prolonged labor for Cheryl. I was frightened, helpless as I watched. The doctor performed some hand-nudging in the tense silence, and I prayed with every breath. I asked God to allow my son to be born safely and healthily, and to allow me to live long enough to see him into manhood. On that day and the eighteen years that followed, God answered that prayer. When the attending delivery nurse handed Derek to me, he was a purplish color, as he cried healthily and proceeded to pee all over me. Fortunately, he's treated me much better since that moment.

*\*\*\**

As Daryl and I worked diligently as managers, there was moderate success for our clients. My sister landed a limited, three-day role on the soap opera, *General Hospital*. Several other clients were able to get one-time supporting appearances on network television shows, including *Hardcastle & McCormick* and *The A-Team*. One client landed two scenes as a prostitute with no lines, in *City Nights* (1984), an action-comedy starring Burt Reynolds and Clint Eastwood. Those moderate successes didn't lead to a windfall of income for me and Daryl, as we still struggled to sell the three-picture, HenDonPax scripts.

However, by the mid-1980s my brother, Brian, moved to the West Coast, playing college football at Santa Barbara City College. Importantly, another calling beckoned him at that time: hip hop music. I was surprised by the skills he developed in writing and "spitting" rhymes. The popular phase of rap at that time emanated from Run-DMC, Young MC, and MC Hammer, offering dance and party-style rapping. In the late 1980s, the music industry was transitioning from a more cultural-political style that emerged with KRS-One and Public Enemy to a more aggressive, confrontational language that surfaced with gangsta rap. My brother emerged somewhere in between those overlapping strains in hip hop, and for some A&R people, he was too "soft" and not "gangsta" enough. Listening to Brian's tapes, Daryl was excited, insisting that we add him as "Sweets the MC" to our roster of talents. So, with our roster of actors and a rapper, we had a range of talented performers. The only thing we needed was that one break.

It was at that point that Daryl approached me with a financial proposition. His pitch was that we could get $75,000 in two days, which would allow us to complete an album for Brian *and* provide initial seed money for an action script I'd written, titled *The Final Contract*. I was excited with the offer and the possibilities. However, the red flag was in the details: Daryl had a relative who was a member of one of LA's street gangs. This relative and his gang sold illegal items, and they would loan the money to our management company to hide some of their illegal income. So, there it was—an answer to the prayer of getting money. Daryl said we would have a year to repay the loan with no interest. In that year, he argued, we could launch our projects. He saw my reluctant face, but told me to think about it overnight.

I didn't sleep much that night, nor did I tell Cheryl about the business opportunity that Daryl pitched. As I looked around the darkness of our little Inglewood home, I reasoned that this was the chance to finally move ahead in the film and music business—to move my wife and son into a better environment, to get away from the teaching jobs. After all, thinking back to my year of working at the Century City law firm, White people accepted various "business connections" to reach success. How many successful people in the entertainment business had been capitalized by questionable sources? How many pastors in the large churches I drove by had formed an allegiance with one devil or another in the name of the Lord? How many years of hard work had I invested to gain success?

I entered my son's tiny bedroom and watched him sleeping in the crib. I felt compelled to give him more than a life of dancing on quicksand when it came to financial security and dreams. And then I remembered the prayer. The one I lifted in the delivery room, holding my crying child as he took his initial breaths. I prayed for God's protection of my son and to give me the years to see him grow into manhood. Yet, I was contemplating a deal that might put him—and Cheryl—in a direct collision with danger.

"No, Daryl, I can't do it," I told my partner the following night. "There are too many what-ifs in the deal. If we don't pay that money back, what'll happen? If the gang's filtering money into our business, at what point would they demand more involvement in our company? If something goes wrong, what if they came after Cheryl and Derek?"

Daryl was disappointed, but he accepted my decision. He reasoned aloud that with all the projects we had—the talent management, the music, the film scripts, the television license—*something* would fall into place. He agreed we would stay on track and move forward with what we were doing. I heard him. Watched his face. And I knew he was saying his words for my benefit rather than speaking from a sincere heart.

In May 1987, Derek was a year old, and I was thirty-five. During weekdays, I made the ninety-minute, one-way commute to Pasadena, holding down a tenure-track position at Pasadena City College. I managed to move from the part-time history position to a full-time appointment in the English Department, teaching five courses each week during an eighteen-week semester. It was a blessing to get into a tenure-track position at the college level, but I was still hungry for my writing and film efforts to surge forward. At the same time, I continued driving back and forth to Santa Barbara for the board meetings for the television station. On one trip, a board member mentioned Fithian Press, a publishing company located in Santa Barbara, so I submitted my novel, *The Shadows of Truth*, to the editor.

Abruptly, Cheryl left her position at the Beverly Hills children's hair salon. I was surprised, but I encouraged her to pursue her coworker's offer to start a business partnership and open their own salon. I told her we could borrow money against the house, but to my surprise, Cheryl didn't want to pursue the deal. Instead, she took a part-time job with a cosmetics company, working several days a week setting up and maintaining store displays.

Painfully, another phase entered our relationship at that time, a roller coaster of discussions that deteriorated into arguments. I heard comments that echoed previous relationships—I wasn't expressing love and feelings as she wanted. I was surprised as I felt we were in love as much as we were before—I knew I was. So, we agreed to visit a marriage counselor, but there was something underneath the surface that wasn't articulated during our sessions. Something present in our arguments, yet elusive. I adjusted to make certain we spent more time together. I committed myself to *dating* Cheryl again—the two of us out for dinners or movies and day trips away. I was lost to what I *wasn't* doing, but I was committed to our marriage.

At the same time, the television station application took a brutal turn. After years of competition, the FCC encouraged the competing groups to merge and restructure as one, which placed more pressure on my group. In fighting erupted as one member argued that his Santa Barbara family history dictated that he should be in charge of our group's decisions. At the same time, Floyd Little sold his car dealership, getting a better business deal pulling him out of state. My years of driving back and forth between LA and Santa Barbara for scheduled *and* emergency meetings were all for nothing. My allegiance to the group and the golden fleece of owning and running a new television station eroded painfully.

The decaying opportunity of the television license also issued a final breaking point in my relationship with Daryl. Our business partnership was fading. Our friendship dried into crumbled pieces and blew away like debris in a cold windstorm. So, my life and relationships were shifting in ways that were unexpected. And there I was—dancing on quicksand again. Desperately attempting to find my footing but slowly sinking instead.

\* \* \*

*The Shadows of Truth* was accepted for publication by Fithian Press in Santa Barbara. On that drive to meet with owners and editors John and Susan Daniels, I was excited. It was my version of having a baby delivered after years of carrying this manuscript. When we began our discussion, John and Susan were relaxed, extremely well-read people who appreciated a variety of literary forms, and they had such positive feedback about my manuscript. However, John had a request—he wanted to change the title to *The River Woman*. His perspective was that the new title captured the pivotal character emerging in the history of the novel's story.

On the downside, Fithian Press wouldn't pay an advance—but it was nothing new for me not to have money. Also, Fithian Press was a small, independent business, so there wouldn't be a budget for extensive promotions—nothing hurtful since I planned to launch a Los Angeles campaign through the network of people I knew. There was still much work to be done with revisions, proofreading, and editing, but I was on track toward the destination I desired. I lingered in the fulfilment of the hard work that brought me to that step of publication. I certainly had earned it, but the marketing process remained. Getting the novel into the hands of readers was still a challenge—a new area for me to learn and navigate.

\* \* \*

The canyon opening between Cheryl and me grew wider. Her part-time job wasn't something she wanted to maintain, and she wanted to be at home with Derek full time. I understood, but I still needed a little help financially with our monthly budget. Unexpectedly, Cheryl also surprised me with her announcement that she ideally wanted to have *five* children. My response was—why? My argument was that we needed to be the best parents possible for Derek, and we needed a stronger financial base before discussing enlarging the size of the family. She disagreed and professed that having a large family was what she really wanted. However, I made a point that we didn't need to have five kids—like her parents did. That comment led to another argument, which wasn't the last one.

In my private thoughts, Cheryl had morphed into a different person. She was not the woman I dated, married, and loved. We seemed to be moving at different paces in different directions, the conflicts becoming more frequent. I was in an unfamiliar, confusing valley in my life. Similar to characters in a play, Cheryl and I were beginning to exit the stage of our marriage, following cues coming from outside of our relationship. The breakdown in our union wasn't making sense, and no possible solution was present and within reach of my breaking heart. And as romantic notions of rescue and salvation drifted from my thoughts, I was haunted by the sad survival statement shared by a character in August Wilson's *Fences* (1987): *"You got to take the crookeds with the straights."*[4] Arriving at that reasoning was one step, but to implant the perspective into my crumbling world was something quite different.

Yes, the "crookeds" were unavoidable in life, as painful experiences cut deep inside. Somewhere in my human limitations, I rejected the lethal incisions that disfigured the life I knew. I desperately wanted to lean into the "straights," clutching all the affection that Cheryl and I once shared. Instead, I was at a cliff, raising clenched fists at the sky and falling to my knees in desperate prayers. Yet, as sure as the sun rises and sets without my permission and control, the "crookeds" that touched my life seemed inevitable.

\*\*\*

My brother Brian's music career as Sweets the MC was not advancing at the pace we all wanted. On his part, Sweets the MC was ready to make a shift into producing his own music, as well as any talent he might come across. He relocated from Santa Barbara to LA, committing himself to making a successful future in music—both in front of the microphone and behind his producer's 8-track production board.

Daryl and I both supported my brother's new direction. However, Daryl and I had a bigger problem, which surfaced during a heated argument. In his anger, he insisted he was still busy raising money for our company, but in his honesty, he finally admitted to selling drugs on the regular behind my back.

In the years that we worked together, I never saw Daryl using or selling drugs, but I knew that I didn't want Cheryl, my son, or my brother to be targeted due to some faulty drug transaction. After years of friendship and our

---

4 August Wilson, Fences, in *Cornerstones: An Anthology of African American Literature*, edited by Melvin Donalson, New York: St Martin's Press, 1996, p. 514.

business partnership, I had to walk away from Daryl, despite my affection and admiration for him. It was an emotional decision that left me in tears.

\*\*\*

Dana Plato was a familiar name and television personality due to her role on the weekly comedy, *Different Strokes*. When I, along with my project team, met her at her home in Chatsworth, she was very pleasant and sociable. She was petite and looked fragile as she busied herself with her young son, Tyler, and she and I chatted briefly about raising energetic little boys. Meeting her musician husband, Lanny Lambert, I was impressed with his home studio. He allowed us to listen to one of the pieces he was developing, as he played his rock guitar with a take-no-prisoners attitude and control.

My road to visiting Dana and Lanny's home was an interesting detour from my poetry, fiction, and screenplays. It began when a friend, Black producer Conrad Bullard, introduced me to the three Black men who came together to develop an animation project to encourage kids to avoid drugs. In the 1980s, following President Ronald Reagan's War on Drugs initiative, First Lady Nancy announced her "Just Say No" to drugs campaign. Cocaine was *the* popular drug, and the introduction of the highly addictive crack cocaine surfaced in public conversations and national headlines. The same public conversations neglected to assess the disproportionate arrests of and prison time for Black and Brown people using and selling crack compared to the lenient treatment of some White people selling and using powder cocaine. Additionally, some news outlets—and the Reagan administration—didn't evaluate the connections between drug prevalence in the inner city and Central American politics shaped by the involvement of United States government officials.

Conrad and the three Black men wanted to target the younger generation with their anti-drug message, and with the help of a fourth Black man, named Chaz, the plan was to have Dana host the animated children's series *The Fresh Kids*. Chaz indicated that he was Dana's manager, and he could persuade her to host the show which would help her public image. Despite his claim of being her manager, the whispers from the three Black men suggested something more of a party relationship between the two.

As for me, I was asked to be the story editor-writer on the project due to my sale of a *Dennis the Menace* cartoon episode—"The Backyard Band"—to DIC Entertainment, televised in 1985. I would develop the show's bible, containing the character descriptions and episode plots that centered on the friendship and positive values of the Fresh Kids that enabled them to reject drug use. Eventually, we struck an encouraging note, as one of Conrad's contacts led to our submission to NBC's Children's Programming for its Saturday morning lineup. We waited during that painful phase of hope for NBC's decision. Finally, the news came: Children's Programming decided to develop a show that would feature actor Don Johnson as its host. Why? Our group was told that Don Johnson's popular drama series *Miami Vice* (1984-1989) brought success *and* criticism of its drug-related plots, and the actor was looking for a way to boost a positive, anti-drug image through children's programming.

Conrad wanted to push the project forward, but then the three Black men bickered over the next best step for the animated stories, which led to arguments about who actually owned the characters. I knew the animation project was doomed as the partnership of the three Black men collapsed.

In those final days of my attachment to *The Fresh Kids*, I never saw Lanny and Dana again. It was the evening news that carried the tragedy that became Dana's life. I never knew the details of her background, nor was I privy to the spiraling sadness that led to her death. But for two, maybe three times when we met at her house, she and Lanny were always gracious and friendly, both seemingly riding a wave to the shores of success that they sought in their marriage and careers.

\* \* \*

As I weighed the heaviness of my faded marriage and my fears of being a single parent to my son, I committed myself to fighting any circumstance that would leave my son parentless. No matter the degree of tragedy in my broken marriage, I wouldn't abandon my pledge to being the best father possible. I knew that if I remained faithful to my dreams and my belief in divine guidance, I could and would survive. There was an avalanche of prayers, an endless waterfall of tears, and long nights filled with headaches and insomnia. And as I journaled, I used my writing to give shape to an unrecognizable sadness that had become my life.

That sadness became depression, and that depression possessed me when my crumbling marriage reached the lawyer phase. That phase was prompted by Cheryl's announcement that she was planning to relocate to Houston, Texas, to live with her grandmother—*and* she was taking Derek with her. I rushed to find a lawyer, which was a challenge with my tortured income. Luckily, I came across an attorney who had graduated from Brown University. An older man nearing retirement, he charged me a modest retainer of $1,000, which would set me back about two months from getting my own apartment.

From there, the unsettling negotiations developed. The pendulum of demands and agreements about the material and financial issues of a marriage. I was on a cliff, wanting to jump and be done with conversations and arguments that ruptured my spirit. The cumbersome paperwork, legal meetings, and day in court led to a judgement: Cheryl would remain in the LA area—keeping the house, the most recent car we purchased, and receiving $500 a month from me for Derek's support until he reached eighteen. Since she wasn't working full-time, I was responsible for paying for the car and some of the house bills. Derek was just two years old, and, importantly, I insisted on having him with me once a week—every other weekend, and every other Wednesday. Those payments and visitation schedules became our basic agreement and my new life schedule—which would continue for the following sixteen years.

Eventually, I found an apartment on Jasmine Avenue in Culver City, a small municipality near west Los Angeles. The location gave me quick access to the busy morning commute to Pasadena City College, and it allowed me a twenty-five-minute drive south to the Inglewood house to pick up Derek.

Adjusting to my new single-dad life was difficult. I constantly ached to be with my son. It was a tedious, difficult road I followed, but I promised my two-year-old son I would never leave him. My thoughts circled back to him non-stop—wondering how he was doing, missing his smile and the "Derek sounds" that were unique to him. My divorce and the loss of material things broke me into small pieces, but my son needed me. And of all the things I desired, I needed him. He gave me the courage and hope to face my uncertain future.

\*\*\*

With the publication of *The River Woman* in 1988, I immediately began writing the screenplay based upon that novel. I received encouraging responses to the novel, particularly around Pasadena as I did readings and participated on panel discussions about race relations. At one of those functions, I was approached by Gayle Anthony, a Black freelance journalist who praised my novel to the point of embarrassment. In one of her efforts to get the novel to a wider readership, she wrote a critique of the novel that was published in the December 1988 issue of *Players* magazine. *Players*, a national magazine, was the Black version of *Playboy*. It wasn't my first choice for reaching readers, but I welcomed the opportunity. Gayle wrote a wonderful full-page critique with my photo as an insert.

By the time I finished writing the screenplay, I was encouraged by various writers to submit it to the Nicholls Screenwriting Fellowship, an annual competition that searched for new screenwriters, providing a fellowship to write and serving as an introduction to agents. To my pleasure, I made my way through the first cut of hundreds of scripts to eventually reach the quarter-final round of inclusion. Although I was hoping to be a finalist, I was pleased with making it as deep into the competition as I did.

I received several calls from agents indicating their appreciation of my writing and encouraging me to submit something *new* in the future. However, there was one call that excited me—an agent wanted to meet with me to talk specifically about *The River Woman* screenplay. On the day of the appointment, I drove forty minutes north from my Culver City apartment to Hollywood, taking La Cienega Boulevard to Fountain Avenue. I parked in a narrow driveway of a modest house with the agent's cottage office in back.

The White agent, in his late forties, was energetic and loquacious, and he introduced a younger White male assistant. The first fifteen minutes of conversation were enjoyable as we discussed the influences and sources for my script's complex plot. Shifting to a discussion about our favorite films, the exchange became more exhilarating. However, the conversation evaporated painfully when the agent said, "This is an original and terrific script you wrote, but . . . I can't sell it as it is."

"I . . . don't understand," I heard myself saying.

"I can't because your protagonist is a Black woman. Can't sell a script with a Black woman in the lead."

"But . . . you said it was a good story," I countered. "It's original."

"Yes, it is, but in this business I'm in, I need something I can sell. So . . . perhaps you can rework the script . . . change the lead."

"But the story's about a Black woman journalist . . . her ancestry and the slavery in her family's past."

"I know, I know," he insisted.

After that, I was angry. I was deaf. I saw his lips moving, but I heard nothing. It was the late 1980s, and the same racist platitudes strangled my ability to breathe the success I sought. Was it this one agent, or was he one of the many? Soon, I was in my car, driving home to Culver City, and appropriately, catching every red light along the way.

\* \* \*

In the desert of my Pasadena City College teaching, there was a refreshing oasis that appeared on the department's bulletin board: an announcement about the dean's lecturer-in-residence, a one-year visiting position in the UCLA Department of English's Writing Programs. The Writing Programs offered composition courses to strengthen undergraduate skills in reading, analyzing, and essay writing that intersected various disciplines. I applied, interviewed, and was accepted as one of two visiting lecturers. The opportunity offered me the chance to break the five-day monotonous routine at Pasadena City College and get back to a university campus. The added benefits would be taking the thirty-minute public bus to the UCLA campus from my Culver City apartment, eliminating the busy, ninety-minute commute to Pasadena. Importantly, changing up the rhythms in my life offered a healing treatment to my post-divorce ailments.

One of the early lessons at UCLA was the reinforcement of the belief that scholarship was defined by a PhD and an academic tome rooted in *high theory* with its concomitant, inscrutable language. But I had discovered through my previous experiences on various campuses that intelligence wasn't necessarily rooted in obscure texts or irrelevant chapters birthed by research and abstract ideas. For me, intellectualism wasn't about concealment, but about revealing and concretizing those issues, ideas, and strategies for self-enlightenment *and* for motivating others. Over the years, some of my colleagues supported my meditations about the intellectual world, but those inhabiting a Research 1 institution, such as UCLA, had already succumbed to the traditional notions of the hierarchy of academia. The truth *was* and *is*—some of the most intelligent people I ever encountered did *not* have a PhD behind their names, nor were they ever awarded a grant, fellowship, or book contract.

\*\*\*

As I began my journey at UCLA, I saw Cheryl once a week when picking up Derek. She and I formed a respectful relationship due to our shared love for our son. However, I was surprised when she sold the Inglewood house and moved to an apartment in Fox Hills, an area with young Black professionals. We had discussed holding onto the Inglewood house as a future gift to Derek, or as a means to pay for his college education. Then, a year or so later, she announced that she was getting married. Her future husband, Braxton, worked at LAX as a mechanic for one of the major airlines. When he and I met, we discussed the reality that I would still be present in Derek's life. He understood, and we agreed to communicate about all things dealing with Derek. However, I was caught off-guard by the announcement that Cheryl and Braxton would be moving to Fontana, a growing community fifty miles east of Los Angeles. The affordable housing in Fontana made the move a smart choice for them, but, for me, it meant a two-hour drive one-way to spend time with Derek.

I was able to maintain that visiting schedule during the first year I was at UCLA, but then I was awarded a second year as a visiting lecturer-in-residence. To maintain my consistency in Derek's life, I moved from my Culver City apartment and, through prayer and supplication I eventually bought a small house in Mira Loma, which was a ten-minute drive from Cheryl and Braxton's Fontana house. I was proud to qualify for my three mini-bedroom and two-bath house on my own. However, I was deeply in debt again, committed to a mortgage and the need for a new vehicle to drive the miles that had become part of my commute back and forth to the city.

\*\*\*

Despite the busy commuting and teaching schedule, I juggled my campus obligations with my creative projects. *The River Woman* novel would never be a "bestseller" without national marketing, newspaper ads, or magazine reviews, but it was still selling locally at bookstores and at readings that I would give. So, I leaped into my next novel, *A Room Without Doors*, the story of a Black father and his son migrating from the Deep South into New England. It was told through the son's perspective as he created a family of friends—Jewish, Chinese, and White. By the winter of 1993, I had written and revised fourteen chapters of the manuscript, sending the pages off to the Sandra Dijkstra agency near San Diego. During that time, I had two short stories accepted for publication: "The Promise" in *Emergences*, a UCLA publication, and "Voices" in the *Words of Wisdom* journal, an East Coast publication.

Being a father, writer, professor, and commuter was exhausting. Each area was demanding, and I sometimes lost focus on the freeway, forgetting where I was going and in which direction. Life became a treadmill that accelerated at a hyper speed, and all I could do was hold on and keep moving.

\*\*\*

In the two years I spent at UCLA, I met four impressive men of contrasting qualities along the personality spectrum—and one woman who changed my life completely.

The initial person I met was Mike Rose, a member on the interview committee when I first applied for the visiting lecturer position. Mike was a professor who was well known on campus and in the academic field of education. His book, *Lives on the Boundaries: Struggles and Achievements of America's Educationally Underprepared* (1989), made a major impact in the education field, followed by ten additional books that he wrote and/or co-wrote while receiving numerous fellowships, grants, and awards. He was the epitome of what a major university desired in a professor—a popular professor and a Scholar who remained a researcher and writer over the decades of his career.

However, Mike possessed an additional trait often absent from other academics: he didn't flaunt his celebrity Scholar status. In the twenty-six years that we remained friends until his death in 2021, Mike's humor and humility underscored the best of what existed among educators. His support and insight helped me navigate my two years at UCLA and long after, as he encouraged me to maintain my dreams. Mike was that listening ear who always took the time to keep me grounded and focused on the writing that was important to me, not on the trappings of academia.

In a similar manner, Teshome Gabriel was an outstanding Black scholar and professor in the UCLA School of Theater, Film and Television. We met during the first summer that I taught the composition classes in the campus's Academic Advancement Program. An Ethiopian-born cinema expert, Teshome taught a critical class in World Cinema that demanded students to rise to levels of analysis that challenged and stimulated their intellectual growth. In one of the many conversations we had, he assessed his distinguished recognition in film studies.

"Mel, it's all bullshit," Teshome said over coffee. "This is just the White institution's way of setting their pretentious requirements as the model for intellectualism."

Teshome understood and addressed the scholarship expected of him at a Research 1 institution. However, we often talked about the decades of Black actors wearing the screen masks of the clown and buffoon in order to navigate the movie industry that limited the growth and recognition of their talents. Similar to Mike Rose, Teshome never began a conversation with his academic credentials. However, his book, *Third Cinema in the Third World: The Aesthetics of Liberation* (1982), helped me in my later book-length study about Black film directors.

On the other end of the academic spectrum, I first connected with Jess Mowry over my campus phone. He reached me through the Sandra Dijkstra Agency where I had submitted my work, and as it turned out, his first book of short stories, *Rats in the Trees* (1990), had been published by John and Susan Daniels, my editor-publishers in Santa Barbara. With the agency and publisher in common, he was open to talk with a fellow writer.

Jess had an interracial background due to his Black father and White mother. His voice was deep, and he spoke slowly in articulating his thoughts. From his Mississippi background, Jess was raised in Oakland, California, and his childhood through adolescence had been rough and hard-edged. His writing focused on that urban scape that often smothered adolescent hopes, destroying the spiritual and physical lives of his characters. But at the time of that first call, he was at a curious intersection on his career path—a former homeless kid and gang member turned author being offered six-figure deal by Disney Productions to write the screenplay based upon his third published novel, *Way Past Cool* (1992). The book was doing well with critics and the reading public, and with that introduction, he asked me for my thoughts. I was humbled that he would have such confidence in my perspectives without ever meeting me face to face. I told him that despite the current fascination with 'hood films, such as *Boyz N the Hood* (1991), *New Jack City* (1991), and *Juice* (1992), Disney would sanitize his story to make it more "appropriate" for its targeted audience. It wouldn't be the worst thing that could happen, but the movie would certainly be different from the presentation of the Oakland street life that he wrote. By 2020, Jess had written nineteen books, and he remained committed to uplifting street kids and providing a look into a world they didn't create but had to survive. Over the years, we remained friends, encouraging one another as we wrote our truths across blank pages.

In contrast, at the beginning of my second year of teaching at UCLA, I had a student who I recognized but couldn't place initially. It took a couple of days of reading the class roster before his family's name connected. Sean Astin was one of those young actors who followed his parents into the entertainment business. He had come to prominence in a number of television and big screen films, and with his wife, Christine, in my class as well, they brought dedicated and often confrontational perspectives to class discussions. As a proud Christian, Sean never held back on his comments, especially against homosexuality. In several classes, we battled verbally about his Bible belief against homosexuality and my Christian acceptance and defense of homosexuality and feminism. We counter-punched and exchanged interpretations of verses that kept the class engaged—and I loved it! Sean won praise on the big screen for starring in the titular role of *Rudy* (1993) and years later as Sam in the *Lord of the Rings* series.

\*\*\*

In addition to the men I met during the two UCLA years, my life was changed by one remarkable woman. Toward the end of UCLA's fall quarter in 1992, I crossed paths on campus with Beverly Tate, a beautiful Black woman who showed little interest in me. A high school teacher at the time, Beverly was one of fifteen secondary teachers receiving a year-long fellowship from the American Council of Learned Societies (ACLS), with the organization's initial meetings being held on the UCLA campus.

A week after our first introduction, Beverly tracked me down to gather information on African American images in movies. From there, we met and talked, and met some more, sharing our divorce histories and commitment as single parents to our sons. Both our parents had migrated from the South—Tennessee for her folks and Georgia-Florida for mine. Beverly was intelligent, independent, a devoted educator, *and* she was an undeniable bibliophile. But the location of her Simi Valley condo from my Mira Loma house would require a more than two-and-a-half-hour drive west one way. We had that "geographically undesirable" distance that broke up some LA-area relationships. However, we continued to edge closer through phone calls, dinner dates, weekend movie nights, and tennis matches. After a series of moves and counter-moves, we continued sharing the various hills and valleys of past experiences. Importantly, we intersected at our perspectives about parenting, religion, arts and culture, careers, race, and politics.

Eventually, Beverly traveled with me to Cape Cod, meeting my family and tribe of friends. Soon, thereafter, I suggested that we move in together in her condo. Moving in with a single mom was a new challenge, and for her, having to accept my crazy schedule as a single dad effected our "together" time. Between our work obligations and my daddy schedule, we stepped into an unfamiliar world. Yet, we both took the leap, and during the next few years, we grew closer as we listened; loved; argued; attended academic conferences; and traveled together.

After knowing one another for several years, I did the most romantic thing ever at that time in my life. In July 1995, as Beverly and I drove for a weekend in San Diego, I told her to look inside the glove compartment. She removed an envelope that contained the end results of months of my secret planning: two tickets to Maui and a three-night stay at a resort hotel. She released a flurry of questions, and in anticipation, I had answers. From LAX, we flew into Kahului Airport, arriving at the Maui Prince Hotel at Makena Beach. After dinner that night, I gave her a ring and proposed. She replied "Yes," and to her question of "When?" I replied, "Tomorrow afternoon." The following morning, we purchased our Hawaiian-inspired attire, and by the afternoon, we met the minister, a woman cleric I had contacted through letters and phone conversations. The minister brought forms for us to sign, her portable music box, and the photographer/witness, and Beverly and I were married on the grassy park overlooking Makena Beach.

It was a singular, unforgettable weekend. I was very much in love with Beverly, and my leap into marriage again was based upon our distinctive relationship. We both had experienced the "crookeds" in marriage, but we took a step forward, focusing on the "straights" of the relationship we would build together. Learning from our past experiences, our maturity and faith gave us hope.

CHAPTER THIRTEEN

## Promises and Prayers

During my second year at UCLA, I was approached by a representative of St. Martin's Press to serve as the editor of an African American anthology. Representatives from established publishing houses were common and expected faces on campuses—promoting a company's current publications and searching for new pitches for undergraduate textbooks and scholarly research in progress. In her late twenties, Krissy Masters was a rep younger than most who frequently visited UCLA's Department of English and Writing Programs. She claimed she had gathered information about my background from Pasadena City College to the UCLA campus, and she commended my varied teaching and writing experiences that would contribute to a younger vision for an undergraduate anthology.

Years had passed since anthologies about Black authors appeared on bookstore and library shelves in the late 1960s and 1970s. By 1995, there was a need for maintaining and updating the breadth of the growing African American Literature tradition. The task was daunting: reading and researching; collecting original materials; writing editorial text and biographical information; gathering permissions from authors or their estates; and organizing all introductory and end information. The completed anthology—*Cornerstones: An Anthology of African American Literature*—would include ninety-nine authors and 144 selections. Beginning the project while at UCLA allowed me access to campus libraries, but returning to Pasadena City College in the fall of 1993 with a heavier teaching schedule impacted my available time for the anthology.

So, I applied for a sabbatical for the 1994-95 academic year, and it was approved, providing the time needed to pursue the anthology. My 1001-page anthology covered various historical periods, authors, and genres, and I completed all of the critical and historical assessments and biographical materials myself. After the years of researching, editing, and writing, I was extremely proud—and exhausted. Published in 1996, *Cornerstones* contributed to an academic and popular recognition of a body of creative expressions from generations of Black authors. I was proud of that tradition, as I still worked to have my creative writing included as a significant author within that tradition.

As I journeyed through the many stages and years of developing the anthology, I also wrote and completed my novel, *A Room Without Doors*, and began looking for an agent. With multi-ethnic characters searching for their well-earned places in America, the novel explored topics of family, friendship, and interracial relationships. After rejections from numerous agents, the novel finally found acceptance with the Marie Brown Agency in New York. I was ecstatic, knowing that the novel was accepted by the best literary agency headed by a Black woman.

However, after a year of submissions to major publishers, *A Room Without Doors* wasn't selected for publication. One publisher suggested that there were already numerous books about Black father-son relationships—which was a lie. Perhaps the publisher was thinking about that relationship appearing in children's literature, but my novel wasn't targeting that readership. More emphatically, how many published books were still being placed on bookstore shelves about White father-son relationships in various genres? Another publisher indicated it might be interested if I rewrote the novel to focus more on the New England environment without the Southern racism included.

I was frustrated and disappointed, hoping the novel would find access to a wide readership. The rejection of my novel was a familiar déjà vu nightmare, as the powers in charge always found *something* missing or placed some impediment that prevented publication.

\* \* \*

After Beverly and I married, we lived at her two-story condo in Simi Valley, a bedroom community of about 120,000 people, located about thirty-five miles from downtown Los Angeles. Black folks were perhaps 1 percent of the population, and her primary reason for buying and living in the area was to provide the safest environment possible for her son, Adam, away from the big-city realities of crime and gang activity. I understood, which mirrored my support for Derek's mom and stepdad moving east to Fontana to obtain a house and a safer environment for Derek and his siblings. However, in 1993, when Beverly began teaching in the English Department at Pasadena City College, we discussed buying a house in Pasadena.

At the same time, the aftermath of two events convinced us it was time to leave the small city of Simi Valley. The first occurred during 1991-1992 when the Rodney King high-speed chase and subsequent police beating dominated the news. Although Mr. King's 1991 physical attack was captured on video, the four accused officers were found not guilty by a jury trial held in—Simi Valley. There was a toxic cloud of attention hanging over Simi Valley, and the majority White population always seemed to be watching me and Beverly to see if we were watching them. It was a peculiar, uncomfortable atmosphere.

The second event was in 1994, when the 6.7 Northridge earthquake shook Beverly's second-floor condo without mercy, leaving the whole building red-tagged for a week as FEMA and the Home Owners Association sorted out financial issues. The Northridge epicenter was about twenty miles east of Simi Valley, where over fifty people died. It was a four thirty a.m. wake-up quake that convinced us that another space would be a better choice.

So, we searched the Pasadena area for a new home, eventually settling into a small, two-bedroom house with a family room and a backyard. The house was located in foothill town of Sierra Madre, the village contiguous to the east of Pasadena. Sierra Madre was a bucolic setting with a Black population of less than 1 percent, and its most notable claim was serving as the setting for the film, *The Invasion of the Body Snatchers* (1956). However, the location allowed us a ten-minute drive to our jobs on the PCC campus, reducing my freeway travel time for my once a week visit with Derek.

\* \* \*

Settling into the Pasadena area offered another bonus—I connected with Wilfred "Pepie" Samuels, my friend from my University of Iowa days. By the late 1990s, he had served as a professor at several universities, planting firmly at the University of Utah's Department of English and serving as chairperson of the African American Studies program. Although originally from Costa Rica, Pepie was raised in Pasadena. Receiving a call on my campus phone, he confessed he saw my name on the PCC English Department faculty listing, and our reunion was as smooth and effortless as if only days, rather than years, had passed.

Pepie was a member of the American Literature Association (ALA), an academic organization dedicated to researching and writing about the significance and influence of American authors across the decades. Pepie was the president of the African American Literature and Culture Society, one of the many subgroups that comprised the ALA. With an annual conference each Memorial Day weekend, and many smaller symposia throughout the year, the ALA offered an avenue into the current research and publications about American literature and culture. Over the next ten years, Beverly and I remained active, presenting papers at conferences scheduled in various locales.

In addition to the participation and traveling we did through the ALA, Beverly and I also attended a conference of the Collegium of African American

Research (CAAR), which was an international group of scholars who conducted research and critical writings on various aspects of African American culture. The organization revealed that White scholars outside of America were more enthusiastic and curious about Black culture than White American scholars. So, we attended CAAR's conference in Liverpool, England, which included a tour of the International Slavery Museum situated at the Liverpool docks. The museum emphasized the city's role in the Transatlantic Slave Trade, highlighting the participation of both the country of England and individual British citizens.

During one ceremony at the museum, the publication of the *Norton Anthology of African American Literature* (1996) was honored. Black scholar Dr. Henry Louis Gates, Jr., the book's main editor, was present and spoke about the significance of the museum and his anthology, emphasizing the inextricable connection between the Black African diaspora and the oral and written traditions comprising African American culture. My book, *Cornerstones: An Anthology of African American Literature*, had also been published in 1996, and at the completion of the ceremony, Dr. Gates and I shared a brief discussion about the challenges of editing a literary anthology.

I was pleased that my anthology was on bookshelves nation-wide. And as Beverly reminded me, the lasting accomplishment of *Cornerstones* was that it was instrumental in revitalizing the significance, complexity, and relevance of the African American literary tradition. Beverly was correct, and I was proud to have contributed to that literary and cultural tradition.

\* \* \*

By the late 1990s, my friend, Reggie McDowell, was the manager at the Sheraton Universal Hotel in Los Angeles, and for years, he had been a listening ear to my efforts at writing and filmmaking. Due to his hotel's location, several television and film celebrities resided at the hotel. Reggie met numerous people in the entertainment business, including his friend, producer Jackie George. Jackie and I were comfortable with one another from the beginning. She had taken an impressive journey through the movie business, working on films that starred popular names. However, as a woman, she had to navigate the gender minefield, where men owned the arsenal of power and decision-making. Fighting consistent barriers, her filmmaking bio included a range of movies that gave her contacts and real-time experiences in feature films. She had worked in various capacities as a producer on *Born in East LA* (1987); *Die Hard 2* (1990); *Out for Justice* (1991); *Demolition Man* (1993); *Batman and Robin* (1997); *Eye of the Beholder* (1999); and *The Cheetah Girls* (2003), and more.

As Jackie and I talked about the story and feature film possibilities of *A Room Without Doors*, she suggested we might find an appreciation for the project with Greystone Films, an independent company. Agreeing to work together, Jackie and I wrangled our way into Greystone Films to meet with executive producer Bill Winston. Bill had a background in radio, which was affirmed by his resonant broadcaster's voice. He was cordial and engaging, describing years of experience on film projects. Working as an assistant to noted actor Robert Duvall from the late 1980s to mid-1990s, Bill served as a co-producer on the feature film, *A Family Thing* (1996), which starred Duvall, James Earl Jones, Michael Beach, and Irma P. Hall.

When Bill read *A Room Without Doors*, he liked my script, but he indicated that his company wasn't in a financial position to buy or option it due to the completion and release of the company's first family movie, *Lunker Lake* (1998). So, with no possibility of Greystone Films funding the feature film, Bill suggested that he and I work together to develop the project with Jackie George serving as the line producer once we went into production.

It was new territory for me to actively participate in a producer's capacity, since writing had always been my focus. However, Bill encouraged my casting ideas, asking my thoughts on Michael Beach in the lead role of the father. I definitely supported Mr. Beach as the strong father, based upon his memorable performances in the films *One False Move* (1992) and *Soul Food* (1996). So, Bill got a copy of the full script off to Mr. Beach for the part.

At the same time, Bill sent me a contract to my home fax machine that detailed our business relationship regarding the film. I shared the document with Jackie for her feedback. The contract's particulars included the major points: my co-producer credit; my writer's credit; a writer's fee to be negotiated between $75,000-$150,000; a fifty-fifty split of the net profits between me and Greystone Films. I was orbiting in an atmosphere of the most high joy!

As the project simmered on low flames for the following months, Beverly and I were invited to attend Greystone Films' Christmas party at a popular restaurant in Santa Monica. Bill introduced us to his wife and then disappeared into the exuberant throng of 200 guests filling the restaurant. I met Mr. Beach and had a pleasant chat, discovering that he was from Wareham, Massachusetts, a small town about forty minutes from my Hyannis roots. We spoke about *A Room Without Doors*, and he admitted that he hadn't committed to the project yet as he was still reading the 140-page script.

At that point, Mr. Beach was pulled away into another conversation, and Beverly and I settled at a table with actor Tom Bower and his wife. Mr. Bower had recently appeared in the race-related drama, *White Man's Burden* (1995), with John Travolta and Harry Belafonte. But Mr. Bower had become popular for his role as Marvin, the airport basement supervisor in *Die Hard 2* (1990). He was a thoughtful, articulate man who was putting much of his time and energy into working with stage theater projects in Santa Monica.

Unquestionably, it was an enjoyable night. There were numerous actors and celebrities present, and I was confident that the project was still heading in a positive direction. As I waited during the next few months, good news developed in the Scholar area of my life. My book proposal for the study of Black film directors was accepted by the University of Texas Press. I was excited to have the opportunity to develop a critical book that intersected with my efforts in filmmaking. So, the research and development of that text was my parallel universe of writing, as I explored the racial, cultural, and business elements of developing and directing feature films for the big screen.

At the same time, I was contacted by an old friend—Black producer Conrad Bullard. He passed along information about a possible writing job with John Horne Entertainment, a new Black production company launching its way into feature projects. Horne Entertainment was located on Wilshire Boulevard in Beverly Hills, inside the building where *Hustler* magazine had its administration offices. Horne Entertainment was developing a film titled *Unconditional Love*, and the company wanted a novelization of that film's script. The novel would serve as a marketing tool to give the movie a wider audience, and Conrad had recommended me to write the book.

By February 1998, *A Room Without Doors* hadn't moved forward with much speed. However, Greystone Films released its second feature, *Left Luggage* (1998), starring Isabella Rossellini. The film made it into the Berlin Film Festival, and Bill Winston planned to travel to Germany to attend. The day before he left, he shared that he attended a special awards dinner hosted by Showtime Cable TV. In attendance was Black director Kasi Lemmons, and he asked her to direct *A Room Without Doors*. She was unavailable to participate in our film, but she suggested a new direction going forward—to make *A Room Without Doors* first as a short film to attract investors for the feature-length version. Ms. Lemmons wrote and directed the short film, *Dr. Hugo* (1996), as a prelude to writing and directing her captivating feature, *Eve's Bayou* (1997). Brad suggested we follow the same plan of action with *me* as the writer-director of the short film version of *A Room Without Doors*. I was surprised and flattered, but I felt the impact of the original story might suffer if made as a thirty-minute film. Yet, I understood that to serve as director would give me a major opportunity to move deeper into filmmaking. Without much convincing, I proceeded to transform my 140-page screenplay into a thirty-page script for a short film.

In a rush of meetings, Bill and I discussed the shaping of a short film, weighing which plot elements needed to be included. Bill liked my ideas, and he spoke with Pearlena Igbokwe, who was the head of development at Showtime. (Years later, she moved to NBC's Department of Drama Development before becoming the first Black African woman president of Universal Television). Pearlena encouraged the short film version, informing Bill that the film would have to be completed by the fall in order to qualify for Showtime's Black Filmmaker's Showcase.

In early March 1998, things began to be—*peculiar*. Bill and Jackie had some disagreements about the characters in the short, and Bill's low rumble of displeasure grew louder with his insistence that Jackie avoid the film's creative aspect and simply serve as the line producer. Typically, a line producer took charge of hiring crew members, maintaining the film's budget, and keeping the production on schedule. I awkwardly found myself in between the two of them, attempting to keep things positive and peaceful.

The plan was to shoot the short film in 35mm film to provide the most polished, professional visual quality. Jackie developed a budget and shooting schedule—$61,000, which was about $30,000 over what Bill wanted. So, looking for ways to cut cost, I followed up on some possibilities: getting an Eastman Kodak film discount; using my Sierra Madre house as the main set; using my next door neighbor's house for production headquarters; rewriting scenes and locations; and eliminating some characters.

Jackie and I convinced Michael Beach to participate in the short film, and with Paulette's help, I reached out to veteran Black actors Dick Anthony Williams and Lloyd Roseman. Dick was a veteran performer whose resume included numerous films, including *The Lost Man* (1969), *The Anderson Tapes* (1971), *The Mack* (1973), *Dog Day Afternoon* (1975), *Edwards Scissorhands* (1990), as well as a plethora of television credits. On his part, Lloyd had performed in numerous community theater stage projects.

As Bill was busy completing his obligations for Greystone Films, Jackie stepped up and took charge of some of the hands-on duties—in particular, reaching out to her connections for the necessary crew, including director of photography, sound, gaffer, script supervisor, makeup, wardrobe, props, and sound editing, and importantly, the director of photography and the first assistant director.

Jackie took the big leap into negotiating our pay scale—"Favored Nations," a policy that all participants in the film, including Michael Beach, would receive the same daily salary. Somehow, Jackie massaged the budget down from $50,000 to $20,000. My significant hurdle was getting Beverly on board for using our house as the main interior and exterior sets.

Throughout the entire shoot, Michael Beach was wonderful to work with. Despite the modest size of the short film, he approached our project with professionalism, interacting with the other cast members and crew without an inflated ego or special considerations. In addition to Michael, we had veteran Black actors Dick Anthony Williams, Shelley Robertson, and Lloyd Roseman. Completing the cast were four younger actors: Ron Robinson, Alissa Ann Smego, Darius Rollins, and my twelve-year-old son, Derek.

On his part, Bill Winston disappeared and was not communicating. I knew he was out of town and looking for funding, but previously he would connect and update me. But suddenly, it was—silence. So, we pressed forward, knowing that we had a window of time to have our major star and to have the film completed in time for submission to the Showtime competition.

From there, I recruited my brother, Brian, to compose the original music. He had been honing his skills as a music producer while working a full-time job at a Hollywood sound equipment company. Jackie brought on Black actress Cynda Williams to co-write and sing her song, "With You," over the end credits. Cynda had been gaining popularity and attention with her impressive performances in *Mo' Better Blues* (1990) and *One False Move* (1992).

Bill was still unreachable, and I was nervous. We had a talented group of people in front of the camera, as well as a mix of experience and newcomers behind the camera—including myself as I studied and prepared to direct the project. The only thing we didn't have as our shooting schedule crept closer—full funding. I contacted Reggie McDowell and asked him to invest in the movie. He provided $2,000, but we were still $18,000 short the week before the scheduled shoot. I was a gaggle of nerve endings during sleepless nights.

Then, a couple of days before the shoot, I finally heard from Bill. He had health issues—the shingles. He had pulled back from all of his work, travel, and friends. Even as I was glad to hear from him, I was fuming, explaining that Jackie had done the heavy lifting to bring cast and crew together. Bill's response was that we should postpone the shoot, arguing that he was still actively seeking money. I insisted that we couldn't postpone, as we had people—including Michael Beach—who had locked in their schedules for our shooting calendar. Bill was angry because he felt that Jackie and I had taken the film project from him, deliberately cutting him out. In his anger, he said he wouldn't deliver the funding he had already raised. I shared the phone discussion with Jackie, and she was furious at Bill for holding back the money two days before the shoot. She had put her reputation on the line, calling in favors and making promises in order the bring in the crew.

Then, the day before shooting was to begin, Bill faxed me a *copy* of a $10,000 check from his funding source. It was his proof that he had found an investor, but he wouldn't be providing the money to me. I endured a new level of stress. It was a palpable, living monster that shadowed me at first. Then, in a sadistic manner, the creature attached itself to my chest, allowing me to breathe just enough to suffer. The joy of writing and directing my first film dissolved into a swamp of regret, as the days and hours of work during the past year brought me to a ledge of a breakdown. And somewhere between insomnia and desperation, I had only one possible strategy that slowly came to me.

I had already convinced Beverly to allow us to use our Sierra Madre house for the actual shoot with furniture being moved, strangers storming throughout the house, and the interior uninhabitable for twelve hours for each of the five shooting days. But the more difficult request to Beverly—to allow me to take $13,000 out of our $15,000 savings (we had to keep something in the account to keep it open). The moments of silence between my request and her answer aged me several years. And when her positive voice touched my ear, I took a breath—she stuck by me.

I, then, asked Jackie to carry the weight of being both the line producer and producer to keep me immune from the inevitable problems, anxieties, and confusion on the set that would develop. To keep me away from the nervous energy at my neighbor's house where makeup, wardrobe, and eating services would be situated. I needed her to take on the craft services role, ensuring that she had food and drinks available while I concentrated on the performances of the actors and the communication with my director of photography, Eric Goldstein, to develop the visual quality the film needed. I asked Jackie to convince everyone that their payments would be available at the end of the shoot, even as we faced the post-production needs—film development, editing, sound design, coloring, and the titles for opening and end credits.

Then, I reached out to John Horne Entertainment, getting a commitment from the company that I could receive a down payment of the $5,000 promised for writing the novelization of the film *Unconditional Love*. And I promised I would have the first draft of the novel to the company within a week. Basically, that meant I had to write the novel during lunch breaks in the five-day shoot and then late into the evenings after filming. So, with Reggie's investment, our savings, and the writing of the novel, I would cover the film's budget.

The actual shooting days were long and challenging. With the magical work of my film editor, Tina Imahara, the film took the professional shape and appearance I'd hoped for. Once the music, end credits, and theme song were laid, we had a 35mm film that we were proud of. We submitted the DVD copies of our film to various film festivals, gaining acceptance and screening in thirteen. These included the New York Independent Film and Video Festival;

the Hollywood Black Film Festival; the Urban World Film Festival; The Black Harvest Film Festival; the African American Film Marketplace; the Hollywood Entertainment Museum Film Festival; the Roxbury Film Fest; *and* the Showtime Network's Black Filmmaker's Showcase. Chosen as one of the five finalists, *A Room Without Doors* was broadcast on the Showtime network with my personal interview shown before the screening.

Making my first narrative film was an unforgettable experience of hard work, mistakes, and accomplishment. At the same time, it was the kind of filmmaking experience that I never wanted to go through again—until next time.

CHAPTER FOURTEEN

# Nights of Dreams, Mornings of Hope

By the summer of 1998, I was both wounded and elated after completing *A Room Without Doors*. At various festivals and screenings, I met filmmakers like me who were working earnestly to advance short works into feature films. I submitted to film festivals, while searching for agents and funding for a feature film.

I was particularly seeking funding to replenish my savings account and to make sure I could support my son's needs as he was moving full speed toward being a teenager. Through one of my contacts, I connected with a "packager" of entertainment projects with venture capitalists. Amadi Njoku, a Nigerian businessman, agreed to meet with me at a hotel restaurant in the West Hollywood area. Having read the materials I forwarded, he was enthusiastic about the feature version of *A Room Without Doors*, though he wouldn't divulge the details about his financial sources. He affirmed that he was the middle man, for which he would get a finder's fee, assuring me that my request of a $2 million budget was within the investment range of his sources.

So, as promised, he got back to me within a couple of weeks. One potential investor he found had questions about the audience, the expected film rating, and the length of time it would take to see returns. I explained what I knew and what I expected, using similar dramatic theatrical films as comparisons for our possible profits. The back and forth continued for several weeks, but the potential investors decided to invest in a "dot.com" company which they believed would offer better financial returns.

So, Amadi approached a second investment group that showed a keen interest in my feature film project. The group came back and wanted to know who would direct the film. Basically, the group wanted me to get Spike Lee. I indicated to Amadi that Spike was already working on a project, and that his documentary, *4 Little Girls* (1997), and fictional film, *He Got Game* (1998), were recent releases that kept Spike *the* go-to Black director. Besides, I argued that *I* knew the story better than anyone, and my salary as writer-producer-director combined would be less than Spike's salary as director. So, the group then came back and asked if I could get Denzel Washington to play the lead instead of Michael Beach. I responded that from what I read in the press, for his lead role in *He Got Game*, Mr. Washington's salary alone was four times the proposed budget for *A Room Without Doors*, and he already had several projects lined up for years to come. After that, there were no further questions, and Amadi Njoku disappeared as well. No returned calls to my messages.

Having weathered the difficulties of completing my short film, I took Amadi Njoku's business journey in stride. Then, a new possibility surfaced when I met with an independent production company with offices in a small North Hollywood building. The three-man company was looking for a Black writer to craft an inner-city gang drama based on the real-life experiences of a former Los Angeles gang leader. The working title for their feature film was *From Cradle to Grave*, and once they indicated a $5,000 writer's salary, I was in. The partners gave me files of biographical information, and along with my own research, I set out to do an outstanding job under a rigid thirty-day time frame. During two additional meetings, I updated and discussed my progress at their office space, knocking out a ninety-page script in a few weeks. I was proud of what I submitted. More importantly, the producers were pleased as well, and when I got my check, I smiled all the way home.

I went straight to my local bank, deposited the check, and told Beverly we would immediately pay our bills from the check to suture the hemorrhaging of our accounts caused by *A Room Without Doors*. A week later, I received a message from my local bank—my checks for our bills were bouncing. I hurried to the bank and showed them the receipt of my deposited writer's check to address the mistake, but . . . the mistake, unfortunately, was the check I deposited. I hurried back to the North Hollywood offices of the independent company, and as I entered the small office space, there was *nothing* and *no one*—except the building owner who angrily asked me where the producers were. They owed him rent, and he swore he would find them and collect. So, it was a slow drive home, where, once again, I had to explain the situation to Beverly.

\* \* \*

By the time the fall semester began at Pasadena City College, I was back in the classroom, teaching one literature and three composition classes. I was weary from the roller coaster experience with the independent film company. Having dozens of student essays coming my way during the semester, I fell into an academic depression, but I reminded myself that to have a steady job was a blessing.

I was, then, contacted by producer Conrad Bullard again, who assured me that he had a unique project he wanted me involved in. It was a documentary project called *African Tapestry*, which would focus on the country of South Africa. It was being funded by Matt Lansing, a Black real estate investor in San Diego. With the connections he had already established with South African filmmakers, Conrad proposed a film to explore the cultural elements within the country despite the oppressive history of Apartheid. He wanted me to be the lead researcher and writer on the project, and he would serve as producer-director. I would join him, his wife Delores, and production manager Bruce Cecil as part of a development team. The four of us would travel to South Africa, searching for archival films in Pretoria; meeting local filmmakers in Johannesburg; and building connections with academics in Cape Town. If our initial trip went well, we would finalize contracts and shooting schedules, and in early 1999 we would return to South Africa to shoot the documentary.

On November 1, Beverly dropped me off at LAX, and our team took our six-hour flight into JFK in New York, connecting with our fourteen-and-a-half-hour flight to Johannesburg on South Africa Airlines. It was a lengthy journey, and one hour before landing, I looked out my window and took in the soft morning light layered atop a tan-colored landscape. In the distance, a union of clouds parted on the horizon, allowing the sunlight to shimmer. Closer to our destination, the landscape transformed into textures as ridges and hills came into view. The colors also changed when the tanned topography became dappled with red, black, and brown swirls running throughout the terrain.

My romantic vision was tempered when one of the passengers—an Indian man—shared with my team that he was traveling to attend his brother's funeral in Johannesburg. His brother, a store owner, had been shot during a robbery, and as he narrated the story, the mournful man warned us to be careful and to avoid Johannesburg's streets at night. Coming from the Los Angeles area with its street gang clashes and the post-LA riot years, my team wasn't frightened, but we certainly reflected on the reality of where we were going. Flying into South Africa at the beginning of November 1998 was a particularly fascinating time. We arrived during the week when the Truth and Reconciliation Commission, led by Bishop Desmond Tutu, released its conclusions for the strategies to unify the country after generations of the Apartheid-related crimes against the Black majority.

We were met at the airport by Constance Beresford, a White South African filmmaker. She was a forty-something woman with short, blonde hair; a lean frame and rugged-looking face spoke of her experience. Through her company called Beyond Films, she flew in and around all parts of the African continent.

Constance and her Black driver drove us to the Courtyard Villas in an area called Sandton, which was considered a "nice area." I saw an abundance of Black people—brothers and sistas with natural hair styles and some in braids, their clothes suggesting their positions in the working class. At dinner that first night, we met Constance's working partner, Pierre, a White filmmaker with a pleasant demeanor, and Tony Wasserman, a garrulous fifty-something White cinematographer, who frequently freelanced for NBC.

Before arriving, Conrad had shared months of discussions with Constance and Tony about our project, receiving suggestions on where to locate personnel and hard copy archives in Johannesburg and in Pretoria, the country's capitol city. As we all discussed the dimensions and goals of *African Tapestry*, I was struck by the comfortable, relaxed demeanor the White filmmakers exuded with us four Black Americans, as all three were confident and experienced.

As the conversation drifted to other topics, we shared our encounter with the Indian man on the plane. Constance then confessed that five months earlier, her brother had been shot—twice in the head, three times in the body. He survived without any brain damage as the bullets exited through his face. He lost vision in one eye and had tunnel vision in the other, *but* he was alive. There was no clear evidence as to why he was attacked, but Constance theorized it was due to his perceived status a successful White businessman driving a BMW.

The following day, Conrad and I were driven to Pretoria, where we spent the first of two days at an archival house. I looked over indexes containing old footage dating back to 1939, while Conrad looked through the most recent materials on South Africa. It was a fruitful exploration as we discussed which pieces might serve our needs for shaping our cultural series. By late afternoon, we were at the home of Jurgen Schadeberg, a White filmmaker and photographer in his sixties. He had been a productive writer in the 1950s, publishing several books about the country. He proudly displayed his small library of documentary films, and he agreed to be interviewed on film for *African Tapestry*.

The following morning, Conrad and I returned to the archival house in Pretoria, continuing our viewing of historical, cultural, and entertainment footage. By mid-afternoon, we were back in Johannesburg, and I was looking for gifts for Beverly and family members. That night, we went to a party—arranged by our executive producer Matt Lansing—at the house of a Harvard graduate currently living in Johannesburg and working for Citicorp. The people attending were of various racial backgrounds, professions, and business connections to American companies based in South Africa.

The next day offered a singular voice I'll never forget. After breakfast, we were gathered by our driver for the day—a woman named Thando Makapela.

She took the four of us in her van to the Soweto Township. In the first few minutes of arriving at the township, I was in a peculiar world where a brutal history was meeting a transitional phase of possible forgiveness. One million Black people living in one square mile!

The look of the place reminded me of rural Georgia in the 1950s with its red clay soil spotted with patches of green grass. Dwellings were made of stacked brick with tin roofs or tiled coverings. In some areas, there were just shanties made entirely of tin from top to bottom to sidings. The people were dressed in clothing that announced their poverty: women wore long dresses with their hair wrapped in scarves, and men wore some version of khaki or denim pants and tops. But there were some younger people—apparently students in school uniforms—adorned in much like the wardrobes in the films *A Dry White Season* (1989) and *Sarafina* (1992).

In the central area of the township, a memorial for the June 16, 1976, massacre in Soweto grabbed my attention. This was the area where an estimated 175 Black students were killed and one thousand injured as they protested the forced teaching of the White Afrikaans language in Black schools. It was a protest met with White policemen with automatic weapons and fixed bayonets. The memorial contained trailer cars with photos of the massacre placed around the interior, taken by Peter Magubane. Magubane was a Black photojournalist who worked for *Drum* magazine at the time.

Leaving the memorial, we drove through the township, stopping at a small restaurant called Winnie's Place, which served African foods and a traditional African beer called "Umqombothi." This mixture was made over a one-week period from corn, yeast, and malt that was cooked together, left to ferment, cooked again, and then fermented again. Then, the beer was placed in a bowl-like container and served by a woman who tasted the drink first to show the men it was poison-free. The beer was served at room temperature—thick and gritty on the tongue, with a pungent odor similar to that of urine.

Traveling through the township, I was struck by the physical conditions—the shanties and outdoor markets selling vegetables, fruit, and chickens, as well as the dozens of people who didn't show desperation and sadness on their faces, despite lives framed within physical limitations. I particularly wondered about the children that I saw—their dreams and possibilities. I thought about my son, Derek, and what kind of hope he would find if he were locked within this kind of environment. As a parent, what do you tell your child about the truth of their lives when chained to the township? How would we fashion that environment within our documentary while giving the people living there the dignity they deserved?

On the way back to our villas, Conrad needed a bank, and Thando found one that she felt would meet his needs. Waiting in the van, my team members and I reflected out loud about our day in the township, and we drifted back to the Truth and Reconciliation Commission's findings and suggestions, which were published daily in newspapers. We turned to Thando and asked for her thoughts about forgiveness and amnesty of those who did wrong during the Apartheid rule.

There were several moments of silence. At first, I thought that she possibly didn't hear the question we asked. She turned and looked at us, and her face hardened into a mask of anger.

"Never!" she growled. "I will *never* forgive them!"

The rage in her voice was palpable. Concrete and unyielding. Then, she told us a story we weren't expecting.

*Years earlier, Thando lived with her mother and brother, all supporting one another financially. Her brother was able to get a job as a driver for Winnie Mandela. With her husband, Nelson, still in prison, Winnie was under observation by the White authorities, who monitored her movements and associates. One night, the authorities came to Thando's house and took away her brother. Despite the pleadings of Thando and her mother, her brother was taken without charges or warrants. The following day, Thando, with her mother, went to the police, attempting to find her brother. They received no answers. The same responses continued for the next two days, as Thando and her mother feared the worst. Then, early one morning, a miserable morning, Thando and her mother were awakened by a loud thud against the front door and a roaring engine as a vehicle sped away. Opening the door, Thando saw an oversized canvas bag tightened at the top by a drawstring. She opened the wet bag, and inside she found her brother's dismembered body, his remains mangled into bloody pieces.*

No explanation. No one held accountable. No one found guilty. I was locked deeply within her words, her emotions, her intensity. I was paralyzed by what I heard. In the heavy silence that possessed the interior of the van, I finally whispered—*Jesus!* Part disbelief, part prayer!

The remainder of that day was lost to me. Late into the night, I was possessed by the strangest mood. The reality of what had happened to so many Black people—to so many human beings—locked me inside a deep depression. Then anger. I wanted to reject what I felt, particularly the hate. I didn't sleep. Couldn't sleep. The details of the Black history that I taught to students over the years surfaced in my thoughts—the Middle Passage, the chattel slavery, the Reconstruction Era, the migrations of hope, the lynchings, the marches, the Black Power Movement. And though I only knew Thando for two days, her personal experience struck me with the same collective impact of the horrors of racism that filled those books and essays from which I taught and reflected.

The next day, we prepared to visit the city of Cape Town, but we were cautioned by our Johannesburg friends to fly there instead of driving. The two-hour flight would be more expensive, but it would be safer and less exhausting than the fourteen-hour drive. The flight allowed Conrad and Bruce to discuss the proposed six-week shooting schedule at the end of January, as Bruce considered the budgetary needs for the pilot show and various episodes. When we touched down at Cape Town International Airport, we were met by Gee, our White South African driver who spoke both English and Afrikaans. In her early twenties, Gee was a filmmaker who grew up in Port Elizabeth. Just beyond the airport, we passed a Black township called Crossroads, partially in view from the main highway. We were told that Crossroads was just one of several Black townships in Cape Town.

Gee drove us directly to a scheduled meeting at a government estate to meet Ronnie Kasrils and his wife, Eleanor. The estate was a compound that had several living quarters spread out within its grassy landscape, and the compound itself was situated in back of the mountain range—including the imposing Table Mountain, a looming presence which stood over three thousand feet high, and Devil's Peak, which was a bit shorter. It was a truly singular, beautiful view of a natural scape that defied description.

The Kasrils were White, but they had worked with the African National Congress, a political organization that challenged the Apartheid system. After Mandela's release from prison and his transition into power, Ron Kasrils was appointed as the Deputy Minister of Defense for South Africa. The Kasrils hosted us for lunch, and they were warm and engaging, obviously comfortable being around Black people. Our discussion undulated from the *African Tapestry* documentary project to Ron Kasrils memoir, *Armed and Dangerous*.

It was an afternoon that passed too swiftly, and Gee took us on a route across the mountains that allowed us incredible views of some coastal communities. We found our way to the coastal point, and Gee explained we could see where the Atlantic and Indian Oceans met one another. From that natural beauty of South Africa, we traveled to our residence at a Holiday Inn. After dinner, our evening walk around the area led us to a jazz venue, where we listened to an accomplished Black quartet.

The next morning, we took a two-hour boat ride to Robben Island, touring the prison where Nelson Mandela was incarcerated. The guide at the prison was named "Speech," and he had himself served thirteen years for conspiracy and traveling across the border without official papers. He gave the details of a usual day of working at the prison, and the visit included two sobering moments. The first was stepping inside of Mandela's cell, where I stood in the middle, outstretched my arms, and touched the opposite walls—it was more of a closet than a cell. The second was the visit to the limestone quarry, where the prisoners awoke every miserable morning to break up the white, sun-reflecting stones and carry them from one location to another—all day long, back and forth. Busy work that had no purpose other than physical pain and tedium. The quarry was hell with bright sunlight and monotony. Nelson Mandela spent eighteen of his twenty-seven years of imprisonment there on Robben Island.

When we returned to the mainland and Victoria Market on the oceanfront, we played tourists to soften the head-pounding hours on Robben Island. We added a forty-five-minute drive to another tourist-commercial area called Stollenbosch, where we enjoyed more food and wine at the Spear's Winery. We topped the day off with another stop at Signal Hill, on another side of the Table Mountain landscape, which was just as fascinating as the previous day. I was struck by the sheer beauty of the area, its unique assault upon my senses, a moment of breathlessness and wonder. And I considered the incongruity of how such a beautiful place could harbor such a mockery of life as Apartheid.

On our last full day in Cape Town, Gee drove Conrad, Bruce, and Dee to the archives at the University of the Western Cape, about forty minutes outside of Cape Town. On their way out, they dropped me off at the University of Cape Town in the city. Sitting on a hilltop location, the campus was comprised of older buildings with newer ones springing up in between. My goal was to simply make connections that might be useful when we continued to research for the documentary project. Unannounced, I entered the African Studies Center and spoke to the secretary who indicated that the director would not be in that day, so, leaving my college business card, I told her I would forward information about *African Tapestry*. Afterwards, I explored the campus a bit more before taking a minibus ride back to the hotel to meet the team.

We flew back to the United States on the morning of Monday, November 10, enduring the first, lengthy leg of the journey. For the return trip, the layover was at Miami International Airport as we waited for two hours before connecting to our LAX flight. I was disconnected from any normal perception of time, mentally weary and physically exhausted.

It was comforting to finally reach home to see Beverly and Derek. But it took several weeks before there was any room in my head for thoughts beyond South Africa. Consequently, it was disappointing when, a month later, I learned that the funding for the documentary was falling short. Specifically, Conrad had agreed to allow Matt Lansing to take 50 percent of the funds raised for

*African Tapestry*. This detail was never shared with me before I committed to the documentary series. With that agreement, Conrad would have to raise double the amount of the estimated budget to provide a financial base for the project. Again, I was disappointed in Conrad and that funding structure. It would be impossible to initiate a January start for the project.

I really respected and thought highly of Conrad. I saw him as someone who was skillful and accomplished, someone who knew so many people in the entertainment business. However, I also knew that I wouldn't commit to another project with him. It was a decision I needed for my own creative and personal health. So, as I moved back into the classroom—adjusting my focus to lecturing, correcting papers, holding office hours with students, and attending meetings—I wondered how long I would survive the disappointing winds encompassing the creative and cinematic worlds.

I didn't know the answer to that thought, but I knew that I would never forget the ten days I spent in South Africa.

\* \* \*

Although Beverly and I had our house in Sierra Madre, I still owned the house in Mira Loma. During mid-week visits with Derek, I frequently cooked dinner and shared the evening with him, often staying overnight to make certain the property was maintained and that the utilities were in working order.

On one overnight visit, after returning Derek to his mother's home and ending a "good night" phone conversation with Beverly, I showered and eased into bed, nodding off as the television newscast filled my ears. But it was a brief nap. I woke abruptly when I felt the hard pressure in my right side. The pressure became a dull pain that wouldn't subside. Over the next several minutes, the pain instensified—a deep stabbing from an invisible blade. The tormenting eruption was so severe I levitated above the bed. Like the little girl in *The Exorcist*, I lost control of my body as agony possessed me, jerking me back and forth like a Black ragdoll. I rolled onto the carpet. Attempting to get to my feet, the brutal jolt paralyzed my efforts. I screamed, crawling from the bedroom, along the hallway, toward the kitchen for the wall phone. Losing my mind to the agony, I gritted my teeth. Took deep breaths. My fingers dug into the carpet. Slowly, the intensity subsided and morphed into a dull throbbing in my side.

The visit to my doctor led to a referral to Dr. Schlossberg, a urologist. My symptoms and scans told a story that was quite familiar to him: kidney stones. With Dr. Schlossberg's detailed information about four types of stones, he needed me to capture a stone for analysis. At work on campus, I carried a miniature basket in my briefcase and eventually caught a stone as it passed painfully with my urine stream. Dr. Schlossberg's analysis was that I had calcium oxalate stones, resulting from my constant intake of dark colas with high sugar content; spinach; broccoli; salt; and chocolate with almonds. Like a modern-day Moses, Dr. Schlossberg delivered his basic dietary commandments: thou shall *not* drink caffeinated dark-colored colas and tea, nor eat brocolli, nor consume high-sodium foods! Thou *shall* drink more water each day! As I recited the commandments, I recounted the years of driving the freeways while sucking down colas as my primary travel beverage.

Having that knowledge was enlightening, but my system remained vengeful, as kidney stones continued to appear. Dr. Schlossberg, like a gallant knight of the medical roundtable, fought the stones that assaulted my urinary tract. His weapon of choice was a combination of scans that identified the location of the stones and an outpatient procedure called lithotripsy. The procedure used sound waves to break the stones into small particless, allowing the miniature pieces, *sans* pain, to leave the body in the urine stream.

Beverly served as my corner person each time I fought the stones, helping me to get back into the ring of my work and writing routines. She was the Mickey to my Rocky, and she kept me honest about a more conscientious diet, loaded with an increased water intake.

However, nothing prepared me for the doctor's announcement that a scan revealed one stone had lodged itself into the wall of my bladder. That was the source of the continual throbbing and discomfort I felt. Dr. Schlossberg concluded that he would perform endoscopic surgery to remove the stone. He explained he would complete the procedure using *only* a local anesthesia. Due to the doctor's careful description, I *intellectually* understood the problem and the procedure required. However, there was nothing—short of hypnosis and/or brain removal—that could have prepared me for the procedure.

On the assigned day, when I entered the doctor's chamber of horrors in my drafty hospital gown, I came face to face with "Nurse Marquita de Sade," a sour-looking White woman with an angry disposition and, no doubt, a history of broken relationships. Her fixed frown was chiseled with loathing, as she ordered me onto my back on the cold table. This woman had no knowledge of kindness nor sensitivity. There was no color in her eyes or warmth in her voice. She was irritated with life in general. She barked the first step in the process: "*Local anesthesia.*" She lifted my gown, grabbed my penis in one hand, and with the other hand, she globbed a blue-colored liquid around my abdomen and around the base of my penis. She squeezed and rotated my penis like it was a gear-shift in a rickety, broken-down truck. She was no Picasso, as she painted and layered the blue goop over my body. Then, she barked another order: "*Wait.*" Where the hell would I go—a barefoot, half-naked Black man with a blue-colored penis?

Dr. Schlossberg finally entered the room and spoke briefly to Nurse de Sade. She moved to one side of the table and narrowed her hateful stare at me. I figured she stood ready to choke me to death if the process failed. Narrating aloud as he went, Dr. Schlossberg inserted a thin, lighted tube with a camera into my urethra, edging it forward into my bladder. Along with the camera, there was a miniature claw that would grab and retract the stone from the wall of the bladder. I felt my body tensing at the intrusion of the thin, foreign object, and the top of my head felt close to exploding. Even with the anesthesia, the thin tube felt like a pointed chisel being driven into my soul. It was beyond torture. In an eternity of seconds, I faintly heard Dr. Schlossberg's voice: "*Got it!*" The recoiling of the tubing was quick but magnified in the severity of my torment.

As Beverly drove me home after the procedure, I couldn't describe the ordeal, and she was thoughtful enough to allow the silence to cushion the ride. For all my years as a writer and priding myself in my communication skills, I was speechless. Yet, in my head, I fought against a thought that forced me to face an unwanted truth. At the junction of being in my mid-forties, my body was changing, and aging was a new reality. Although my photos carried the image of my colored hair and mustache, wrinkles were claiming areas of my face, and my body ached a bit longer after my regular gym workouts. Like a well-tuned jalopy, I was still moving with occasional creaking, even as my mind was sharp, focused, and filled with ideas and themes I wanted to share across the page. Unlike my writing of poetry and prose, I had no control over the rendering of this aging narrative affecting my body.

\*\*\*

My parents lived very full and notable lives in Hyannis during the late 1970s to the 1990s. Mama D earned some notable distinctions, including her roles as the vice president of the Cape Cod NAACP for ten years and a charter member of Hyannis' first town council for three years, to name some of her achievements. On his part, Papa D headed the Freedom Fund Committee for the Cape Cod NAACP and served a twenty-six-year membership in the Hyannis Rotary Club. My parents had made a remarkable journey from their Southern roots to constructing thriving, fulfilling lives for decades in Massachusetts. When they retired, they journeyed back and forth between Hyannis and Mira Loma for several years, spending springs and summers on the East Coast and falls and winters at my house in Mira Loma. With their four grandchildren—my brother

Brian's three and my one—in California, the decision to move permanently to the West was an easy one.

My parents made that final move in 1998, and the plan was for them to stay in the Mira Loma house on Tamarack Way, which worked well for them financially, while placing them ten minutes from Derek and his mother's family. When I drove weekly to visit Derek, it became a visit with my parents as well. They found a welcoming church, made friends, and enjoyed their new Southern California residence.

\* \* \*

In 1998, I interviewed for and received a position as a contributing editor for a new men's magazine. When I found that the inaugural issue would feature essays about the editors and their relationships with their fathers, I knew exactly what I wanted to write. *Code: A Style Magazine for Men of Color* was a polished publication that targeted a male readership with feature stories, interviews, commentaries, celebrity profiles, and photographs that emphasized men's fashions. When I told friends that I received a salaried position and that *Hustler* magazine created the publication, the smirking comments automatically slid into jokes about naked women. But during the time that I worked with the publication, there was no required assignments or any pressure to develop anything salacious or erotic. And my boss, the managing editor, was a White woman.

My essay for the July 1999 premiere issue was titled, "My Father's Son," a two thousand word reflection on the values and shaping of my masculinity by my father. Although my father never received the academic education that I had, he was one of the smartest men I knew. It was no easy task being a Black man in America, but Papa D had survived the onslaught of pernicious arrows that targeted him from all directions. I comprehended how my father's sacrifices translated into opportunities and choices that I had in my life. My article meditated on Papa D's life journey, as his individual story was emblematic of Black manhood in America. A manhood challenged by a racist history and distorted ideals. American society maintained a siege on Black men, destroying bodies and spirits with duplicitous attitudes, excessive incarceration, and psychological and physical violence.

I wrote additional essays for the next two issues of *Code*, and I was pleased with my handling of nonfiction. However, at an early morning meeting with the general editor, she informed me that I was *fired*. Catching me by surprise, I waited for the punchline to the joke, but she insisted that I *knew* why I was being dismissed. Assuring her that I had no clue about anything that prompted my dismissal, she returned a stern stare and asked me to leave. It was a mystifying morning, and to this day, my termination remains unexplained. I was frustrated as I became a pariah, a visible untouchable walking the office hallways.

It was the most peculiar ending to an experience that I thoroughly enjoyed. Abruptly, by January 2000, *Code* magazine ceased publication. I was saddened that a monthly periodical that reached out to working class *and* professional Black men alike failed to connect with its core audience. However, "My Father's Son" became an essay—and later a poem as well—that found its way onto numerous internet sites. I had completed something of sustained value to celebrate my father and other Black men like him.

\* \* \*

I met David Massey and Rodney Hooks in the late 1990s while attending a film festival where we each screened our shorts films that we directed. It was encouraging to intersect with two Black filmmakers who, like me, were ready to take the next step into features. David had a distinguished background as a graduate in the producers program at the American Film Institute. He received well-earned attention when he was nominated for an Academy Award in the Best Live Action Short Film category for his film, *Last Breeze of Summer* (1992). He went on to establish his film company, UCE Productions, which produced faith-based short films, and in later years, he produced and directed notable documentaries and fictional short films.

On his part, Rodney worked as a first assistant director and assistant director in feature films, such as *Legal Eagles* (1986), *Deep Cover* (1992), *The Meteor Man* (1993), *House Party 3* (1994), *The Seat Filler* (2004), and *Akeelah and the Bee* (2006), and television series, including *Falcon Crest* (1985), *Matlock* (1986), *The West Wing* (1999), and *Night Stalker* (2005).

The three of us also connected with a fourth Black professional, Raymond Forchion. Ray was an actor, screenwriter, and a casting director as he navigated the movie and television worlds with accomplishments in front of and behind the camera. Perhaps his most-viewed role at the time was his portrayal of OJ Simpson in the television movie, *American Tragedy* (2000), but he appeared on television series, such as *Ellen* (1996) and *Will and Grace* (2000), with many additional shows thereafter.

In the years that followed our initial meeting, David, Rodney, Ray, and I critiqued and supported our writing and pitching efforts. For me, the additional reward was that the three of them were down-to-earth brothers who weren't caught up in the Tinseltown posturing and vain glitter. So, we met, talked, encouraged, and finally worked together on a short film that I wrote and directed, titled *Performance* (2008).

*Performance* followed a Black woman journalist who wrote hip hop articles for a national magazine under the pen name Alex Feinstein. When she received the assignment to write about an aging, Black male performer from 1940s studio movies, she discovered some similar stereotypical Black imagery within past and present popular culture. Importantly, she learned about the humanity behind the older actor's screen roles.

With Rodney's help, I approached Art Evans for the lead role. I had much respect for Art, following his memorable roles in the films *A Soldier's Story* (1984), *Die Hard 2* (1990), *Tales from the Hood* (1995), *The Great White Hype* (1996), and *Metro* (1997), as well as numerous appearances on network television shows. Art was such an easy actor to work with, and his balanced mix of the professional and the personal helped to galvanize his on-screen connection with the lead actress, Nisa Ward.

During our auditions for casting, Ray and I were impressed immediately by Nisa's reading. She skillfully connected with the character and improvised convincingly when prompted. Out of the numerous actors who read for the protagonist, she stood out. Nisa went on to appear in several feature films, including *Middle of Nowhere* (2012), *The Fate of the Furious* (2017), *Widows* (2018), and *Birds of Prey* (2020).

I learned some important lessons from my earlier directing of *A Room Without Doors* and applied that experience to my second effort. As a producer, I confidently found and negotiated the two major settings for the film, and working with my multi-talented Black director of photography, Keith L. Smith, we arrived at a lower budget by shooting on high-definition video rather than 35mm film. Keith's skills behind the camera were impressive, as he worked as a cinematographer on dozens of short and feature films.

*Performance* was completed in six days, and the final film was accepted and screened at twelve film festivals, including The Texas Black Film Festival; The Hollywood Black Film Festival; The San Diego Black Film Festival; The Beverly Hills Film, TV, and New Media Festival; and the African American Marketplace-Los Angeles. With the inclusion of the film in the numerous film festivals, accolades about my writing and directing showered my ego. More importantly, however, I had confidence in writing and directing that resulted from years of projects, both unfinished and completed. I knew my strengths, as well as those areas that needed improvement. Most importantly, I was still hungry to do more, to go beyond my short film accomplishments and step into feature films. With my developed skills, experience, and partnerships, I expected that future opportunities were moving closer than ever before.

### ***
### My Father's Son

four thirty a.m.,
rushing to the bathroom
to pee through the dim
light sneaking along the hallway,

my ears weighing
the rustling of his jacket,
the sliding glass doors,
the truck's engine dinning,

and pulled by the light,
I edge forward to see him
watching the snow,
the flakes collecting like small debts
against the glass,

daddy, dark and beautiful,
stood tall inside the door,
his shoulders hunched against the chill,
across the broadness of his back
I saw the massiveness of his will,

his eyes colored with stern resolve,
warmed my shivering youth,
sniffling, his handkerchief dabbed
the frost from his nose
and when he smiled
within me rose
the thrill of being his,

daddy smelled like work,
touching my face with a large dry hand,
his muscles taut from mops and pails,
legs, long and aching, would carry him
across tiled floors in donut shops,
over shoe-stained carpets in banks,
the dirty corners of post office halls,
the cubicles of bathrooms, greying and dank,

daddy's jacket, bulky and worn,
was buttoned to the top,
the collar turned against his unshaven face
vast boots with thick white socks
pulled high over his aching calves

*"lock the door behind me and scoot back to bed!"*
and upon his head
he tightened the baseball cap,
beyond the door
he faced the frozen attitude
of a merciless morning

daddy moved, a solitary man, through
drifts of snow,
his large boot prints
marking the places where he had gone,
the truck door slammed,
gears cursing beneath his gloved hand,
lights rolled across the unplowed road,
while daddy, a gladiator, challenged
the dawn from the depths of his inner man

alone, I shivered with guilt,
my mind impressed that he left nothing undone,
and succumbing to sleep,
with my boyish dreams,
I longed to be my father's son

# CHAPTER FIFTEEN

# Wrestling with Despair

By 2003, Beverly was tenured in the Pasadena City College Department of English, and I was a tenured associate professor in the English Department at California State University-Los Angeles (CSULA). The English department at CSULA had twenty-four full-time professors, and I was the *only* tenured Black professor. The good news was that the department's chairperson appreciated my interdisciplinary background and the numerous courses I could teach—larger lectures courses of 110 students in Gender and Sexuality in Popular Culture; to medium-sized classes in African American Literature, Creative Writing, and American Film; and smaller graduate seminars of fifteen students in African American Literature and Fiction Writing. I worked with and directed graduate students completing their master's degrees in English, as well as participating on department and university-wide faculty committees.

From 2004 through 2017, I maintained a steady productivity expected of a tenured professor in the academic arena, even as I continued to chisel out creative work. For me, despite the distinctions between the academic and popular realms, I enjoyed the intersection of the two worlds. I published over ten essays in both academic and mainstream periodicals. I delivered over forty readings and lectures at academic conferences, writing retreats, and radio shows in LA, San Diego, San Francisco, Boston, Salt Lake City, San Antonio, London, and Paris. I had three academic texts published: *Black Directors in Hollywood* (2003), *Masculinity in the Interracial Buddy Film* (2005), and *Hip Hop in American Cinema* (2007). I wrote five unproduced screenplays, while self-publishing two novels, *Communion* and *The Third Woman*; two poetry collections; and two short story collections. Additionally, I completed two stage plays, producing and directing one of those plays, titled *Shout*.

It was a productive phase in my life, and sometimes, I had to force myself to slow down from this need, perhaps addiction, to constantly push myself through my creative expressions. At times, the various forms of writing gave me pathways for digesting the world around me that didn't make sense—a world that didn't rhyme, that didn't percolate with positivity. Yes, I had my Christian faith for spiritual sustenance, but there was no one church or denomination that explained my restlessness and questions about that faith as practiced in the contemporary, racist incarnation of Christian nationalism.

Despite my productivity as a creative writer and academic, there was an aching sense of failure as a filmmaker. The demands from various areas in my life were pulling and tugging me in different directions, and I couldn't produce enough words to explain the unfulfilled space inside, despite the many people who called me the most driven and accomplished person they knew.

\* \* \*

On the CSULA campus, I welcomed the invitation to apply for a position as chairperson of the Department of Pan African Studies (PAS). It seemed the fitting next step in my academic journey, and the shift to administration was a different challenge that beckoned me. It was a very small department with only four full-time members and about eight part-time instructors, depending upon the given quarter. Two of the members, both Black professors, I knew already: Dr. C.R.D. Halisi, who had done a considerable share of teaching and not as much publishing, and Dr. Melina Abdullah, who was quite popular with the Black students on campus, as she served as a pied piper of Afrocentrism. They both had backgrounds in political science, and consequently my background in African American literature helped to round off the variety of course selections the department could offer. The fourth professor was hired as a tenure-track addition, and she, too, had a political science background.

At the time, the university president was also Black and had served in that leadership capacity for nearly thirty-four years. Although he purposely remained a distant but silent defender of the PAS Department, he encouraged and supported me as the PAS leader. However, to my colleagues in the department, he was an "Uncle Tom." I didn't share their assessment, and from my perspective, they didn't know who the real enemy was.

In addition to the PAS Department, there was also various area studies: Chicano/a Studies Department; the Latin American Studies program; and the Asian and Asian American Studies program. As the leader of PAS, when I reached out to the leaders of each of the area studies, they were all enthusiastic to work together consolidating our collective strengths to both protect and grow our area studies. They saw the benefits to the students and the collective strength to protect our areas from frequent budget cuts that could decimate us as individual departments and programs. We four leaders met and conversed regularly, and together we attended a conference in ethnic studies at San Francisco State University, a campus at the forefront of developing and maintaining Ethnic and Cultural Studies in the California State University system. At the same time, I went to the Ethnic and Women's Studies Department at nearby California Polytechnic State University, gathering information about its area studies department—the administrational structure, the course offerings, and the criteria for the BA and MA degrees awarded.

An additional strength to our efforts to join forces as an area studies department was the leadership of Jim Henderson, the new dean of the College of Natural and Social Sciences. Jim was White and a math scholar—a tall, intelligent man with a charming sense of humor. Without hesitation, he supported our cultural areas and our efforts to unite. More importantly, Jim and I became good friends who respected each other, developing an off-campus friendship as well.

By the end of the academic year, we four chairs of area studies called for a group meeting with our respective faculty members. We looked forward to faculty members joining forces to establish a new Department of Ethnic Studies that would provide dynamic academic offerings for our students and for the campus. At the meeting, we shared our suggestions and plans. But—silence. Then, the various faculty members delivered a litany of arguments against a collective department, fearing it would weaken the integrity of each area's individual existence. The faculty members couldn't—or wouldn't—comprehend that alone, each area was exposed to financial cuts and a stagnancy in student and faculty growth.

My fellow chairs and I had worked for most of the academic year to investigate and weigh the benefits of a collective department from various perspectives. We didn't anticipate that the opposition would come from within. It was disappointing and deflating, and as I shared the results with President Rosser, he encouraged me not to give up, promising to work with me to build the PAS Department. However, the PAS faculty were not supportive of me working with Dr. Rosser, and they announced that they wanted new leadership other than Dr. Rosser and myself.

I was stung by the PAS faculty and their inability to comprehend my vision and hopes for the department, but I stepped down as the faculty members desired. The department leadership then went to Dr. Melina Abdullah, who represented a more aggressive agenda, as she would continue to do years later as a founding member of the Los Angeles chapter of the Black Lives Matter organization.

The on-campus battles and disappointments magnified the emotional rupture I felt. Like a seizure that wouldn't stop, I shook from one day to the next, disconnected from people I thought I knew. A year filled with the elusive politics of fighting battles that weren't real, of demonizing people and efforts that weren't oppositional—it all became exhausting.

\* \* \*

Much more devastating than my campus life was the weakening of my marriage. By 2008, Beverly and I had been together for fifteen years, married for thirteen. I became detached. Drifting. Following the purchase of our Mohawk Street house in east Pasadena that Beverly wanted, she was happy. I was disgruntled and restless. I didn't care about the house as she did, and what I searched for could not be fulfilled by real estate.

At age fifty-six, I was frustrated with my academic world, and I hungered to further develop my goals as a writer and filmmaker. I was disappointed that my years of efforts hadn't translated into the life I desired for myself. I wanted something that I felt was so simple—to sustain an academic life that merged with my creative talents.

There were long, painful conversations with Beverly when I tried to articulate my desires and frustrations. I needed a change, a shift from the confines of the quagmire that had become my life. I was a malcontent who needed a parole from an imprisoned life that seemed to be taking from me and not giving something tangible in return.

When I told Beverly that I needed to move out, I knew I broke her heart. She had found what she wanted in her profession and her home. And though she tried to understand by suggesting we rent a room somewhere closer to the ocean for weekend getaways, that wasn't enough to satisfy my longing. It wasn't Beverly who was the problem or at fault in any way. It was *me*.

My restlessness was connected to my sense of failure—on campus and in my creative efforts off campus. The many years spent trying to blend my intellectual and artistic pursuits felt hollow. I kept going in circles, despite the investment of energy, hard work, and commitment. I had failed to meet the expectations I set for myself. I wasn't exactly certain what I needed, but I had to jump off from a professional and personal treadmill that led to frustration. Despite being a wordsmith, I couldn't express in a definitive way the irritation and restlessness that possessed me. I was floating like a windswept balloon—without direction and connection to anything that made sense anymore.

I boxed up my personal items, placing them in a Public Storage unit, and stuffed the most necessary items and clothing into my sedan. I moved in with Paulette during the fall of 2008, into her one-bedroom apartment in Sherman Oaks, just west of UCLA. Paulette was more than generous and supportive of me—listening to my rambling explanations and allowing me to simmer in silence. I wrote, read, and took frequent drives to the ocean which was much closer than the trek from Pasadena. I reached out to my male friends for my social ties and kept up my regular visits with my son and my parents.

By January 2009, I was able to move into my own apartment on Federal Avenue, in west Los Angeles, just south of Santa Monica Boulevard. The one-bedroom apartment wasn't fancy or noteworthy, but I was relieved to have my own place. The apartment's location helped, with a fifteen-minute drive to Santa Monica, overlooking Pacific Coast Highway, Santa Monica Pier, and the beach. My membership to a fitness chain gave me access to several gyms in the area, and the nearby public tennis center allowed me to connect with a weekend group of competitive tennis players. However, my weekends were filled with writing a new novel, *Communion*.

I wasn't able to escape the major reason for my new location: my broken marriage. My self-analysis led to recurring moments of guilt, even as I cherished the freedom to submerge myself into solitude. I was somewhere between "nowhere-special" and "unable-to-be-where-I-wanted-to-be." I ached inside for Beverly, and at the same time, I leaned on the possibilities of what might be a different and new tomorrow. Yet, what exactly did I desire, and what would it look like if it were to arrive? Popularity and praise, financial riches? Was it fame and fortune I wanted, the two gods worshipped as success? Would I recognize perfection through my imperfect vision? Yes, I wanted more than disappointment, but I would only be disappointed if I continued to devalue what I already possessed. I prayed and I drank. I exercised into exhaustion. I prayed and drank some more. I yearned for that peace I found decades earlier while sitting at the Staffelsee in Murnau, Germany. But nothing. No relief.

Beverly decided to divorce me and move on with her life for her own emotional survival. Intellectually, I understood. I had upended her life and shattered the world that she wanted. I couldn't fault her for her anger and her disappointment, and at the same time, I couldn't find any words to make her stay. She had done all that she could do to save our marriage. The suffocating space of my emotional breakdown was *not* Beverly's fault, and I understood that she needed to go on with her life.

My lifeline was diving deeper into my novel, *Communion*, trying to discover in my fictional world something life-saving to grasp. The manuscript gave me a way to purge my emotional extremes through its various characters and the serpentine plot. On weekends, I wrote for hours at the nearby coffee shop, sucking down cups of caffeine as I filled blank pages.

I attended services at a couple of churches, lifting my heaviness toward a lightness I hoped to find. Yet, the churches seemed more concerned about my afterlife, and ministers provided no lifelines to bring me to the shores of recovery. I floated on the confusing waters of restlessness, holding my breath as strong currents dragged me further out into an infinite sea.

\* \* \*

As early as the fall of 2008, the cracks began to show in my parents' health—my mother first and then my father. My mother's diabetes, phlebitis, high blood pressure, arthritis, and neuropathy all cascaded into her life, as well as the difficulty with painful, twisted intestines that called for surgery. Once the surgery occurred, her health took a debilitating turn, made worse by her unwillingness to change her eating habits. And, of course, there was an abundance of medications before she was hospitalized. She begged me to take her home from the hospital, but I reasoned that there was a twenty-four-hour care in the hospital—something that couldn't happen at the Mira Loma house. When the doctor announced an updated analysis of her health with the word hospice, my knees buckled. However, we brought her home with the hope that Papa D could care for her with the support of visiting nurses.

In the following two months, I received numerous pre-dawn, distressed phone calls from Papa D, and I knew what I had to do. My sister was then married, and she and her husband were living northwest of Los Angeles in the San Fernando Valley. My brother was married with three children and had moved to Tennessee. So, I gave up my apartment and the life I was shaping in west Los Angeles and moved out to the Mira Loma house. As difficult as it was, I knew that my parents had sacrificed much more for me. They had, no doubt, given up things that I would never know about.

On February 10, 2010, I received a phone while at my campus office from the visiting nurse in Mira Loma—my mother had died. I fell into an abyss of pain that I never experienced before. The one-hour drive from the university to the Mira Loma house was a painful trek through a thick flood of tears. The eventual paperwork stated that she died of respiratory distress and congestive heart failure exacerbated by hypertension and pulmonary fibrosis. Words on a page. Words at her funeral. Words on her gravestone. And an emptiness that left me wordless.

\* \* \*

Although Papa D found relaxation in his vegetable and flower gardens that he maintained at the Mira Loma house, his high blood pressure and imposing dementia demanded an assortment of medications and weekly visits to his doctor. His significant issue of several was his memory loss. Despite efforts to let him stay at home on his own during the workday, he was incapable of feeding himself and taking his seven medications. The next step of finding a facility was exhausting—the interviews, the visits, and the costs for full care were overwhelming. When finally settling on a facility in the nearby city of Riverside, Papa D's eventual wandering off the premises required that he be moved from a private room in a separate, secured building.

My saddest day was the visit when Papa D and I sat in the facility's outdoor garden, and he didn't recognize me. He called me by a name I'd heard him mention in previous conversations—a boyhood friend he knew in Bainbridge, Georgia. On that day, he talked about something he saw in the distance as he pointed, looking at me while chuckling. *I* wasn't there. I had disappeared, crying as I attempted to conduct a conversation as his childhood buddy. Soon after that visit, the facility asserted his need for hospice care. When I found a space in another facility, his personal room was smaller. On my regular visits, we sat with many others in a large activity room staring at television shows. My appearance raised no particular emotions or recognition. I attempted to carry on something similar to a normal life, but I didn't know anymore what that was.

\* \* \*

Some of my male friends envied my single status. In their minds, my opportunity to meet women on and off campus seemed ideal to them. In theory, their wild visions held some veracity, but after spending fifteen years with Beverly, I wasn't interested in racing into another relationship. As for "playing the field," I saw pretty women daily, but I wasn't motivated to putting in the time, energy, and money. I preferred going home alone to the Mira Loma house—writing or sitting in darkness, listening to music.

Were there available and interested women? Yes. That wasn't the problem. In California, there's no shortage of beautiful women. However, Beverly was the woman I loved. Besides, many women seemed to have taken an oath of allegiance to the league of *non compos mentis*. So, I preferred women friends with whom I would briefly socialize—happy hours, chatting at the gym, or meeting at coffee shops. Being in my late fifties and single was a different kind of script, and I wasn't ready or interested in being a leading man in any woman's life.

\* \* \*

There was no easy way to move forward with my life, but it was important that I took steps in that necessary direction. So, in the spring of 2012, I ventured into a different teaching experience, offered to me by my friend, Dr. Renford Reese, a Black scholar who taught political science at California State Polytechnic

University, Pomona (Cal Poly Pomona). Renford was busy and productive, having published four books at that time, including *American Paradox: Young Black Men* (2004) and *Prison Race* (2006). He invited me to teach a ten-week class in film appreciation at the California Institution for Men (CIM) in Chino, California. The class met once a week in a designated room under the watchful gaze of the institution's guards. The facility itself, with roughly three thousand inmates, was about a twenty-minute drive west from the Mira Loma house. I took the job in order to get outside of myself, which had been the major focus during the recent two years. I hoped that I could possibly lift, in some small manner, the thoughts of those incarcerated men who were surviving their restrictive environment while reshaping their lives.

After a volume of completed forms, emails, and meetings, I organized a class that would use popular films of various genres to explore and discuss a variety of topics, such as manhood, fatherhood, and cultural identities. With popular movies, such as *Die Hard with a Vengeance* (1995), *Mi Familia* (1995), *A Better Life* (2011), *Unstoppable* (2010), and *Contagion* (2011), my approach was to use accessible movies as prompts for meaningful class discussions and essays. This would *not* be a deep discussion into semiotics or the visual representations of existentialism, nihilism, or onanism. The twenty-five men who signed up for the class were White, Black, Latino, and Asian. Their felonious acts landed them into the facility, but I never received a detailed docket about each inmate's background and journey into CIM.

The first two visits to the institution generated a considerable amount of nervousness. Checking in at the front desk with my allocated identification as my briefcase was searched. Then, the buzzing sounds as I passed through three unlocking gates beneath mounted cameras. In the mid-afternoon sunny, spring weather of that initial class meeting, I stood out in my dress shirt, tie, and briefcase. Taking the walkway to the building in the distance, inmates were active in the yard in their orange overalls. I tensed up from my throat to my booty cheeks—glancing at the dozens of watching eyes locked on me. I reflected on the form I signed, acknowledging that in case of any insurrection from the inmates, my hostage status would *not* influence decisions made to recapture control of the facility. It was a wordy way of stating that my life was *not* the priority once I was inside.

At the designated building, I took the stairway to the second floor where the men were assembled in rows of chairs positioned before a portable table with wheels. On top of the table, a television monitor was attached with a DVD player on the shelf beneath. The back wall of the room was a wide observation glass where a uniformed guard watched and listened.

The men were receptive and respectful, never targeting me with attitudes. The screenings and discussions worked effectively, as many of the men had much to say about issues and ideas emanating from the films. By the third class meeting, I felt more comfortable, observing that the inmates had a much better appreciation of the educational process than my university students.

On one occasion, however, I was reminded of an issue that some men had in my class. After the session when we screened and discussed *Mi Familia*, the uniformed guard entered the room from behind the wall of glass. The inmates were gone as I gathered and organized the items for my briefcase.

"So, just so you know," the guard said in a matter-of-fact tone, "make sure your movies don't have scenes like that one."

"Like what?" I asked, confused. "The movie didn't have any violent scenes."

"Yeah, but some of the inmates are in here for pedophilia, and scenes like that . . . well, just don't show them."

I was still unclear until he provided more specificity. Toward the end of the film, a scene emphasized racial and cultural awkwardness when the Latino character—Memo, a law student—brought home his White girlfriend and her parents to meet his family. As the Latino and White families navigated their initial meeting, Memo's preschool nephew rushed into the living room and jumped atop the coffee table wearing only an indigenous head dress. The naked boy was innocently playing as the White characters looked on in shock. The scene functioned as comic relief, but it posed a different kind of significance for the pedophiles in the class. The guard's warning forced me to widen my awareness.

On another occasion, as I was leaving the facility and checking out at the front desk, a young Black inmate had delivered some items before he was buzzed back into the yard. The man seemed so young, so I asked the desk guard his age.

"He's twenty-two, I think," the guard responded.

"Can I ask . . . why is he in here?"

"He was in a ride along with some friends . . . waiting in the car as they went inside a convenience store . . . stole some items, but they killed the cashier on the way out."

"Mm," was all I could say. "How long is he in for?"

"Twenty-five years."

I nodded reflectively. When I was twenty-two, I was completing my first year of teaching high school. And as I thought of the twenty-five years that followed that teaching job, I had opportunities for education, travel, family gatherings, friendships, marriage, and fatherhood. And for the remainder of the evening, I continued to see that young brother's face—nameless with only a flickering flame of life in his eyes. And though I never saw him again before completing the class, he haunted me. Why was I so blessed, chosen, and entitled to have such a full life?

* * *

Thoughts about "blessings" and a "full life" were seeped into my brain. The list of the positives was the much longer one, as well as the privilege I had to be in a position to do such self-analysis. Before leaving Beverly, I had spent too many moments weighing the negative, and I had foolishly interlaced that negativity with our marriage.

Those realizations were major reasons for me reconnecting with Beverly. We actually began communicating again when my mother died and as I tried to make the right decisions for my father's welfare. My parents loved Beverly, and she always showed her love for them and my son. She and I began talking over the phone about the health issues my parents faced, followed by an occasional meeting over coffee and tea. We even enjoyed concerts together again—a Sade concert at the Los Angeles Staples Center and a David Sanborn jazz performance at the Catalina Bar and Grill in Hollywood.

Sanborn was my favorite sax player, and on the night of his performance, I picked Beverly up at the Mohawk Street house to ride together to the venue. After a fabulous evening of music, I drove her back to the Mohawk Street house and the unusually chilly weather in Pasadena was exacerbated by extreme wind gusts, as palm branches and swirling pieces of discarded papers layered the streets. Arriving at the house, there was no power, so I went inside to help her light several candles. Without any power, there was also no heat, but she assured me she would be fine.

So, I said, "Good night" and headed out for Mira Loma, but fifteen minutes along the freeway, I pulled over. What was I doing? I couldn't leave her alone in that dark, cold house. It had nothing to do with her capability to take care of herself. She was always independent and resourceful. But at that moment, I felt *wrong* in knowing her situation and leaving her behind. I *was wrong*, realizing that she was the one woman who went the distance with me and my dreams—when other women couldn't or wouldn't keep in step. I drove back and asked her to come with me, and we drove to the Mira Loma house for that night. After that, we shared numerous phone discussions about work, the friends we had in common, and Papa D.

In addition to our appreciation of contemporary jazz, Beverly and I had always enjoyed playing and attending professional tennis tournaments. One of the annual competitions occurred during the summer—the Women's Tennis

Association's week-long event in Carlsbad, California—a two-hour drive south from Pasadena. We were staying at a hotel across from Carlsbad Beach, and on the second morning there, I received a call on my cell phone.

"Mr. Melvin Donalson?" the business-like voice asked.

"Yes, who's this?" I responded.

"This is the Southern California Mortuary and, let me say that we're sorry for the loss of your father."

The man's words pierced my heart, and seconds later, it reverberated in my head. I was breathless—numb. In a clumsy handling of communications, Papa D's hospice facility contacted the designated funeral home and neglected to contact me. When I began to speak, I was already soaked with tears. Beverly waited for me to explain, but I remember only whispering the word: *Daddy*.

Papa D died in August 2013, his death caused by acute cardiopulmonary arrest, acute myocardial infarction, atherosclerosis, hypertension, and Alzheimer's Dementia. I think that at the age of 83, working since he was in the third grade, losing Mama D, and living in a facility that wasn't his home—my father was just tired.

\*\*\*

On Valentine's Day 2014, Beverly and I were married—again. It was my good fortune that after all that I did years before, she still loved me as much as I loved her. Again, we kept the ceremony simple, inviting my sister and her husband Pete, as well as two close friends—Dave Kee and Kate Remo. Following weeks of gathering the necessary paperwork and making appointments, the six of us met at the Beverly Hills Courthouse for our simple but meaningful ceremony in a judge's chamber. After our post-ceremony lunch with the six of us, Beverly and I drove south to San Diego for the weekend. The simplicity of it all was the beauty of it all. I was a fortunate man in finding once more what I had walked away from years earlier. I had lost my parents, which shook me deeply, but gaining Beverly's affection and trust again was priceless.

\*\*\*

In 2015, when I was approached on the Cal State-LA campus to become the director of the First Year Experience (FYE) Program, I didn't hesitate for too long. The position would take me out of the classroom and would remove me full time from the English Department where I had become increasingly irritated by the department's priorities.

For me, my aspirations as a "director" had always centered around filmmaking, and so I had to transform myself into a director's role for a program in need of more funding and structure. The foundational objective of the program was to assist, support, and monitor the progress of incoming freshmen to the campus—with the reality that students of color were an important target. The program was voluntary for students, but it specifically reached out and worked with the campus's Educational Opportunity Program (EOP), the English Department, the Math Department, and the University Counseling Services to assist in organizing cohorts—or learning communities—of students transitioning to a university campus from a high school setting.

The person that was key to the success of building the FYE Program was Nancy Aguilar, the administrative coordinator. With her years of experience and her sincere dedication to students, she oriented me to the successes and weaknesses of the program as it existed.

Working with department chairs and various support services, FYE became an efficient resource center for incoming freshmen. Going into my second year of leadership, we won grants from the state university system's chancellor office to augment the campus's funding. Our FYE Program grew from serving 300 students during my first year to over 1, 300 students during the next year.

\* \* \*

In the winter of 2017, I completed my play titled *Shout*, a two-act family drama. A seven-character play, *Shout* explored a family acknowledging and reconciling the life-changing decisions shaped by mangled emotions and misunderstandings. Coming from their multiethnic backgrounds, the characters had to consider the ways in which the dynamics of age, race, and gender had to be endured and carefully weighed in reconciling love.

As I wrote the play, I knew I had to direct it, envisioning the characters, stage, blocking, and lighting as I developed each scene. But as I moved closer to committing to the project, I knew I had to also function as the producer—organizing the funding, selecting the theater, and promoting the play. When I told Beverly that I was going to mount the play by following film director Robert Townsend's credit card plan for funding *Hollywood Shuffle* (1987), she wasn't enthusiastic about that strategy. However, she supported and worked with me on the project.

Then, I reached out Juan Carlos Parrilla, a former grad student who had become a friend. Juan Carlos was a writer himself, and he taught playwriting at the Casa 0101, a theater situated in Boyle Heights, a predominantly Latino community. I also recruited Vique Mora, another former student and friend, who agreed to be the script supervisor and production assistant. My friend Ray Forchion and his assistant, Rose Marie, took the lead on the auditioning process, as we needed four women and three men, representing Jewish, Black, White, Latino, and Japanese American characters.

After a month of searching for a venue, I found the Fremont Theater with its tiered, one hundred-seat space, in South Pasadena. Unfortunately, due to the heavy booking for the upcoming holiday season in November, we could only contract the theater for two weeks of performances, which meant the box office receipts wouldn't lead to any profit. Importantly, before beginning rehearsals, I interviewed and selected skilled people in stage managing; set construction and design; lighting and sound; props; makeup and hair styling; and wardrobe.

Our chosen actors came together in a cohesive, memorable ensemble. I worked effectively with the cast, shaping their characters from the page to the stage. Our performances soared as each audience praised both the talents and the themes that the play revealed. And after five months of scouting venues holding auditions, rehearsals, and performances, I was exhausted. As we totaled the box office returns, I was hundreds of dollars in debt. But *Shout* was one of the most creative and satisfying experiences I ever had . . . and I was happy.

\*\*\*

As I was developing *Shout*, I was drafting my novel, *The Third Woman*. I was swinging the creative pendulum back and forth between the two forms. Whenever I returned to one genre or the other, I would do so with a freshness that summoned my best efforts. *The Third Woman* had been simmering inside me for a long time, the urgency of the piece emanating from the experiences of the women I had known over the years who survived sexual violence.

In researching essays, books, and articles—both earlier and contemporary publications—I gathered a range of experiences and responses that would make my novel relevant and of interest to readers. I explored numerous websites of activist groups, such as the V-Day organization, and governmental agencies that offered information and statistics to update the current issues regarding studies and investigations about sexual crimes. I self-published the novel in the fall of 2015. It was the best novel I had written at that point in my life, and it was certainly the most relevant one.

\*\*\*

My poetry always served as a charging station to my writing and film interests. Between lengthier projects, I dove into the deep waters of verse to test my swimming skills with language. Over the years, I had submitted poems to various publications, but in 2017, I decided to gather new poems into my self-published volume that I titled *Revelations*.

In 2018, I was reading my poetry in public again. At that time, I was approached by Gerda Govine, a well-known Black poet in Pasadena, to join a group of poets she was organizing for public readings. Responding to the city's decision to celebrate the creative arts, Gerda obtained funding to form the Pasadena Rose Poets. During the next two years, I participated with this group of ten poets in readings throughout the city. The ethnically diverse collective of poets—African American, Jewish, Asian, Latino, Armenian—created works that ranged in content, style, and tone, and it was invigorating to read aloud and interact with audiences again.

By the fall of 2019, the *Pasadena Rose Poets: Poetry Collection* was published, and it contained nine of my poems. Two of the Pasadena Rose Poets went on to edit a separate publication, *The Altadena Literary Review*, in 2020, which included two of my poems. Additionally in 2020, I was invited to write a poem, "Outbreak," and the "Afterword" for a timely anthology, *When the Virus Came Calling: Covid-19 Strikes America*, edited by Pasadena author and editor, Thelma T. Reyna. The book was released in December 2020, featuring poetry and nonfiction, and the collective works explored the health challenges and political reactions to COVID-19.

\* \* \*

*Love* is an overused four-letter word, christening everything from romantic relations to friendships. When my loss of Beverly folded into the loss of my mother, and then the loss of my father, I sank within the quicksand of self-absorption about what I didn't have and what I hadn't achieved. However, I kept writing and bathing myself in words, emotions, and experiences. Eventually, I saw the afflictions tormenting others who had so much less than me—emotionally, materially, spiritually. Unlike those people, the truth was that my life *wasn't* empty. I had my wife, my son, my extended family, and my friends—my lifelines that gave me value and completion. And then I had the words of creativity that flowed back to me because of those lifelines. Right before me, I had the weapons I needed to wrestle with and defeat despair. I had people that meant everything to me, and recognizing my good fortune, I knew I meant something special to them.

CHAPTER SIXTEEN

# The Echoes of Dreams

I never thought I would be speaking of my friends—my dearest brothers—in the past tense. That realization became my reality when four of my closest friends died during a three-year period: James Tobey (2018); Bill Edwards (2019); Wilfred "Pepie" Samuels (2020); and John Jenkins (2020). These men were brothers who all shaped my life, each adding something immeasurable to who I was and who I became. I often reflected on why I was so fortunate to know them and to have them in my life.

Collectively, they gave me a compass of companionship that provided passages through and sometimes around barriers that singled me out for destruction. Thanks to them, I navigated convoluted pathways that seemed endless in their challenges. With them in my life, I survived the emotional, psychological, and financial storms that bombarded my aspirations. They were my cornerstones, and the solid foundation of their friendship helped me comprehend the depths and incomparable value of brotherhood.

I could not and did not attend any of their funerals. It wasn't only because their services were held at a distance in Hyannis, San Francisco, Salt Lake City, and Lewiston, Maine. They had all traveled a lot further with me in our friendships. The truth was that I wasn't that strong. I couldn't find within me the strength to say goodbye a final time. So, I hid away from the ritual ceremonies and the awkward dialogues with those attending. I withdrew and kept my sorrow to myself. I survived in the only way that worked for me: keeping them alive inside and letting go only when I was ready . . . whenever that might be.

* * *

When my film partner David Massey shared his idea for *Passage*, I was definitely interested. Although I had recently written two feature screenplays—one drama and one comedy—I was still going through the traditional process of seeking a theatrical agent.

So, while I was busy with the submission process of my two scripts, David and I shared notes, thoughts, and numerous phone conversations to develop and write the script for *Passage*. When we finally had gone through numerous drafts, followed by more rewrites, we had a fictional story about the clash between two Black African cultures in 1600. We shaped a thirty-minute short film that David wanted to shoot on his homeland turf in the Virgin Islands.

David and I co-wrote and co-produced, while he directed the movie, working with our friend, Keith Smith, as cinematographer. As David broke down the script into a reasonable budget, I began the daunting task of connecting with and following the over-complicated paperwork process required by the Screen Actors Guild (SAG). We wanted to use professional actors, as well as the seasoned department heads that we had worked with over the years—for camera, wardrobe, music, editing, and sound. After reassessments and reliance upon promised favors, David came up with the necessary funds to cover the budget.

Even though dialogue was purposely minimal in the film, the physicality and facial expressions of the two lead characters required skilled actors who could emote and capture the viewer's attention with expressions and gestures. Fortunately, our casting step delivered two actors—Noel Arthur and Robert Okumu—who carried the film with their captivating performances. For budgetary reasons, I remained stateside while David led cast and crew to the Virgin Islands for seven days of filming. The post-production phase—editing, sound, music, titles—went well, with each area contributing to the film's polished and engaging aspects.

Although we submitted *Passage* for the Best Short Live Action Film category of the Academy Awards, we didn't make the short list. I understood David's quest for a nomination, but for me the awards were not the most important goal. Certainly, a nomination would have propelled our filmmaking efforts forward, but I was proud to have been a writer-producer on such an accomplished film. With David's efforts, we were able to get *Passage* screened for cast, crew, and friends at the Charlie Chaplin screening room at the Raleigh Studios on Melrose Avenue in Hollywood, and then on the big screen at the Laemmle Monica Film Center in Santa Monica. David and I knew that we had accomplished something of value that carried important cultural and historical information even as the film entertained through the action, tension, and rewarding ending. *Passage* was accepted into seven film festivals that year, energizing my creativity and confirming that I belonged in the world of filmmaking.

\* \* \*

At sixty-eight, I completed writing a new novel that would fall into a popular genre, and I began researching and sending queries to literary agents. After a year and several months of submitting, the Steven Chudney Agency accepted my novel, *KillProof*, an action-thriller story with a Black woman protagonist. I purposefully stepped into a popular genre with a twist on the lead character. The reviews I read about novels that were being published and marketed in the thriller genre appeared to be variations on a particular storyline: White women protagonists dealing with anxieties or addictions. My protagonist, Bree, was a Black woman with anxious moments, but she didn't succumb to those situations. She was intelligent, self-reliant, and passionate, while being a loving mother and daughter—and a kick-ass adversary.

However, I couldn't transform the publishing world that catered to its perceived audience while genuflecting to "celebrity" authors who continually received publication. Rejection after rejection, I had become more realistic about writing and the publishing industry, but sadness still lingered. When I began writing *KillProof* and having primarily academic and self-publications behind my name, I knew the popular reading world knew nothing about me.

At the same time, I knew that the keepers of the keys that placed words, books, and thoughts into the public arena weren't infallible. I knew the marketing component of published works relied upon systems of the same book, with an anomaly sporadically appearing to prompt yet another system of "sameness." The powers that worked those systems hadn't changed much, and for those powers, there was no urgency to derail the train of treasures that led from print to bookstores, online vendors, the big screen, and small-screen streaming services.

Following a year of submitting, my agent couldn't find a publisher for *KillProof*. I experienced that sinking feeling that always came with writing projects that began with hope and possibilities but ended up in the quicksand of disappointments.

Recovering from the years of writing *KillProof* and the rejection that followed, I leaned into a 2019 observation by Black film director Ava Duvernay: "*For me, it's a question of the way we pursue our creative dreams. There is something in our culture that says your dream . . . has to happen immediately and all at once, and that is destructive to the creative spirit. I just embraced the idea that this was going to be a gradual exploration of the thing I was interested in – making films – and gave myself permission to go slowly.*"[5] Over the years, I found that "patience" was a difficult pill for me to ingest. It seemed imperative to inhale and hold my breath until given permission to breathe again. However, as dif-

---

5. Ava Duvernay, "Ava Duvernay . . . Daring to Dream," in Industrialscripts.com/ava-duvernay-quotes/

ficult as it was to accept, in the process of bringing a writing or film project to completion and recognition, at some point *waiting* was an essential element.

\*\*\*

"You have prostate cancer," Dr. Kim told me.

I was immediately deaf. I saw his lips moving and felt the tears streaming down my face. I was locked inside a suffocating cabinet of solitude mortality. Two weeks earlier, following a high PSA score, Dr. Kim had taken ten painful snips from my prostate gland to determine how urgent my situation was at that stage. Rather than waiting over several months to see if the PSA score would increase, I decided to move forward with addressing the situation.

Reading a booklet with details and photos and watching numerous YouTube videos about various treatments, and I opted for the external radiation therapy. I followed up with Dr. Goy, an oncologist, who explained the details of the radiation process. My treatments would be scheduled for weekday mornings over a five-week period—a total of twenty-five sessions.

The twenty-five treatments were scheduled to begin in January 2022. So, during the following weeks, I began to organize for my death—just in case. I gathered insurance policies, bank account numbers, information about credit cards, and written instructions for a memorial gathering rather than a costly mortuary funeral. I completed paperwork about "willing" my body to the University of California-Irvine medical school. And essential to all that I did, I continued to write.

I loved writing. I needed writing. As I recognized before, it was and is both an addiction and therapy all at once. Writing allowed me to soar with my senses, even as my common sense anchored me to real experiences. It was both freedom and reality—a unique "free-ality" that served as the cornerstone of who I am. *Writing* is my Polaris, luminating the commonalities and extremities in my existence that could only be expressed in the affirming words: "I am here, and I have meaning!"

\*\*\*

Early in my five-and-a-half weeks of daily external radiation treatments, I lapsed into self-pity, particularly the day I spent my seventieth birthday on the treatment table. I was weary with commuting one hour each way between the cancer center and home, as well as complaining about my restrictive, high-fiber diet to keep my lower track empty. Sitting in the clinic's near-full waiting area of men and women of various ages and racial backgrounds, I was a member of a club I didn't ask to join.

Then, midway through the required weeks, two people forced me from my valley of self-pity. First, there was a White man I'd seen regularly in the waiting room. He appeared weary, perhaps a few years older than me, and on one occasion, he claimed a vacant seat next to me. We slid into a conversation before he committed to his phone messages. He shared his diagnosis, and assuming his age, I asked about his retirement activities. With a distressed expression, he confessed that he was only sixty-two and was years away from retirement. He was a building inspector for the city of Anaheim, and each day following his cancer treatments, he rushed off to work a full-time shift. As he shared his responsibilities, his voice carried a weariness. He was trapped between dealing with cancer *and* the financial responsibility to his family.

The second person I noticed was a girl about twelve-years-old who was guided into the waiting area in a customized wheelchair by two adults. The chair's seat was positioned higher than most and fixed at an angle, enabling the girl to recline. I assumed that the adults were her parents, though most days, she was attended only by the woman. I didn't walk across the waiting room to pry or interrogate the preteen, but each day she showed a similar fixed expression—neither pain nor joy. And I wondered what type of cancer she had. Why was that child sentenced to a life of disease? How long would her life extend after the treatments at the center?

Moving forward into my sessions, I decided I wouldn't waste time meditating on the "why and what" of *my* condition. I was determined to maintain an attitude that allowed me to be positive. I was weary of my treatments and daily schedule, but no one had to guide me in and out in a wheelchair. And my twelve-year-old memories revolved around my family, friends, and moments of laughter during my Cape Cod summers—not daily visits to a cancer center.

My final radiation treatment was in February 2022. Beverly and I celebrated by driving to the beach and walking the surf. The warm sun bathed my face, and the music of the ocean waves filled my ears. I was content to be at that step in my life regardless of what might come in the future. Two months after the radiation treatments, I took another PSA test. I was quite pleased that my PSA had dropped down from 4.1 to 1.4.

\*\*\*

There are passages in my life that developed like a well-written script. At other times, there were maddening frustrations and losses that hung as dark clouds over any of my efforts to reach the light of success that I sought. But such is the challenge for those who dream beyond the satisfaction of today and who seek something more fulfilling for tomorrow.

The people who intersected my life gifted me with a fullness that inspired and sustained my teaching, writing, publishing, and filmmaking over decades. Being held in affection by so many people was a blessing that lingered on the remarkable. Whether I deserved such deep caring from others was questionable, but I never doubted the love showered over me by family and friends. Truth was—that love fueled and sustained my teaching, writing, and filmmaking. And despite the various disappointments, financial challenges, political frustrations, health issues, and personal losses, I have had a fulfilling life. I've navigated a creative world that often collided with an academic world, and despite that conflict, I've remained a Creative and a Scholar.

As I balanced the often-conflicting identities of a Creative and a Scholar, I have had fulfilling experiences that were uniquely mine. I have lived long enough to recognize and appreciate that any unachieved goals were still a part of my remarkable journey. As a Dream Warrior, the ongoing fighting and confrontations were as essential as the dream itself. Dreams inspired me to leap and dive into the ocean of tomorrow, even as they required me to swim the threatening tides of age and time. Did I get weary? Absolutely—often and painfully so. Dreams, however, emanate from the essence of who I am and who I want to be. Dreams became the sustenance of my unique identity. For me, dreams shaped my purpose and inspiration for living.

\* \* \*

## "Dream Warrior"

Dreams have entered my life as melodies
layering the air that colors my skin
with notes of images and syllables of sound,
inspired words flow from deep within

the serenade of lingering doubts and fears,
and the tangled rhythms of what can be,
the mystery of embracing while letting go,
the haunting fears that struggle to be free

and when I dread the unseen, distant end
that hides far behind a shadowed wall
I wrestle the process of where to begin
and embrace the words that explode from within

# Bibliography

Duvernay, Ava, "Daring to Dream," Industrialscripts.com/ava-duvernay-quotes/

Hurston, Zora Neale, *Their Eyes Were Watching God*, New York: Harper Collins Publishers, Inc., 1990.

Mays, Benjamin E., *Born to Rebel: An Autobiography*, Athens, Georgia: The University of Georgia Press, 1971.

West, Cornel, "To Live is to Wrestle with Despair," in libquotes.com/cornel-wet/quote/lbs9y1x.

Wilson, August, *Fences*, in *Cornerstones: An Anthology of African-American Literature*, edited by Melvin Donalson, New York: St. Martin's Press, 1996, pp. 469–517.

# About the Author

**Mel Donalson** received his BA from Bates College and his PhD from Brown University. He edited *Cornerstones: An Anthology of African American Literature*, and he's published essays, short stories, poetry, novels, a play, and critical books on American film history, including *Black Directors in Hollywood*, *Masculinity in the Interracial Buddy Film*, and *Hip Hop in American Cinema*. He wrote and directed the short film, *A Room Without Doors*, which was screened on Showtime's *Black Filmmakers Showcase*. Additionally, he wrote, produced, and directed the short film, *Performance*, which aired on the Aspire Network, and was a writer-producer on the short fictional film *Passage*, which was screened at the Pan African Film Festival in Los Angeles.

www.ingramcontent.com/pod-product-compliance
Lightning Source LLC
Chambersburg PA
CBHW011955150426
43200CB00016B/2912